A Naturalist
Along the
Jersey Shore

Joanna Burger

A Naturalist Along the Jersey Shore

*Drawings by
the author*

Rutgers University Press
New Brunswick, New Jersey

Library of Congress Cataloging-in-Publication Data

Burger, Joanna.
    A naturalist along the Jersey shore / Joanna Burger.
      p. cm.
    Includes bibliographical references (p.) and index.
    ISBN 0-8135-2299-4 (cloth : alk. paper). — ISBN 0-8135-2300-1
(pbk. : alk. paper)
    1. Natural history—Atlantic Coast (N.J.)   I. Title.
QH105.N5B87   1996   95-52724
508.749—dc20   CIP

British Cataloging-in-Publication information available

To my husband, Michael Gochfeld, who shared these adventures with me.

To our children, Debbie and David, who helped me see nature through fresh eyes.

To Anne and Alex Gochfeld, who steadfastly encouraged me to write of my adventures.

And to my parents, E. Melvin and Janette Burger, who showed me plants and animals when I was a small child, and always encouraged and supported my interests in nature.

Contents

Fall Changes

Winter Solitude

Signs of Spring

Preface

Ever since I can remember, I have loved the shore. Growing up on a farm in upstate New York, I marveled at the flocks of white birds that descended on our fields at planting time. "They're seagulls," my father told me. I conjured visions of waves and beaches stretching to the horizon. Through cold northern winters, I waited for the birds' return and, although we could ill afford their damage to the planted seedlings, I hoped they would remain. After a few weeks, however, they departed for their northern breeding grounds in Canada. There were songbirds in the woods and fields, of course, but it was the gulls that fascinated me.

Soon I began to pore over books in search of the identity of these gulls, and for information on where they lived during the summer and where they went each autumn after they left our farm. Images of them flying in flocks over white-capped waves, and photographs of them standing on cream-colored sand, drew me to the shore, at least in my daydreams.

Although I lived only 125 miles from the coast, it was over ten years before I even glimpsed the ocean, and another fifteen before I finally was home amid the marshes, sand, surf, and raucous colonies of seabirds that fringe the Jersey shore. Since 1972 I have lived in New Jersey, within 25 miles of the broad beaches of Sandy Hook. From the comfort and safety of my home base as a research and teaching professor in the Biology Department at Rutgers University I could travel to the shore whenever I had a free afternoon, an entire day, a weekend, or a summer.

And so I have spent over twenty years exploring the Jersey shore, from the Arthur Kill and Sandy Hook to Cape May, from salt marshes and back bays to the gleaming white beaches. I have enjoyed all seasons, from the dead of winter to the wonders of spring, and finally to the complexity of the summer season. New Jersey has a bad reputation throughout America. After all, we are the most heavily industrialized and most densely populated state. We have more than our fair share of unfortunate environmental conditions. Visitors often see nothing beyond our intensely altered environment. Yet, our state has more beach frontage per square mile than any other.

I love the Jersey shore, from its white sand beaches and vibrant green salt marshes to its bustling communities. Although I share with thousands of others an appreciation of its wild and wonderful diversity, I also enjoy the solitude of remote salt marshes and deserted beaches. This book describes some of the organisms, natural communities, and ecosystems that one finds along the Jersey shore.

In this book I write about the plants and animals that characterize and define the Jersey shore, of the shore itself and where it came from, of the changes that we humans have made along the shore and will continue to make, and of the possible effects of global climate change. This book is for those with an interest in wildlife, nature, and the never-ending cycle that comes with each season. May it help others to see the wonder and magic of life along the Jersey shore.

Whenever I am in the field, or later in the dim light of a flashlight or lantern, I often make field sketches to capture the essence of observations. I include these to give a feel for all sides of the naturalist's experience here.

Although I write about the Jersey shore, I have also wandered the shores of nearby states, and the organisms and communities I describe are not unique to New Jersey. They are common to the salt marshes, beaches, and back bays from Northern Massachusetts to the Carolinas. Many of the organisms go farther north, farther south, and to coastal areas beyond, and I have studied them from Maine to Florida.

For several years, from April to August, I lived in an old duck-hunting shack on Clam Island in Barnegat Bay, opposite Barnegat Lighthouse, which served as a beacon in calm and stormy weather. The shack is gone, burned down by kids having a summer party—but memories remain of the early mornings when herons and egrets perched atop their tiny bushes and of the swirling gulls mobbing a peregrine searching for food. I have lived on other islands, and spent years surveying the birds of coastal New Jersey, as well as studying the behavior and ecology of many other birds and reptiles. We read so much nowadays about the destruction of rainforests and coral reefs, the threat of extinction, and the loss of biodiversity. It is important to realize that understanding biodiversity begins at home.

Funding for my reasearch has come from the New Jersey State Endangered and Nongame Species Program, the New Jersey Office of Science and Research, the Fish and Wildlife Service of the U.S. Department of the Interior, the U.S. Environmental Protection Agency, the National Institute of Environmental Health Science, the National Institue of Mental Health, the National Science Foundation, the Hudson River Foundation, Penn Foun-

dation through The Trust for Public Lands, the Environmental and Oc-
cupational Health Sciences Institute, and Rutgers University. I thank M.
Cooper, of UMDNJ–RWJ Medical Resources, for the maps.

Over the years I have shared the Jersey shore with a number of companions and travelers, and I thank them now. Two people have accompanied me
in many of my experiences, either in person or through reminiscences: Michael Gochfeld and Fred Lesser. Michael has visited all my dilapidated field
cabins, tents, and study sites, patiently helping with fieldwork, discussing research ideas, and providing helpful criticisms of my science. He has been my
constant companion, in life as well as along the shore. Fred has shared my
travels through Barnegat Bay, first ferrying me by helicopter to my isolated
hunting shack on Clam Island, and then piloting our boat through the bay
even in the densest fog, to distant islands where skimmers and terns nest on
small, fragile lines of salt marsh wrack. Surely no other person knows the bay
so well, the creeks so intimately, or the salt marshes so completely. Words can
never express my delight and gratitude to them both.

Others have shared my experiences along the shore in New Jersey and
nearby New York: Carl Safina has been both a student and a friend, and I
still value his knowledge and his feel for the fishes that form such an important part of the food web. Larry Niles has also been both a student and
a friend, and I appreciate his unique perspective on wildlife management
and its relationship to landscape ecology. Many of my graduate students
have enriched my knowledge of the organisms they have studied, and I have
learned from each of them: Tom Lemke, Pat Slavin, Lynne Miller, Doug
Gladstone, Mary Fitch, Wade Wander, Gary Shugart, N. Kotliar, Brook
Lauro, Kathy Parsons, Greg Transue, Bill Boarman, John Brzorad, Kevin
Staine, Steve Garber, Tom Fikslin, Jorge Saliva, Jacques Hill, Dave Shealer,
H. May, Susan Elbin, Laura Wagner, Nellie Tsipoura, Malcolm Martin,
Mandy Dey, E. Stiles, J. Stout, and B. Palestis. I look forward to many years
of friendship and interactions with them, and eagerly follow their own
journeys through research, teaching, and conservation.

Bob Loveland walked the shores of Delaware Bay, and helped me see the
wonderful lives of horseshoe crabs. Pete McLain and Dave Jenkins provided
help and advice on colonial bird management. Betsy Jones provided a
unique perspective on the lives of the injured birds she lovingly cared for.
Bert and Patti Murray, and Charlie and Mary Leck have been companions
through my science journey. Colin Beer, Bob Paxton and Sarah Plimpton,
Carl Safina and Mercedes Lee, and Betsy and Jim Jones all provided beach
houses, wonderful company, and expert field experience during my research with beach and marsh-nesting birds.

Jim Jones spent many hours with me on Barnegat Bay, sharing his unique knowledge of the bay and of boats. He was always game to go in search of breeding birds on the salt marshes, and I had only to call and say I was on my way to have him rev up the boat, stow the push pole for those very shallow waters around some of the islands, and pack the cooler with just the right refreshments. I miss him when I wander the bay, but his ashes rest comfortably on Pettit Island, amid the nesting terns and skimmers he loved so much.

For nearly fifteen years I have had the good fortune of serving on the New Jersey Endangered and Nongame Council, the advisory body to the Endangered and Nongame Program of the Division of Fish, Game, and Wildlife. I have enjoyed my interaction with all the council members and program personnel over the years, and have learned much from them. I especially treasure the friendship and knowledge of Rich Kane, Jim Applegate, and Robert Shomer, who have shared most of my tenure on the council. Any group that contains veterinarians, teachers, researchers, conservationists, and private citizens provides a unique combination of perspectives on the conservation and management of all wildlife; and I thank them all.

Three teachers profoundly affected my view of nature and my role as a scientist: Miss Richards, Meg Stewart, and H. B. Tordoff. I treasure their wisdom.

Several people have provided valuable comments on earlier drafts of the manuscript, and I am grateful: Ken Able, Caron Chess, Wayne Crans, Mike Gochfeld, Robert Jenkins, Bob Loveland, Dave Shealer, Carl Safina, and Joe

Piping plover on wrack. Males are on outside, female in middle.

Seneca. I would like to thank my editor, Karen Reeds, and the copyeditor, Robert Brown. Several other people have provided data or insights on the shore or animals mentioned: Dary Bennett, John Burger, E. Melvin Burger, Sr., E. Melvin Burger, Jr., Roy Burger, Tim Casey, Jim Dowdell, David Fairbrothers, Steve Handel, Charles and Mary Leck, Elizabeth Johnson, Jan Larson, Bert and Patti Murray, Don Riepe, Dale Schweitzer, Ted Stiles, Pat Sutton, Guy Tudor, and Robert Zappalorti.

Guy Tudor and Michelle LeMarchant, Ted and JoAnn Male, Dan and Aileen Morse, Bernie Goldstein, Jim Kushlan, and Patty Gowaty encouraged me to write of my adventures and to include my field sketches, and this book is partly due to their love and encouragement. Tik o, my forty-year-old parrot, stood faithfully behind my shoulder as I wrote these lines, chewing up passages that he found particularly irksome.

My family has also shared in my adventures along the shore: My husband, Michael, has been my soulmate during my fieldwork for over twenty years. Our children, Debbie and David, have spent hours with us on beaches and marshes around the world, often in search of nesting colonies of seabirds. I hope these memories are as dear to them as they are to me. My brothers and sisters, and nieces and nephews shared my love of nature over the years. My second parents, Alex and Anne Gochfeld, loved to hear of these adventures, and encouraged me to lay them to paper. Finally, I learned my love of nature from my parents, E. Melvin Burger and Janette Vivien Male Burger: they taught me how to observe, how to appreciate what I observed, and how to share it with those I love.

"You got to be on the bay to see a day born, back on the mainland you just see the sun come up."
—Old Bayman, years ago, from: Miller, P. 1994. *The Great Sedges* (Ocean County Cultural and Heritage Commission)

The Shore
Community

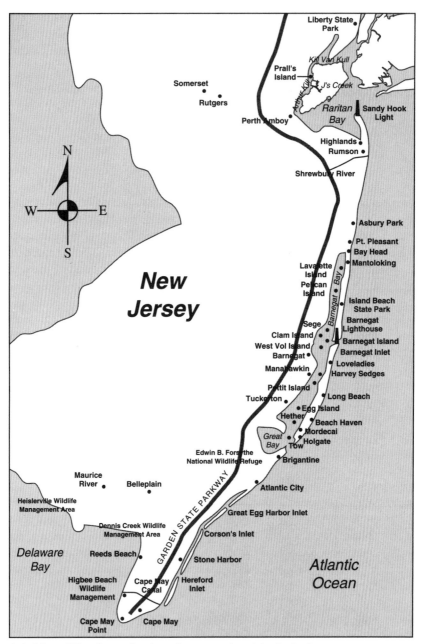

1.1. Map of New Jersey showing places mentioned in the book.

1

Where Did the Shore Come From?

From Maine to Florida along the Atlantic coast there is a fragile ribbon of rocky shores, barrier beaches, and green salt marshes. A series of barrier beach islands absorbs most of the force of the ocean's wave front, but the entire coast is a living thing, shifting ever so gradually from year to year. At the tip of Florida, and farther to the south, the coastline is guarded by mangrove swamps. The sea pounds the shoreline, breaking up rocks, moving sand from place to place, cutting new inlets, closing old ones. Every day the tides go in and out, making imperceptible changes that over time result in large changes. The very shape of the land itself is altered over the centuries. The earth is dynamic, undergoing massive transitions over geologic time as a result of volcanoes, earthquakes, violent storms, movement of glaciers, changes in sea level, and continental drift. Nowhere are the changes more rapid and more evident than along coastal margins. For it is here that the violent forces of the sea meet the land.

The face of our coasts results from the interaction between glaciation and sea levels. When large quantities of water are tied up in glaciers, less is in the oceans, and sea level is low. As glaciers melt, the water makes its way to the ocean, and gradually the level of the sea rises. The continental shelf under our coastal waters is broad or narrow, as sea level slowly rises or falls.

About 50,000 years ago the Laurentide Glacier moved down from the Canadian arctic and covered the northern part of the United States. Eventually the glacier reached its southernmost point in Central New Jersey, where the melting of the massive sheet was balanced by its advance, and the ice sheet went no farther. In its path it pushed boulders, rocks, and soil, and these were deposited at the southern limit of the glacier.

Then the climate changed, the earth warmed, and the glacier began to melt. As the glacier melted, it receded for thousands of years, leaving rocks and debris in its path. Meltwater flowed from the leading edge of the glacier, carrying soil and rocks over the land. The land was soggy, as water flowed rapidly in tiny rivulets. Here and there large pieces of ice remained, but eventually they melted also. The soil was blown by winds because no plants held it in place.

Torrents of water flowed into the sea, and sea level rose. Land freed from the enormous weight of the glacier rose up. Finally the glacier was present only in the far north, and the rapid changes ended. The advancing sea slowed, the land stopped rising, and plants slowly colonized the mud and rock exposed by the dying glacier. The final retreat of the Laurentide Glacier occurred about 10,000 years ago, and our coastal ecosystem was born.

Cores through the peat along the Atlantic coast indicate that there was a rapid fall in sea level about 20,000 years ago, followed by a rapid rise in sea level until about 7,000 or 8,000 years ago when the seas began to stabilize. Barrier islands arose at this time, but sea-level rise was still too rapid for salt-marsh formation. When sea-level rise slowed about 4,000 years ago, the marshes along our Atlantic coast were established. Most marshes are only about 3,000 or 4,000 years old, although a few are as old as 11,000 years. Marshes can only develop when sea-level rise is very slow.

The problem of a rising sea level looms again because of human-induced climatic change leading to global warming. Before the current threat of rapid sea-level rise, the sea was gradually rising at a very slow rate of a millimeter or so a year. It rose by only about four inches a century. Marshes are capable of keeping up with this gradual rise by building themselves up. It is a slow process, this making of land by the mixing of decaying salt-marsh vegetation and blowing sands. This slow buildup is called accretion, and some marshes can have accretion rates of two to three inches a year. The marsh grasses can keep pace with sea-level rises only when they have a constant supply of sediment to mix with decaying organic matter to form peat.

It is a race between the rising marsh and the rising sea. New Jersey marshes have an accretion rate that exceeds current rises in sea level, but states along the Gulf Coast are losing land every year. There the land is subsiding, and with slowly rising sea levels, the land is being inundated at high rates. Louisiana loses several hundred acres every year.

Although long-term change in sea level due to glacial melting and land subsidence or rising has played a role in coastal development, short-term fluctuations in water levels also affect coasts. There are wind-driven waves that have periods of seconds or minutes, as well as diurnal tides. Seasonal and yearly changes in barometric pressure, temperatures, and salinity influence the density and volume of coastal waters, making them rise and fall relative to the land. Sea-level changes are greatest in the summer and lowest in the winter. Changes in geomorphology, such as development of a sand spit or dredging, also affect water levels and tidal ranges. Storms cause sudden changes of ten to sixteen feet above normal tide heights. There is a lag between the period of maximum wind, and the highest water levels, and this lag may be up to fourteen hours.

It is the tides, however, that most characterize the shore and the organisms that live there. In contrast to the water-level changes mentioned above, tides are remarkably regular. There are two daily tide cycles along the Atlantic coast, with a period of slightly over twelve hours each. As you go farther north along the Atlantic coast of North America, the range in tide heights increases. The tides along the Gulf of Mexico, for example, are less than a foot, while those in Maine may be fifteen feet. Even within a geographical area there is great range in the tidal heights over the year. The tidal range is greatest during full and new moons, and the highest and lowest tides occur near the summer and winter solstices.

It is relatively easy to predict tide heights at the ocean edge, but it is very difficult to predict them in back bays, tidal marshes, and along rivers such as the Hudson and Delaware, where water levels result from a complex set of interactions. These interactions include local topography, distance from inlets, size of the inlet, sediment supply, vegetation, winds, and the amount and form of the land between the sea and the marsh. When the winds blow in the direction of the tidal flow, the tides may be very high, but when the winds blow in the opposite direction, high tide may never reach the marsh. The study of tides is a whole science in itself.

Marshes that are far from the mouth of inlets often have tidal ranges that are far smaller than the marshes close to the inlets. By the time the high tide has reached these distant marshes, it has already reversed near the inlet, and waters are flowing back to the sea.

The land-ocean interface along most of the Atlantic coast consists of a series of barrier beach islands that fringe estuaries and coastal bays (Figure 1.2). Salt marshes line the inner parts of the estuaries and bays, where they are protected from the open ocean. Barrier islands are found throughout the world, varying in size and number with sea-level changes, tidal range, geomorphic features, and climate. Worldwide, barrier islands account for 10 to 15 percent of the world's shorelines, but the percentage is far higher in New Jersey. Barrier islands can develop where there is a low to moderate tidal range, along coasts with low profiles, with gentle offshore currents and plenty of sediment for deposition. Most of our barrier islands were formed 6,000 to 7,000 years ago, but their shape is changing constantly. Still, their presence provides protection from the surf, necessary for salt marshes to form.

Sand dunes, on the other hand, form at the edge of the sea, on both barrier islands and the mainland. They form wherever sand is deposited on land, and can be blown and shifted by the wind. Thus sand dunes can be

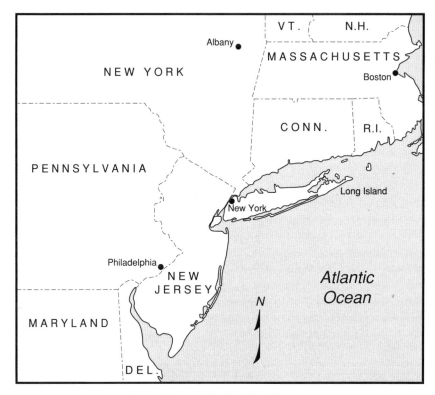

1.2. Map of Middle Atlantic showing barrier islands.

much older than barrier islands themselves, and their longer history means that plants and animals have had longer to adapt to these habitats.

The structure of the land varies as we make our way across the beach from the open ocean, crossing the dunes to the back bays. The habitat, and the plants and animals living there, also change. The transition between zones can be abrupt, and in only a short distance we can move from open, shifting sands devoid of vegetation to a dense maritime forest of cherry trees, holly, cedars, and poison ivy. The leading edge along the ocean experiences high winds, large amounts of moving sand, and high rates of salt deposition. Beach and dune soils are usually lacking in organic matter, nitrogen, phosphorus, and potassium. Salt spray is a primary source of nutrients for barrier-island vegetation, although most of the salt from ocean spray is deposited within five hundred yards of the water, and nearly half of the salt is deposited within fifty yards of the sea. These conditions, so benign and inviting to the summer bather, provide an inhospitable landscape that few plants can tolerate.

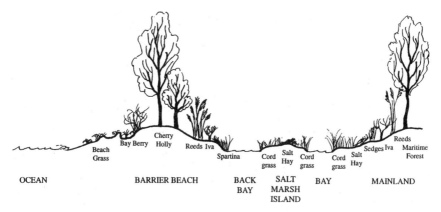

Cherry
Bay Berry Holly   Reeds Iva   Reeds
Beach   Sedges Iva   Maritime
Grass   Spartina   Cord Salt Cord   Cord Salt   Forest
                                             grass Hay grass   grass Hay

OCEAN   BARRIER BEACH   BACK   SALT   BAY   MAINLAND
                                             BAY   MARSH
                                                    ISLAND

1.3. Schematic of vegetation changes from sandy beach to marsh to uplands.

Sand movement, an important feature of barrier islands, depends upon position on the dune, angle of the dune or island, wind speed and direction, and the frequency, intensity, and seasonality of storms. Shifting sands can alter the height of a sandy beach or dune by up to twenty inches in a year. Windward edges of the dunes lose sand through erosion, while the apex and lee slopes of the same dune receive the sand as accretion. The base or swale of dunes often remains static, and it is here that vegetation first gains a firm foothold.

Not only does the shape of a dune change over time, but whole dunes can also move, shifting slowly with winds and blowing sands. Swales are overtaken by moving dunes, vegetation is killed, and new swale habitats between the shifting dunes are invaded by colonizing vegetation. These changes can be rapid, occurring within a few years, virtually before our eyes.

Even more acute are the effects of washovers that also change and rearrange vegetation, as well as the sand. Some plants can withstand washovers, and are adapted to periodic inundation by salt water, but others die or wither away. Animals living in interdune swales also vary in their response to washovers. Some die, others thrive, and some simply move. Washovers also carry large amounts of sand over the dunes onto the back side of barrier islands or onto salt marshes. As the marshes are built up by sand accumulation, and the dunes are rebuilt or shifted along the ocean, the whole barrier island may move gradually inland. The frequency and strength of washovers increase with sea level rise, and as long as the rate of sea level rise does not exceed the rate of marsh and dune development, the island will remain. It will simply move inland.

There is a predictable pattern of land forms, plants and animals as you move inland from the sea (Figure 1.3). Sandy beaches on barrier islands,

1.4. Tidal wrack line showing (left to right): clam, shark vertebrae, scallops, razor clam, whelk egg case, mussel, skate egg case, crab leg, and algae.

barren of any vegetation, occur where the surf pummels the land. These beaches may be narrow or wide, depending upon the availability of sand, the forces of the wind, and the presence of high dunes. Although at first sandy beaches seem uniform along the Jersey coast, there are many subtle variations in form and structure on any given beach. On some, the beach rises ever so gently to the foot of the dunes; on others the rise is steep, and the beach is narrow. Wide open expanses of sand are broken by washover areas where small tidal pools remain for days. On others, the sand is smooth and unbroken by tidal streams or pools.

At the high-tide line a wrack of stranded seaweeds, driftwood, shells, egg cases, dried fish, dead marine invertebrates such as horseshoe crabs, and other treasures lie baking in the sun (Figure 1.4). Dead animals attract ants and flies, which in turn attract foraging shorebirds. These little microcosms usually have anthropogenic treasures as well: the tiny toy soldiers of twenty years ago have given way to plastic Ninja Turtles, beach balls have given way to Frisbees, a variety of different dolls have given way to Barbies, all dressed alike. Only plastic pails with tiny shovels, balloons, and baseball caps have remained the same. Above the wrack line may be another, older wrack line left by the high storm tides of last winter.

The foredunes may be shallow or steep, but they are all stark or only lightly vegetated with beach grass and an occasional seaside goldenrod. Beyond the foredunes is an interdune swale, where the sands are more stable. Here other grasses, sedges, and forbs grow, and sometimes there are a few shrubs such as beach plum or bayberry.

Secondary dunes are behind the foredunes. These dunes are more stable because they are not exposed directly to strong oceanic winds and persistent salt spray. They probably formed centuries ago. Often shrubs grow here, intermixed with grasses and perennial forbs. Behind the secondary dunes some beaches have a maritime forest or shrub thicket. In New Jersey this upland zone can be narrow or quite wide; and the trees can be short shrubs or massive, dense trees. In some places, where the barrier beaches are narrow or highly developed, the shrub or forest zone is gone.

Behind the maritime forest is the salt marsh, adapted to periodic tidal inundation, free from the direct force of the ocean waves. Salt marshes only develop behind barrier islands or in the mouths of rivers where there is some protection from waves. Waves prevent the sediments from forming a stable substrate necessary for the establishment of salt-marsh plants. As tidal currents carry sediments into bays and estuaries, the speed slows, and they can no longer keep soil in suspension. Sediments gradually build up where the waters are calm, and underground grass rhizomes invade, resulting in little lines of cordgrass growing from the established marsh.

Although salt marshes appear level, they are not. The inner, older parts of the marsh are slightly higher, for they have had longer to accumulate sediment and peat. Sometimes there is a higher lip along the edge of salt-marsh creeks, where soil has been deposited with high tides. Tidal waters carrying sediment push over the creek banks, are slowed down, and deposit the sand along the edge. A tall variety of cordgrass grows along these banks, providing hiding places for clapper rails that slip through the marsh searching for fiddler crabs.

The higher elevations of the marsh are flooded less frequently, and are submerged for shorter periods of time. The reduced amount of water reaching the high marsh brings in less sediment, and accretion slows. Pools within the marsh develop because some places have not received quite enough soil for cordgrass to become established. These are filled by high tides and by heavy rains, and eventually small fish are carried in by excessively high tides, but if the pools are high within the marsh, they may dry up when the summer sun evaporates the water. These temporary pools cannot support fish, and become breeding places for salt-marsh mosquitoes. Shorebirds gather around these high pools to forage for insects and other invertebrates when high tides have covered their usual foraging places.

Estuaries and bays separate the barrier islands from the mainland. Many of the bays and estuaries are wide, and are dotted with small salt-marsh islands that are exposed to tides each day. The mainland is also fringed with salt marshes, and these can be very extensive, depending on the slope of the land. Eventually the salt marshes give way to uplands.

There is a striking zonation of plants in the Jersey salt marshes. There is low salt marsh, flooded at every tide cycle, covered with cordgrass, and high salt marsh composed of salt hay. Cordgrass grows on the low areas of the salt marsh that are regularly inundated, whereas salt hay grows where there is less salt water intrusion. Compared to the coarse, stiff, thick cordgrass, salt hay is delicate and low growing, usually less than two feet high. The stems are so fine that the grass generally falls over, forming soft swirling mats that offer inviting places to rest, even to the most jaded of folks.

Where there is even less tidal flow, small patches of spike- grass are nestled in the higher spots with the salt hay. Spike-grass is short, and often has a pale gray tinge. On spoil piles left by mosquito ditching there are bushes such as marsh elder, although these shrubs normally grow at the very upper edge of the marsh where there is little salt intrusion. Black grass and switch grass also grow in this zone of little tidal inundation. Where freshwater enters the marsh and where there is no tidal flow, cattails and reeds (*Phragmites*) grow. Although people have argued for many years about whether these reeds are native to North America, their pollen has been found in sediment cores from salt marshes in Connecticut dating from at least 3,500 years ago.

Many other plants grow in each zone, although they are far less common. The number of different plant species, or species diversity, increases as you go higher on the marsh. Only four or five salt-tolerant species can live in the lower elevations, where cordgrass grows. In the intermediate zones where salt hay and spike-grass grow there can be ten to fifteen species. In the upper border of Jersey salt marshes there are over a hundred species of plants that include asters, goldenrods, marsh mallows, pinks, and many species of grasses, sedges, and reeds.

The marshes are dissected into infinite patterns by creeks that vary from a yard to dozens of yards wide. From the air, their meandering patterns and graceful curves provide a lovely green-and-blue tapestry. Unfortunately, many of the high marshes of New Jersey have been altered. One of the most profound changes, the draining of marshes with "mosquito ditches," took place early in the century. It changed both the habitat and the geometry of the marsh, superimposing stark rectangular patterns on the once-meandering maze.

Many high marshes have disappeared owing to their susceptibility to filling and development. Since the border of the high marsh gets very little tidal flow, it is easier to fill, easier to dike, and easier to rationalize its destruction. Still, New Jersey has over 245,000 acres of salt marsh scattered along its coasts. Once considered wasteland to be tamed and drained, salt marshes are now appreciated on their own merits: not only for the diversity of life they spawn, protect, and nourish, nor for the number of fish that migrate here each summer, but because the salt marsh protects the uplands from the power of the sea. Marshes act as a storm buffer, able to soak up and retain over 300,000 gallons of flood tides before they reach the mainland. Marshes are pollutant filters, removing contaminants in runoff waters through percolation and biologically recycling them through organisms. Salt marshes are some of the most highly productive regions of the world, rivaling many forms of agriculture. The average *Spartina* marsh produces between one and two pounds of above-ground material per square yard each year, and the very high marsh areas with reeds and cattails may produce between three and six pounds of vegetation per square yard per year. Remarkably, the below-ground production of roots and rhizomes can be three to four times greater than the above-ground production. Salt marshes, with their associated tidal creeks, bays, and estuaries, are also one of the most productive areas for human food. Acre for acre, pound for pound, these coastal zones produce more food in the form of fish and shellfish than fields of corn, wheat, or other crops.

Walking across the marsh, one can tell something about the elevation merely by identifying the grasses. Cordgrass grows only where there is daily or almost daily tidal inundation. Small patches of salt hay amid the cordgrass indicate slightly higher places. Where bushes grow in the middle of the marsh, there are dirt piles left by ditching or some other human alteration. A patch of reeds indicates no tidal inundation, except at extremely high storm tides. The Jersey marshes are a mosaic of different patches, and a variety of animals live in the different zones. Birds often select their nest sites based on the predominant vegetation, which signals the probability of tidal flooding.

Although we notice the zonation in flowering plants, there is also zonation in algae, and this zonation is an important part of the salt-marsh food web. Certain species of algae are associated with the different salt-marsh communities. For example, the algal layer beneath the tall cordgrass that grows along the creeks is mainly diatoms, while on the higher cordgrass areas filamentous algae abound. There is less algal cover beneath the dense salt hay because little light filters through. High light intensities favor the growth of lush filamentous algae carpets, whereas diatoms can survive in low light.

The invertebrates we see as we walk across the marsh, called macroinvertebrates, change with the shifting vegetation zones. Fiddler crabs are more common along the lower reaches of the marsh, where there is daily tidal flooding of a lush mat of algae. There are many fewer crabs and other burrowing animals on the high marsh. This may be due to the lower frequency of flooding, required for feeding in some invertebrates. Snails and small isopods, however, are often more common on the high marsh.

Fish are generally excluded from most salt-marsh ponds and pools, except those with tidal connections. During very high tides mummichogs and sheepshead minnow colonize the larger pools. They can be encouraged to live in these areas by the construction of ditches that connect the pools to small tidal creeks, thereby preventing them from drying out. Fish are beneficial on the marsh, at least from a human perspective, because they eat

1.5. Muskrat eating vegetation on bank of marsh creek.

the larvae of salt-marsh mosquitoes before they emerge and descend on barrier beach or mainland communities in search of human blood.

Birds also use the marsh according to the vegetation zones, which reflect tidal flooding. No species regularly nest in the lowest areas of the marsh, for their nests and eggs would be flooded out by tides, and would die from exposure to salt. Several species nest in the high marsh or higher areas of the low marsh, including gulls, skimmers, terns, shorebirds, ducks, geese, and sparrows. Although the gulls, terns, and skimmers usually feed over the open water of bays and the ocean, the other species feed on the marsh or along the tidal pools. Herons, egrets, and ibis, as well as crows, blackbirds, and a few other songbirds, nest among reeds or bushes, and they usually feed in the marshes or in the nearby creeks and bays.

A variety of small mammals live in the higher areas of salt hay, including the meadow mouse, jumping mouse, white-footed mouse, and the masked shrew. Other, larger animals such as raccoon, mink, skunk, and weasel feed on shellfish, bird eggs, young birds, and mice on the marsh, although they spend most of their time in the uplands beyond the marsh. Muskrats sometimes live on the high marsh, although they prefer areas of low salinity, because they eat the roots and tubers of plants (Figure 1.5). In some Jersey marshes they build winter dens of vegetation that may be up to seven feet high, but in other places, such as along the Arthur Kill, they frequently burrow in the mud along the creek.

The creeks, bays, and estuaries that separate the barrier islands from the mainland are an integral and critical part of the coastal ecosystem. It is here that the great diversity of coastal marine animals lives, breeds, or spawns. Small floating, microscopic plants, called phytoplankton, convert sunlight into plant biomass. The phytoplankton, along with the algae, marsh plants, and plants that grow beneath the bay waters are the primary producers. They, along with microscopic animals, form the base of the food chain. Animals that eat these plants, called primary consumers, include the microscopic zooplankton, filter-feeding mollusks like mussels and clams, mud-dwelling worms, shrimp, and other crustaceans. They in turn are eaten by secondary consumers such as fiddler crabs, blue crabs, and small fish. The secondary consumers are eaten by predators that include a variety of fish such as bluefish, stripped bass and weakfish, birds such as ospreys, herons, hawks, terns, and gulls, as well as by people. Many organisms belong to different levels of the food web, but only the plants can convert sunlight into energy. Decomposers are an important, though often little-appreciated, component of the food web, for they recycle the dead biomass by breaking it down into units usable by the rest of the food web. This intricate and complex food web in the bays and estuaries is nourished by the plants and animals that live on the marshes and barrier beaches. The marshes, bays, and barrier islands together form an estuarine ecosystem that is one of the most highly productive ecosystems in the world, and that is essential for the life of the oceans beyond.

2

Birds on Salt Marshes and Beaches

In late February, an unseasonably cold wind sweeps across Great Bay to an endless vista of grass behind Little Beach Island. Along the low edge of a band of *Spartina,* grass stems stand upright, their seeds long ago scattered by winter storms. A few feet away the grass bends, touching the ground in wide, undulating swaths. Dollops of snow remain nestled in low places, shaded by protective patches of grass. Wavy lines of mottled white-and-black eelgrass are strewn at the high-tide line. Farther from the marsh edge, leafless bushes are tangled and broken. A tiny mass of grass resolves into remnants of a nest clinging to the branches, the only indication of the birds soon to come. Last summer a red-winged blackbird fledged three young from that fragile nest, and I expect the redwing and grackle flocks back any day now. The marsh seems lifeless on this nasty day, and the cold has forced even the brant into sheltered coves. This scene could be anywhere along the Jersey shore from Bay Head in the north to Cape May, and up into Delaware Bay. The shore is lined with similar bays and estuaries, each fringed with salt marshes. Tiny salt-marsh islands dot the bays.

Looking over the marsh now, I remember how unvarying I once thought it was, how easy it was to ignore subtle variations in vegetation color, grass height, and ground elevation. I wondered then how so many different species of birds could all use the marsh without clashing over space for nesting and feeding. For many years I have been studying how birds nest in salt marshes, how they divide it up in time and space. In this seemingly homogeneous environment, slight differences in elevation are critical for successful breeding, whether you are a clapper rail or a laughing gull. Over the next few weeks the New Jersey salt marshes will welcome a variety of birds, some will migrate farther north to distant breeding grounds, while others will remain, seeking nesting habitat. Today, not even gulls are in evidence.

Only a few days later the sun melts the remaining snow, and the once uniformly brown grass radiates a sheen of yellow, beige, and brown. On some of the higher salt-marsh islands herring gulls and great black-backed gulls stand among marsh elder bushes, already defending territories and seeking mates. All around there are gulls, some standing alone, others in pairs. The birds in pairs court one another, or sit quietly; but the solitary birds are males that are both defending territories and trying to attract unmated females flying over the colony. Great black-backed gulls manage to take the highest spots, the ridges surrounded by bushes. The dark slate-colored back of the great black-backed bull contrasts with the silver-gray mantle of the herring gull. The black-back has a louder, lower-pitched voice that is raucous and jarring. It is too early for gulls to build nests, but it is not too soon to compete for a territory that will be high enough to avoid tidal flooding and will provide enough cover for their eggs and chicks.

The black-backed gulls are nearly twice as large as the herring gulls, and can win in any direct competition. Fortunately for herring gulls, there are still relatively few great black-backed gulls in New Jersey, and most islands have only five to twenty pairs, compared to dozens or hundreds of herring gulls. All the best nesting places are not claimed by the great black-backs.

Threats from tidal flooding and from predators are two factors that strongly affect how birds use salt marshes. Birds either nest high enough to be above the ravages of high tides, they have behavioral means of avoiding flooding, or they rely on both. To avoid predators, many species carefully conceal their nests, or have eggs and young that are cryptically colored and are thus less visible to predators. Alternatively, some birds nest in colonies and engage in group defense of their nests and chicks. In salt marshes some birds, such as clapper rails, red-winged blackbirds, seaside and sharp-tailed sparrows, and boat-tailed grackles nest solitarily, hiding their nests down in the grass or in the low bushes. Gulls, terns, skimmers, herons, and egrets, on the other hand, nest in highly visible and sometimes dense colonies, ranging in size from only a few nesting birds to several hundred pairs.

During most of February, March, and early April the herring and great black-backed gulls stand silently about the high marsh, or engage in noisy territorial clashes, and courtship. Courtship involves elaborate displays between the members of a pair, and the males courtship-feed their females by regurgitating fish or crabs. As spring advances, displays become more frequent and intense, as if the birds remember why they are there.

Although territorial boundaries have been defended for months, only in mid-April do the gulls begin to select nest sites within their territories. The male shows the female his favorite spot by walking to it, and bending to give a low choking call. He bends down, his chest barely touching the ground, and jerks his chest and head rhythmically back and forth. The female stares down, and then walks to a spot she prefers and gives the same choking display. This process is repeated many times, over many days, before the pair agree on a particular spot, and both perform the choking display together, side by side, later bringing small bits of grass to form a nest cup. Most female herring gulls lay three eggs in late April, though a few may delay their clutches until May. The *Spartina* grass slowly grows taller, and the marsh elder bushes turn green and provide shade and cover for the incubating gulls.

By the end of March or early April the elegant, stately white forms of great and snowy egrets walk the shallow marshes and estuaries, slowly searching for prey. Usually each egret walks alone, looking for small fish in a shallow slough or salt-marsh creek. At dusk, black-crowned night herons stalk along tidal creeks, jabbing at fiddler crabs that scuttle into their burrows in the mud. Gradually the egrets and herons move to the highest places in the marsh where the giant reeds sway in the breezes and the scraggly, short marsh elders grow. They squabble noisily for nest sites, but the larger great egrets manage to secure the highest places in the trees, the snowy egrets are left with intermediate places, and the glossy ibis end up nesting low in the reeds. The black-crowned night heron nests are bulky and substantial, of twigs and small branches, and are commonly located on the ground. Although usually free from tidal threats, egret nests can be blown down by northeast storms and gale winds.

In late April and early May, many other colonial species begin to arrive on the marshes: laughing gulls, Forster's and common terns, and black skimmers. Long before they occupy nesting colonies they fly about the bays, resting on sandbars or the edges of salt-marsh islands. Species that nest solitarily also arrive in late April or early May, but their coming is less obvious because they are smaller, travel in ones or twos, and often are cryptically colored. Boat-tailed grackles and red-winged blackbirds settle noisily in the bushes and reeds. On the top of small shrubs, male redwings hunch forward and spread their wings to reveal their bright red shoulder patches, displaying to the recently arrived, brown-streaked females sitting low in the vegetation.

When laughing gulls arrive in late April they find the highest places on the marsh taken by the much larger herring gulls, and they are forced to find territories on the lower parts of the marsh, or to seek salt-marsh islands where there are no herring gulls. Since there are nearly ten times as many laughing gulls than herring gulls nesting in New Jersey, they have many of the salt-marsh islands to themselves. Even so, they nest on lower areas in loose colonies spread out over the marsh.

The laughing gulls are on the marsh for over a month before they construct nests. During this time they squabble over territories and engage in intense courtship. A lone male laughing gull usually claims a mat of dead *Spartina* stems to use as a courtship platform. He rushes back and forth, defending it against other males, his eyes peering into the sky for unmated females flying overhead. Eventually most territorial males secure a mate, and the courtship displays intensify and lead to mating. They have a special, staccato copulation call that can be heard for long distances. When the males mount, they wave their outstretched wings, flashing the white wing linings like flags. During the month the pair stands in one place for a few days, and then shifts to another. Even when the high spring tides flood the marsh they remain on their territory, walking to the highest spots that remain dry. This allows them to discover the very highest spot within their territory for a nest site, and sometimes in the process they desert their territory and search for a higher one that is dry during high tides. Only after the very highest spring tides do they build their nests. Finally in late May the females lay three eggs.

Common terns, Forster's terns, and black skimmers usually arrive on the marshes in early May, and must contend with the larger and already established gulls. Since herring gulls will eat their eggs and chicks, the terns avoid those islands with nesting herring gulls. Otherwise common terns nest on most salt-marsh islands that are high enough to have patches of salt hay with some scattered mats of dead *Spartina* stems or eelgrass. Terns also pick the highest spots in the marsh, and use *Spartina* or eelgrass stems to make nests.

In most places black skimmers nest on sandy beaches as they do at Holgate, Corson's Inlet, and Hereford Inlet; but in Barnegat Bay, many skimmers nest on salt-marsh islands in colonies with the common terns. The skimmers prefer the eelgrass mats, and since they are larger than the common terns, they can successfully defend these places against the terns, which then are forced to the edge of the mat. Intense competition occurs for the eelgrass or *Spartina* mats because these are the highest areas on the marsh where winter tides have deposited the grass. During the summer, they will be the last places to flood, and are the safest places for eggs and young. Forster's terns avoid competition with the other colonial species by nesting in relatively low marshes with no bushes (preferred by herring gulls), no extensive Zostera or *Spartina* mats (preferred by the common terns and skimmers), and little salt hay used by common terns. They usually nest in colonies by themselves, without common terns or gulls.

These different species of colonial birds can all nest on the salt marsh by partitioning it in time and space (Figure 2.1). Herring and great blackbacked gulls arrive first, followed by herons and egrets, then by laughing gulls, and finally by common and Forster's terns and by black skimmers. Birds that

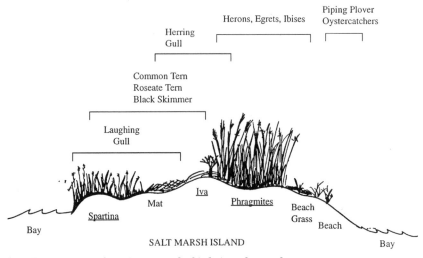

2.1. Partitioning of nesting space by birds in salt marshes.

have established territories usually can successfully defend them against intruders. Thus, later-arriving birds must take the remaining space on islands with already established birds, or they must seek other unused islands.

There is, however, spatial separation in the parts of the marsh they prefer to use for nests. Herons and egrets nest only in the highest places with dense reeds and short cherry and poison ivy trees, while herring gulls nest on the high places with marsh elder bushes. For a short period the competition for nest sites among the egrets and herons is intense, with noisy squabbles, violent jabbing with their bills, and overt attacks and chases. Within a few days, most have settled their real-estate disputes.

Laughing gulls, terns, and skimmers nest in the *Spartina* marsh itself, and if there are no herring gulls the laughing gulls will nest in the high places with bushes. The most intense competition is between common terns and skimmers that prefer the eelgrass mats, but even that is reduced because the larger skimmers can easily win any direct encounters.

I find the same partitioning on the outer beaches, where each species nests in slightly different areas (Figure 2.2). Oystercatchers, piping plovers and least terns nest on the lowest part of the beach, at the foot of the dunes, just above the tide line. They prefer wide, barren beaches with an open view in all directions, so they can see approaching predators. They must select places that are above the high wrack line, or nests will be washed out by high tides. Even so, high storm tides sometimes wash out nests, carrying eggs out to sea or merely displacing them a few yards.

Common terns and black skimmers usually nest in the swales between

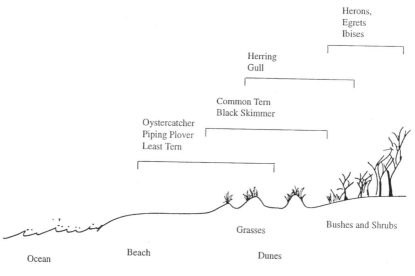

2.2. *Partitioning of nesting space by birds on sandy beaches.*

the dunes. Beach grass, seaside goldenrod, and other beach plants are scattered about, providing shade from the searing sun and cover from heavy rains and predators. They will not nest in dense vegetation, however, for they too must see approaching predators. They nest more densely than the least terns, however, and rely on group defense against predators.

Although laughing gulls do not nest on sandy beaches in New Jersey, they nest in the dunes in other places, such as Florida and Texas. Similarly, herring gulls nest on sand dunes in nearby New York, but these places are too disturbed in New Jersey.

When there are shrubs and bushes fringing the sand dunes, herons, egrets, and ibis nest. They nest near beaches only when these habitats occur on an island where there are no mammalian predators, or when the trees are too high for predators to climb. The larger species nest the highest, leaving the lower places that are more vulnerable to predators to the smallest herons and egrets.

By early June the *Spartina* is green and lush on the salt marsh; the coarser cordgrass by the creek edges is growing tall and dark green while the finer salt hay takes on a yellow-green tinge, and falls in gentle swaths in the higher places. Clapper rails slink softly along the tidal creeks feeding on fiddler crabs, returning to incubate clutches of twelve or thirteen eggs in their domed nests hidden in the tall grass at the edge of creeks. The rails have adapted to tidal flooding by building tall nests, and by retrieving their

2.3. Clapper rail with two chicks on a nest.

eggs or chicks if they are washed out (Figure 2.3). I have seen a clapper rail carry back to its nest six eggs scattered as far as thirty feet away. Once I watched as a very industrious clapper carried nine rail eggs, two belonging to a neighbor, and three laughing gull eggs back to its nest. They are shy birds, and venture out mainly at low tide, to feed on mollusks, snails, worms, and insects, in addition to fiddler crabs.

These marsh- and beach-nesting birds usually feed within a few hundred yards, or a mile or two, of their breeding colonies (Figure 2.4). Herons and gulls feed in the shallow bays and along tidal creeks, Forster's terns feed over shallow salt marsh pools, while common terns feed in the inlets or out in the ocean, and skimmers feed in the tidal creeks and channels. The solitary-nesting species usually feed within their nesting territories in the marsh or barrier beaches.

By June the competition for colony and nest sites is over, and the noises of the marsh are of herring gulls feeding growing chicks, and of the terns and skimmers exchanging incubation duties as the relieved parent goes off to forage. So far the tides have not been exceptionally high, and no nests have been washed out.

Some higher islands are occupied only by herring gulls and black-backed

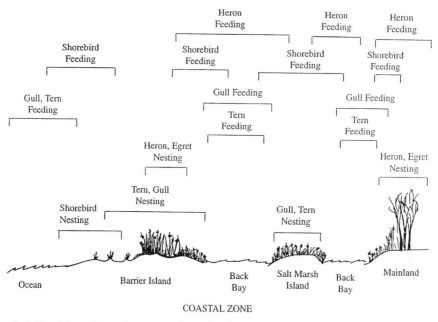

COASTAL ZONE

2.4. Partition of foraging space along the shore.

gulls, while others have laughing gulls, terns, and skimmers as well, each species nesting in discrete groups. The colonies are dynamic, however, and I am saddened by the changes that occur on islands where herring gulls nest with the other species. Herring and black-backed gulls outmaneuver the smaller species for space. Eventually only the larger gulls will remain. In my years on the salt marshes I have watched many colonies switch from all terns and skimmers, to all herring and great black-backed gulls.

The smaller laughing gulls, terns, and skimmers are forced to nest in the lower marshes where the herring and great black-backed gulls are unable to nest. The terns and skimmers nest at the very edge, in low places where they suffer complete or partial washouts in some years. Yet in the last twenty years only once has there been a complete washout of all the tern colonies in Barnegat Bay. Some young terns are fledged every year from some salt-marsh colonies, and that may be sufficient for a bird that can live more than twenty years.

In late June and early July the colonies are noisy and alive with the begging calls of young chicks nearing fledging. With the approach of a parent, chicks jump wildly up and down, flapping their wings and calling vociferously. Here and there a chick practicing flight careens awkwardly into the grass, setting off a territorial squabble, before it runs, flapping its wings, back into its own territory.

By late July the marsh is silent, the nests deserted. The grass is now waist-high along the creeks, and knee-deep everywhere else. A lone clapper rail still skulks along the creek edge, and a few chocolate-colored laughing gull young pick at crabs in the tidal mud. Otherwise there is little sign of the hordes of marsh-nesting birds. A marsh hawk glides low over the marsh in search of mice. Only a few weeks ago his passage triggered a mass of swirling, calling, diving terns to defend their nests. Now they are gone, there are no more small chicks for food, and the hawk once again searches for the tiny meadow voles sneaking through the grass.

Through the winter months the marsh will be guarded by a few clapper rails threading through the brown and battered marsh. It will be invaded by flocks of brant and other waterfowl. But the calls and cries of nesting birds will not be heard for many months.

3

Salt Hay, Glasswort, and Other Commercial Ventures

Coastal areas have always been exploited by humans, and the Jersey shore is no exception. First people came to it as a source of food, then as a waterway to exciting lands beyond the sea, then as a port and center for foreign trade and commerce, and more recently, they came for a pleasant place to live, recreate, and enjoy the pleasures of land and sea.

Barrier beaches and salt marshes have been assaulted from both directions by those wishing to develop the sandy beaches and the uplands. Long ago the Lenape Indians came to the Jersey shore to gather clams and mussels or to fish, but they abandoned the shore in the early summer when the hordes of mosquitoes began to emerge, and were long gone before the biting mosquitoes and greenhead flies blanketed the coast. (Modern New Jersey folks can well understand their plight, and often refer to the salt marsh mosquito as the state bird.) The Lenape came again in the early fall when the cold autumn nights put an end to these seaside scourges. In the dead of winter, when cold winds blew in from the ocean, they again went inland.

The Indians gathered horseshoe crabs to bury as fertilizer for their crops, and saved the tails for spearheads. Trails through the high marsh led to clam or mussel beds, or to good places for spear fishing. The Lenape built traps of sticks and reeds to catch fish. Brush was used to steer the fish along the edge of the marsh, until they were funneled into enclosures. Once the tide fell, the Indians could pull the fish from the shallow water. Several hundred years of Lenape use, however, did not markedly alter the marsh.

Native Americans did not change the water flow along the coast, nor did they try to fill in the marsh. They merely caught the fish and shellfish, hunted sea ducks, and returned to their upland homes to plant crops and hunt deer.

Since the mid-1600s when Europeans first settled New Jersey, the marshes have been flooded or drained, impounded or diked, and ditched or filled. Marshes have been converted into hay fields for livestock; drained to prevent mosquito breeding; filled to provide land for marinas, houses, and parking lots; and polluted by trash, heavy metals, oil, and other chemicals. For centuries salt marshes were viewed as wasteland to be reclaimed, or valuable property to be developed. Only recently have we developed a deep appreciation for salt marshes in their own right, as one of the most productive ecosystems in the world, and as nurseries for the bountiful life of the estuaries and the sea beyond.

Salt marshes were also an integral part of the "life-support system" of the early European settlers in New Jersey. When they first arrived there were few open meadows where livestock could forage, and it was a big job to clear the forest. They pastured their cows on the high marshes where the salt hay grew. Here the cattle were less likely to succumb to marauding wolves. Wolves were once widespread in New Jersey, and bounties, offered for them as early as 1682, were paid until 1750. These natural predators were abundant in the state as late as 1770, and the last wolf in New Jersey was shot in 1855.

Putting livestock on salt marshes was not without problems, for many animals sunk in the mud and mire, and could not be freed. Fencing was costly. The farmers learned to put the cattle only on the highest marshes, where they could avoid the muddy creeks and pools. Still, moving them back and forth among salt-marsh pastures was difficult.

Soon the settlers decided to leave the cattle at home and bring the salt hay to them. At first farmers cut the salt hay in the fall, for the long winter. Then they cut the hay repeatedly for use throughout the year. They used horses in the drier parts of the salt-hay meadows, covering the animals' heads and bodies so they were less bothered by mosquitoes. The horses' hooves sank in the muck, so they were shod with wide wooden shoes. Salt hay was the vital food source that made it possible to keep livestock, and in the early settlement years before the 1700s, livestock was the mainstay of agriculture in New Jersey, for not enough land was cleared for more traditional crops.

Settlers even cut some of the coarser cordgrass, which they called thatch hay, for roofs and for animal bedding. It was soon abandoned as a roofing material because it dried too quickly and caught fire. Thatching was traditional in European homelands where damp conditions prevented fire, but here the air was too dry. Cordgrass remained in use for burial mattresses, or for packing when transporting fragile products, until the late 1800s. Salt hay was put to many other uses by the early settlers. From it they made paper and rope, and they used it for packing material and to stabilize dunes.

In the 1600s the distribution of many towns was determined by the availability of salt marshes suitable for haying. Salt marshes with few creeks and dry paths were highly prized. The salt-hay meadows were often owned by

3.1. Salt hay piles on staddles and hay on gandalow (wooden raft) ready to float out with high tide.

towns, and the right to mow was auctioned off early in the spring. On a good salt-hay marsh, farmers could realize a ton per acre, comparable to what they could produce on an upland meadow that required seeding.

The salt hay was cut and placed on wooden "staddles" to keep it above the high tides (Figure 3.1), which could ruin the hay or carry it out to sea. The tall haystacks were visible all over the marsh. When the farmers needed the hay, or when winter approached, they placed it on "gandalows," or small boats, and floated it home on flood tides.

The early settlers of New Jersey also made use of several other salt-marsh plants. They ate glasswort, a little, watery-stemmed, shrubby plant that grows on the sandier parts of the marsh (Figure 3.2). Young shoots were added to salads, or were pickled for the long winter. When I lived on Little Beach Island I often sprinkled glasswort on salads, but found it is too salty to make up the bulk of a salad. Some of the early settlers called it salt-wort because of its salty taste, while others called it pickle plant. They also discovered marsh mallow, which they boiled to make a mucilaginous substance used to cure dysentery and coughs. Any leftovers were boiled with sugar to make a marshmallow confection appreciated by all. The early settlers admired the rich pink flowers of rose mallow, and soon transplanted them to their gardens (Figure 3.3). Today these plants still grace the gardens of folks along the shore, and these treasures even bloom profusely in my Somerset garden.

It goes without saying that the early settlers thrived on fish and shellfish caught along the shore. Ribbed mussels growing on the muddy banks provided a dependable meal, when blue crabs or fish were hard to catch. The

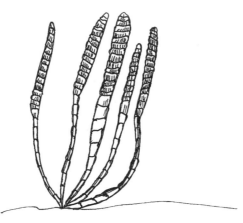

3.2. Glasswort, a small succulent plant that grows on the salt marsh, was used for salads and for pickles.

settlers also hunted shorebirds and ducks that were so abundant during migration. In the fall and winter there were flocks of wintering waterfowl to shoot or trap. Diamondback terrapins were also captured for stews and soups. These estuarine turtles were so common and easily caught that they were frequently fed to slaves or other servants. Lobsters were so plentiful along the Jersey shore that they were considered a trash food, fit only for the lower classes.

The early settlers also learned from the Lenape that crops grew better when Horseshoe Crabs were used as fertilizer, and people flocked to Delaware Bay to gather them in late May. Smaller numbers were gathered at Brigantine and at other places along the shore. Horseshoe crabs were also used as bait in the 1880s for capturing eels. An eel basket, about twenty inches long, contained a smaller inner funnel-shaped basket, with the horseshoe crab bait at one end. The eels forced their way through the open end of the first funnel basket, then pressed through the oak strips of the second basket that allowed them to enter and eat the crab.

English grasses or field grasses were introduced into New England in the 1700s, and their use quickly spread to New Jersey. Forests had to be cleared before the new, soft grasses could be planted, whereas salt hay was there for the taking. As more land was cleared, salt hay became less important. It was easier to plant grass seeds, and horses did not become enmeshed in the mud. Even so, salt hay continued to be used widely until the early 1900s.

In fact, when I first arrived in New Jersey in the early 1970s, salt hay was still being harvested by some bay men, mostly for animal bedding, mulch-

3.3. Rose mallow was transplanted to gardens to provide bright pink color in late July and August.

ing, and topping of hay stacks to keep the upland field grasses dry. It was no longer used as fodder for cattle. Old-timers insisted that salt hay was still used for burial mattresses, replacing the thatch grass. Even today, local residents along the shore use dried salt hay and eelgrass for mulch in their gardens or to protect overwintering plants.

In the late 1700s saltworks were quite numerous along Barnegat Bay. Many were small one-family operations, but others, such as the one at Tom's River, employed several men. They were considered so important that the state of New Jersey deployed two companies of militiamen to protect them in 1776, and the British targeted them for destruction as part of the Revolutionary War effort. Many saltworks in Barnegat Bay were destroyed during the war, but others survived, although they were periodically

3.4. Barnegat Bay sneakbox, with similar duck blind sunk on salt-marsh island.

disrupted by storm tides. Saltworks incapacitated by storm tides usually were repaired quickly, and salt production continued for many years.

Birds along the Jersey coast were always exploited, first by the Lenape Indians, then by the early settlers. At first, birds were killed for local consumption only, and since human populations were low, the resource did not suffer. Gradually, more hunters specialized in migratory birds. Because ammunition was costly, hunters tried to maximize their kills by hunting at night. They crawled along the marsh with a bright torch and grabbed the roosting birds that were dazzled by the light. People became alarmed with the rapid decreases in shorebirds, and night lighting was outlawed in many shore communities. Still the hunting continued.

Duck hunting gave rise to the Barnegat sneakbox, a boat developed in 1836 by Captain Hazleton Seaman of West Creek, New Jersey (Figure 3.4). It is a unique, flat-bottomed boat, covered except for the open square for the gunner. It also has a hatch cover, which protects the inside from rain, snow, falling leaves, and other debris when not in service. Duck decoys were stored in the sneakbox during the winter. Many salt-marsh islands have sunken shooting blinds that resemble sneakboxes, and these too are covered over when not in use.

Some of the greatest devastation along the Jersey shore occurred in the late 1800s, when there was massive gunning of birds for market. New Jersey lies in the middle of the Atlantic flyway, and thousands upon thousands of shorebirds, waterfowl, and other birds migrate along the shore each spring and fall. For two hundred years the settlers hunted shorebirds and waterfowl for their own use, content to kill only what they or their neighbors could eat. Then a market began to develop in the cities, and a demand for ducks and shorebirds was born. Shooting shorebirds became a business. There was a profit to be made. Special boats were developed with long, large-bore shotguns; dozens of shorebirds or ducks could be felled by a single shot. This was the same era that saw the demise of the passenger pigeon.

The demand for birds for food continued, market-gunning was in full stride. Then a new scourge enveloped the coast. It became the fashion to festoon hats, shawls, and coats with bird feathers. White was a particularly fashionable color, and any bird bearing white feathers was fair game. Gulls, terns, and shorebirds dropped from the skies in droves. Soon women wanted larger and larger white feathers, and the plumes of egrets and herons were highly prized above all others.

Not content with a feather of two, milliners added whole wings, and finally whole birds to hats. It was not unusual to see a hat with a whole tern or shorebird, along with dozens of other feathers. The demand from Europe and the United States was insatiable, and gunners appeared along the entire Atlantic coast. Now the guns were more efficient, boats were more available, and ammunition was cheaper than it had ever been. Unable to rely only on migratory birds, plume hunters sought out nesting colonies. Within a few years in the 1870s and 1880s shooters nearly eliminated most egrets, herons, gulls, and terns. Long before there was legal protection, the birds became too scarce to make hunting worthwhile, and plume hunting was largely abandoned.

The great flocks of shorebirds had all but disappeared from the Jersey shore, they fell to the hunter's guns early. Soon herons and egrets disappeared, followed by rapid declines in gulls and terns. The destruction was happening all along the Atlantic coast, in marsh after marsh, on beach after beach. Many species were eliminated entirely as breeding species from one state after another.

At the turn of the century the National Audubon Society was formed, largely to protect our dwindling herons and egrets. These magnificent birds were in danger of disappearing from our coastal environments forever. Laws were passed that protected migratory birds, and treaties were signed with Canada and Mexico. Persecution stopped, and most of our coastal species were protected from further hunting.

Gradually, as bird populations increased in the less-populated southern states where market gunning was less severe, the birds spread north again, taking over their former breeding ranges. Slowly the populations of herons, egrets, ibis, gulls, and terns began to increase along our coasts, finally re-colonizing New Jersey in the 1930s and 1940s. Today these species are an integral part of coastal ecosystems, but for want of a fashionable hat, we almost eliminated them forever.

The most conspicuous alteration of the salt marshes came with the realization that draining the marshes partially eliminated standing water, thereby reducing the number of mosquitoes that could breed. The salt marsh mosquito is a small but formidable creature. After the discovery of mosquito-borne diseases at the turn of the century, it became feared as something more than merely an annoyance. New Jersey has the dubious distinction of being the birthplace of marsh ditching as a method of reducing mosquito populations. Mosquito ditching began in New Jersey at the turn of the century, but it was practiced most widely during the Great Depression.

Following the First World War, large gangs were put to work digging ditches across the marshes of New England, New York, and New Jersey. Almost no marshes escaped the Civilian Conservation Corps or the Works Progress Administration. In almost all of our marshes the characteristic patterns still remain of straight, parallel ditches running from the upland edge of the marsh to the larger tidal creeks. The ditches, usually spaced 115 to 230 feet apart, were designed to remove pools and standing water from the marsh. Draining the marshes became a major societal goal. By 1938 almost 90 percent of the tidal wetlands from Maine to Virginia were ditched.

Ditching had an immediate and massive effect on our salt marshes: it dried many of them, shifted the vegetation from low-salt marsh vegetation to high-salt marsh vegetation, and changed the population of animals that could live there. Ditching enhanced the growth of high-marsh plants at the expense of cordgrass. Where the workers deposited soil from the ditches, high-marsh grasses and woody bushes moved in. Although some songbirds could use these bushes for nesting, the traditional salt-marsh species such as gulls, terns, sparrows, and clapper rails were forced out. Their populations declined. The masses of shorebirds that fed on the low-marsh pools were gone.

The removal of standing water from the marshes not only controlled mosquitoes, but it also reduced the number of other invertebrates and birds that fed on the mosquitoes, and it eliminated the algae and other vegetation that grew in these pools and ponds. No longer could salt-marsh minnows survive on the low marsh, and they are an important part of the complex food web. Dozens of changes went unnoticed until the 1960s.

In the last thirty years New Jersey has lead the nation again, this time in developing techniques to control mosquitoes without draining the marshes, and in restoring marshes by blocking some of these drainage ditches. Several people working for the Department of Fish, Game and Wildlife and from Rutgers University, in conjunction with people in the local mosquito commissions, developed a method of mosquito control known as "open marsh water management."

Open marsh water management eliminates breeding sites for the salt marsh mosquito by restoring the normal tidal water regime on the marsh, and by opening the mosquito breeding pools to tidal movement. Once the pools and pans are exposed to regular tidal flow, fish move in, and the fish eat the mosquito larvae before they emerge from the water surface. When needed, ditches are not cut in straight lines, but emulate the natural curves to open a creek or pond to tidal flow. The resulting muck, or "spoil," pulled from the marsh is broadcast widely over a large area, and few high-marsh areas are created that aid the invasion of high-marsh bushes such as marsh elder or sea myrtle. Wherever possible, earth-moving equipment moves over the marsh and creates meandering ditches that resemble natural salt-marsh creeks. Water control, rather than water drainage, is the key to present mosquito control.

Pesticides were used to control mosquitoes for about twenty years. Then the rising cost of pesticide application, as well as public concerns over repeated use of pesticides, led to greater implementation of water management. Studies of marshes where open marsh water management has been applied show that fish species composition is similar to that of unaltered marshes. This type of water management also results in fewer adverse effects on feeding and breeding birds. Shorebirds, clapper rails, and songbirds can once again find places to feed on marshes altered only by open marsh water management, and breeding sites are available again for these species.

Just when the marshes were beginning to recover from the devastation of ditching, they are being polluted by a variety of heavy metals, petroleum hydrocarbons, and other chemicals. Salt marshes are particularly vulnerable to oil spills because tidal flow continues to bring oil onto the marsh long after the initial spill. Cordgrass is usually the hardest hit because it forms the front edge of the marsh, where most of the oil washes on shore. A massive oil spill, such as occurred in the Arthur Kill in January 1990, kills outright all the cordgrass along the creeks, where most of the invertebrates live. In the Arthur Kill, some 20 percent of the salt-marsh vegetation was killed by the 1990 oil spill. It destroyed the habitat for many invertebrates that form the basis for the food web. Fortunately, that oil spill occurred in the winter when the vegetation and marine life were dormant; the effects from an oil spill in the summer would be far greater.

Heavy metals such as mercury, lead, cadmium, and tin are pollutants that are ubiquitous in the estuaries along the Jersey shore. To be sure, pollutant levels are higher in the New York Bight and in Delaware Bay than anywhere else in the United States, but heavy metals are present in tissues of birds everywhere I have sampled along the Jersey shore. Although some heavy metals are naturally occurring in the soil, by far the greatest input to our coastal estuaries comes from human-generated, called anthropogenic, sources.

Mercury, lead, and cadmium cause a variety of problems for animals and humans. Very high levels, of course, can be fatal, but lower levels cause a variety of physiological, morphological, and behavioral abnormalities. Even low levels reduce reproductive success for most invertebrates, fish, and birds. More subtle effects include slower reaction time, making the birds more vulnerable to predators, or less able to catch their own food. Heavy metals, such as lead, can affect the ability of young chicks to distinguish their parents from others, and they get killed by neighbors they unwittingly approach.

With the banning of leaded gasoline, the levels of lead in our coastal waters have decreased, with similar decreases in the tissues of marine organisms. Although levels of lead in terns nesting in the New York–New Jersey area decreased from the early 1970s to 1989, they have started to increase again. The cause of this increase in unclear, but it bears watching. Currently, some birds in the New York–New Jersey harbor have lead levels in their feathers that are similar to those that cause behavioral abnormalities in the laboratory.

Similar regulations on mercury have decreased the level of mercury in coastal waters. However, we all have to worry about changes in atmospheric heavy metals. The global levels of mercury have tripled over the last one hundred years and are expected to triple over the next hundred years. Atmospheric mercury is deposited over the earth and makes its way into the aquatic food chain.

Other pollutants such as DDT and PCBs occur along the Jersey shore. DDT is less of a problem today than twenty-five years ago, because of its ban in the early 1970s following the realization that populations of fish and birds which were top predators had declined or crashed. After the public was alerted by Rachel Carson's controversial book *Silent Spring* in the early 1960s, it took nearly a decade before this widely used pesticide was banned. Carson warned that unless we acted, we soon would have no raptors, no fish-eating birds, and no top predatory fish. We did react with laws and regulations to ban the use of DDT. Some DDT is still present in our coastal ecosystems because of its long persistence, and migratory fish and birds can pick up DDT from their tropical wintering grounds, since the pesticide is widely applied elsewhere. PCBs continue to be a problem for many of our coastal ecosystems because of their former widespread use in so many electrical devices, and their persistence. Like DDT, PCBs are resistant to degradation, and they bioaccumulate in organisms high on the food chain.

There is concern for heavy metals, DDT, and PCBs, and oil in marine

3.5. Blue crab used heavily as food by early settlers, and still harvested today.

ecosystems because of their detrimental effects on wildlife. Like eagles, peregrines, bluefish, herons, and terns, humans are also top predators. We eat fish, shellfish, and ducks that concentrate these pollutants, and we are vulnerable to the same physiological and behavioral effects. Although many states, including New Jersey, have issued some advisories or warnings regarding the consumption of fish and shellfish, these warnings often go unheeded, because they are not taken seriously, or the risk is deemed small, or they are not made available to the consuming public. In heavily urban areas, many people do not read English, and thus advisories posted near fishing sites are ignored. I have found that people fishing and crabbing along the Arthur Kill are exposed to higher levels of contaminants through consumption of fish and blue crabs than are deemed safe by our regulatory agencies (Figure 3.5). Such levels pose a direct health risk, particularly to pregnant women.

Over the last ten years, there has been increasing concern over the role of PCBs, DDTs, heavy metals, and other toxics because they act as environmental estrogens. This means that these chemicals bind to the estrogen receptors in the body, resulting in either the feminization of males or the masculinization of females. Environmental estrogens have already been linked to a number of behavioral and reproductive effects in birds, including decreased parental care, embryo inviability, behavioral abnormalities of the chicks, and lowered reproductive success. Similar problems have been reported in mammals. These effects have been clearly demonstrated in both the laboratory and in the field. Although much more tenuous, environmental estrogens have been linked to both breast cancer and decreased sperm counts in humans. We may be just at the point where we are seeing more subtle, but potentially more lethal effects of toxic chemicals. Once again, birds served as the early warning signal.

Of all our coastal ecosystems, marshes are particularly vulnerable to pollutants because they receive daily tidal flooding. This provides an avenue for repeated exposure not available to sandy beaches, sand dunes, and barrier beach uplands or forests. Any pollutant issuing from a given source is quickly spread throughout bays and estuaries, and then is carried by tides to marshes, where it is incorporated into the biota, or is buried in the sediments. Either way, it circulates through the ecosystem, ultimately finding its way to the fish and shellfish that we eat.

The "salt prairies" have served us well, providing food for our livestock and for ourselves since the early settlement days. They are part of the nurseries that nourish the bays and estuaries, and the ocean beyond. They form the basis of the food chain, and are some of the most highly productive ecosystems in the world. They serve as nesting areas for birds forced to abandon the barrier beaches. More recently, their ability to shield the land from violent storms and tides, and to cleanse our environment from pollutants, has been recognized as a valuable function in its own right. Moreover, we are beginning to use organisms that live along the shore as sentinels or indicators of exposure to environmental toxics, for like the other organisms along the coast, we also are vulnerable.

4

Is Global Climate
Change a Threat?

Change along the shore is inevitable. The sheer force of the sea has been changing the shape of the shoreline for eons and will continue to do so indefinitely. Sand is picked up from one beach and deposited on another; inlets are cut by the force of the waves in one place, while others are filled in. Some changes are apparent from one year to the next. A wide expanse of beach may all but wash away over the winter, or an island may find itself suddenly a peninsula. Other changes are more subtle, occurring over decades.

I love to look at old maps of New Jersey from even a century ago. Inlets are in slightly different places, the barrier islands have enlarged or shrunk, the shapes of the barrier islands and marshes are different, and some marsh islands disappeared altogether, while others are much larger (Figure 4.1). Lighthouses that once stood on the edge of an island now stand in the middle, Coast Guard Houses are surrounded by maritime forests rather than the open sea (Figure 4.2). In general, the tips of barrier islands are most vulnerable, particularly where inlets are narrow and the currents are stiff (Figure 4.3).

Superimposed upon these changes are those that occur on a geologic time scale. The forming and receding of ice ages altered the amount of water in the oceans and on land in the form of glaciers, with profound impact on the location and shape of the shore. This cycle too will continue. The final retreat of the Laurentide Glacier some 10,000 years ago started the development of our coastal salt marshes and barrier islands.

The slow, inevitable movement of the continents riding on the broad tectonic plates that underlie our land masses also alters coastlines, although over millions of years. This continental drift will continue. North America is drifting westward, albeit very slowly.

Natural, geological forces are not the only ones that affect our shoreline. Global change in the form of land-use change and climate change are also important forces that shape coastal ecosystems. These natural forces that shaped the coast could once act without any barriers, but now our shores

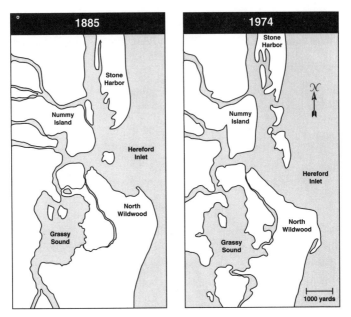

4.1. Map showing changes along the shore at Hereford Inlet. Drawn from U.S. Coast and Geodetic Survey map of Cape May (1885) and NOAA Nautical Chart 825C-SC for Intracoastal Waterway.

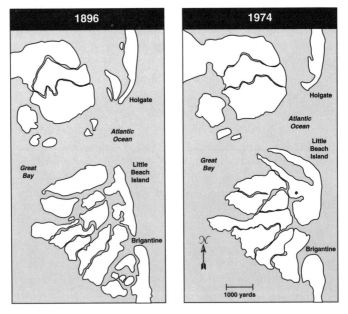

4.2. Map showing changes along the shore at Little Beach Island. Drawn from U.S. Coast and Geodetic Survey map of 1896 (Egg Harbor map) and NOAA Nautical Chart 825C-SC for Intracoastal Waterway.

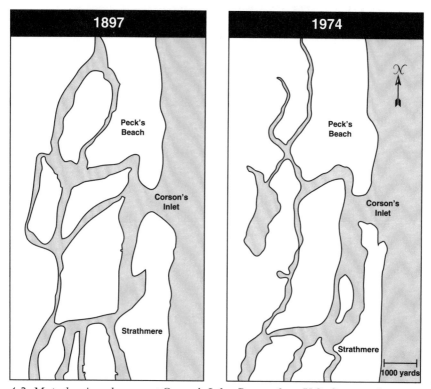

4.3. Map showing changes at Corson's Inlet. Drawn from U.S. Coast and Geodetic Survey map of 1896 and NOAA Nautical Chart 826-SC for Intracoastal Waterway.

are littered with houses and marinas, with jetties, bulkheads, and other structures meant to preserve the coastline as we know it. The force of the sea is stronger than our jetties and bulkheads, and the Army Corps of Engineers spends millions of dollars each year shifting sand from one place to another, building new jetties, nourishing beaches, trying to restore the coast as we want it. Yet every year the sea reshapes the sands according to its own plan.

Another man-made threat looms on the horizon: global climate change. Climatologists have warned us that the increase in so-called greenhouse gases will lead to global warming by preventing excess solar energy from escaping back into space. Greenhouse gases include carbon dioxide, methane, and chlorofluorocarbons (CFCs) such as freon and nitrous oxide. In the hundred years since the industrial revolution, CO^2 has increased by 25 percent, and this rise is likely to continue. There has been an average increase in global surface temperatures of up to 4 degrees F. over the last one hundred years.

Using sophisticated mathematical models of atmospheric processes, climatologists have predicted global temperature changes of 5 to 9 degrees F. over the next century. If the climate models are correct, the earth will not only be warmer in the next one hundred years than it has been during the last million years, the change will also have occurred more rapidly than any other on record. Many profound changes will occur. Global warming would result in changing rainfall patterns and melting of some glaciers and polar ice caps. This additional water from melting ice would flow to the seas, raising sea level several feet.

Although often referred to as global warming, a climatic change toward higher temperatures is by no means a foregone conclusion. Even if the change is in the direction of warming, the earth will not warm uniformly, nor will a place warm uniformly over the year. Some atmospheric scientists believe that changes in landscape structure have already affected local and regional climate, and that this effect is equal to or greater than the changes predicted by increases in greenhouse gases. That is, there is a feedback loop between local or regional climate and vegetation. When an area is entirely and uniformly vegetated, the reflection of light and heat from the land surface is less than it would be if the land were covered with sidewalks or devoid of vegetation. Changes in reflectance, called albedo, affect not only the local temperature, but also rainfall patterns. This is particularly true of coastal regions where there is a ready source of water for evapotranspiration.

Whatever the direction of the climate change, the change will not be uniform throughout the world, or even throughout the United States. Climate change will result in changes in humidity, changes in precipitation, and changes in temperature. One possible result of climate change is sea-level rise because the polar ice caps will melt.

Climate change is difficult to demonstrate because our historical temperature records are limited, and long-term data are available for only a small number of sites. One consequence of global change, sea-level rise, is easier to demonstrate. Apparent sea-level rise, however, is a result both of increases in the level of the sea and the subsidence of the land. At the same time that changes in sea level are occurring, there are changes in the relative position of the land. Land can either rise (accretion) or fall (subsidence). Land rises through the process of accretion, whereby soil is added to the top of the land and incorporated into the peat or humus.

I am often asked "What will sea-level rise do to New Jersey?" "Should I sell my beach house and move inland?" and "Will the birds all disappear because they will have no place to nest?" The long-term answer to these questions is, of course, "it depends." But the short-term answer is that at present the accretion of land on New Jersey's barrier beaches and salt marshes is more than adequate to ensure that our barrier islands and salt marshes will march ever so slowly landward, keeping well ahead of any currently predicted sea-level rises.

There will be changes along the shore, to be sure, but these changes are the ones that have always occurred. The dunes will shift, salt-marsh islands will come and go, and sand will be blown from one beach to another. The very shape of salt-marsh islands will change, as will the shape of sand spits and inlets.

The longer answer is that it depends upon whether the global change is toward warming or cooling (less or more water tied up in glaciers), whether the effects of increased greenhouse gases are in the predicted direction, whether the effects of increases in anthropogenic greenhouse gases are sufficient to cause the predicted effects, whether the land is subsiding or rising at a particular locality, and whether accretion can keep up with changing sea levels.

The rate of sea-level rise is accelerating due both to natural and human-induced causes. Climatologists generally expect that anthropogenic global warming could raise sea level 10 to 60 inches in the next century. One of the impacts could be loss of coastal wetlands. The inundation of adjacent uplands would enable new wetlands to form. If there is available land, then barrier islands and salt marshes will march inland, and the coastal ecosystems will be preserved. The ability of wetlands to move inland requires that this land be available and undeveloped. Sufficient land still exists in the United States to accommodate these changes, but we are quickly using up that land.

In many countries, such as the Netherlands and China, wetlands are already squeezed between an advancing sea and the land being protected. People then build elaborate dikes to hold off the sea. The United States should develop a policy that protects some land above the salt marshes that will be available for the landward migrating coastal zone.

In considering the question of sea-level rise, it is important to remember that tidal salt marshes develop owing to the interaction between sea-level rise, tides, accumulation of organic and inorganic sediments, and growth of the salt-adapted grasses. Thus salt marshes have developed due to accumulation of marine sediments in protected bays and estuaries, submergence of upland areas in direct response to sea-level rises, and accumulation of fluvial sediments associated with river delta systems.

Most of our current salt marshes were formed about 4,000 years ago when there was a reduction in the rate of sea-level rise from an inch a year, to less than half inch a year. Since that time, the coastal marshes have continued to build. However, sea-level rise seems to have accelerated in the past century, perhaps equivalent to the rise that took place over 4,000 years ago. In the last one hundred years we may have lost nearly 50 percent of our tidal wetlands, but most of this loss was due to the direct activities of people, not to any changes in sea level. Clearly the rate of salt-marsh loss due to human development must cease if we are to leave a suitable buffer of accreting salt marshes to protect our coasts.

Since each salt-marsh ecosystem has its own set of factors controlling continued development, it is impossible to predict shifts without examining each marsh separately. For accretion to occur, there must be both a healthy marsh and the presence of sufficient sediment to add to the marsh through natural processes. This suggests that policies that involve the removal or movement of sand from barrier beaches should be carefully reviewed. These sediments must be available so that the natural process of salt-marsh buildup can occur. If the marsh can maintain accretion rates equalling or exceeding coastal submergence rates, the marsh will remain habitable.

Compared to other ecosystems, coastal habitats have an opportunity to adapt to sea-level rise because they are created by low levels of sea-level rise, and they have experienced sea-level rise throughout their evolutionary history. At present, the salt marshes of New Jersey are accreting at a faster rate than sea level is rising.

Solidly Spring

5

Oystercatchers and
Willets along the Shore

The fog lifts grudgingly, revealing a broad expanse of flattened brown *Spartina* stems, broken only by a small clump of short, scraggly marsh elder bushes. Waves lap softly at the peat edge while the tide slowly rises on a Barnegat Bay salt-marsh island. The mist drifts in and out, the island edge is momentarily visible, but the rest of the world no longer exists. A pair of oystercatchers huddles at the nearby creek edge, their long red bills pointing downward, their dark brown backs making a shadowy outline in the fog. Early April on a salt marsh can be very cold, and as the light rain continues, the fog moves past, occasionally hiding the birds from view.

One oystercatcher bends to probe at a dark oblong object, no doubt a ribbed mussel lodged in the peat just at low tide level. American oystercatchers feed on mussels, marine worms, crabs, and anything else they can find to open. Even with a knife I have trouble opening a mussel shell, but this oystercatcher does it quickly by shattering a small hole in the shell with a few powerful blows, and inserting its strong bill in the hole to cut the strong abductor muscle before prying open the shell (Figure 5.1). I often find piles of mussel shells lying at the creek's edge, silent reminders of other oystercatcher meals.

Not so many years ago oystercatchers were rare in New Jersey, and worth a special trip to see. They were a bird of more southern climes, where they nested on sandy shores. Over the years their numbers have increased, and six or seven pairs may nest on a single salt-marsh island or along a stretch of sand dunes and beaches in New Jersey. The first pair to nest in Maine did so in 1994, so they have continued to spread northward.

In Barnegat Bay they usually nest on salt-marsh islands, shunning the heavily populated beaches. They nest where small strips of sand fringe an island, or on the highest part of the marsh itself, or even on *Spartina* or eelgrass wrack. It is still early, and the pair makes no courtship gestures. They look uncomfortable on this raw morning, but are patiently waiting for warmer weather.

5.1. Oystercatcher cutting open ribbed mussels along salt marsh creek.

As April wears on, the sun warms the marsh, the winds subside, and tiny green *Spartina* stems an inch or two high begin to emerge, eventually changing the brown and beige to a vibrant green. Here and there long ribbons of salt-and-pepper eelgrass, washed ashore by winter storms, form dense, high mats. Masses of dark brownish green eelgrass mats are the fresh material that last summer grew in long thin strands on the floor of the bay, while the pale mats are remnants of debris washed up long ago that have been bleached by the sun for several years. These bleached mats are preferred by birds for nesting because they have lain undisturbed for several years, indicating their relative safety from high tides. If high water had reached them, they would have drifted away, carried by ebbing tides.

At most of the islands we are greeted by the loud, musical piping of the oystercatcher pairs or even trios. The loud staccato calls are given as they defend their space against a neighboring pair. During these aerial piping displays, they chase each other back and forth along the marsh, establishing the boundary, and reinforcing their own pair bond. Sometimes they display on the ground, particularly when two pairs decide to claim the same narrow strip of sand along a salt-marsh edge.

In late April I find the first nest, four lightly speckled eggs in a depres-

5.2. Pair of oystercatchers looking for a suitable nest site in a wet salt marsh.

sion on a mat. The eggs all point inward, the most efficient way for an oystercatcher to incubate them. Like those of most shorebirds, the eggs are relatively large for the birds' body size, because the young are fully developed and precocial when they hatch. They are covered with down, their eyes are open, and they can walk about on their own and feed themselves within hours of hatching.

In New Jersey, oystercatchers are very versatile, and nest both on salt-marsh islands and on the barrier beaches. They nest on white sand amid least terns or black skimmers, or on wrack or a spot of sand or mud on salt marshes (Figure 5.2). They even nest within the cordgrass when they can find a high spot that will not be flooded out. They nest alone, with no other birds within hundreds of yards, or they may nest in the middle of colonies of terns and skimmers. Oystercatchers begin nesting well before the terns and skimmers arrive, indicating that their choice of a nest site is not dependent upon the presence of these other colonially nesting birds.

By early May the marsh is no longer silent. For above the oystercatcher's nest a mass of common terns swirl in the air, calling loudly, swooping toward me on silvery wings, and emitting harsh attack calls. A group of eight skimmers fly determinedly away, barking loudly, and circling back to see if I still remain. They fly in formation, their dark wings barely avoiding each other, wheeling in the sun only to fly off again.

Taking my boat offshore a bit, I wait without moving. Gradually the oystercatchers, terns, and skimmers settle, each landing on its own territory. The skimmers stand on the center of the largest mat. There is room for a few terns at the mat edge, but most are scattered in the marsh grass, where they assemble small platforms of grass stems. The colony returns to relative peace, neighbors display to one another, and pairs continue to court

5.3. Oystercatcher (center) incubating in a tern (bottom) and skimmer (right) colony. Common terns are giving courtship displays.

(Figure 5.3). Common terns burst from the marsh, one bird carrying a fish, another following, and they fly high overhead in a ritualized courtship flight. A male skimmer arrives with a large fish in its bill to courtship-feed his female, she takes the fish, turns, and he mounts her. With the fish in her mouth, they copulate. The male extends his wings to keep balance, for they mate for about a minute.

Even though oystercatchers will nest away from tern and skimmer colonies, they take advantage of the other birds' ability to defend themselves. When a crow or marsh hawk flies across the marsh, the oyster-catchers slip silently from their nests and fly to the edge of the marsh. Their nests are safe because the terns are aggressive and mob the intruder, escorting it out of the colony.

In mid-May clutches of two and three skimmer eggs dot the mat, each in a well-worn depression that serves as the nest cup. The nests are a yard or two apart, and their whitish eggs with dark brown splotches are smaller and paler than the oystercatcher's. On the mat edges and out in the marsh grass the common tern nests have one or two eggs that have dark splotches on a beige or olive background, smaller still in size than the skimmer eggs. In only a few days most skimmer nests will have three to five eggs, and most terns' will have three.

The oystercatcher silently incubates its clutch of four, its mate standing nearby, seemingly guarding the rest of the colony. It is an illusion, however, for the oystercatchers on some salt-marsh islands have systematically eaten all the tern and skimmer eggs. All that remains is a lone pair of oystercatchers and remnants of nests with empty eggs, each neatly slit in half. This colony is peaceful, and the oystercatchers incubate quietly along with the skimmers and terns. When the oystercatcher's mate returns to take its turn at incubation, the skimmers stand to jab at it and call loudly, but otherwise the exchange between the oystercatchers is quiet; and the off-duty oyster-catcher flies off to feed at the water's edge.

Retreating to our boat, Fred Lesser and I continue our survey of the salt-marsh islands in Barnegat Bay. Twice a week we travel the length of Barnegat Bay, counting the gulls, terns, and skimmers on all the salt-marsh islands. Common terns nest on twenty-six of the islands this year, Skimmers nest on twelve , and oystercatchers nest on twenty-one. All but one are salt-marsh islands where the oystercatchers nest on mats; on Mordecai a long ribbon of sand provides space for six or seven pairs of oystercatchers. On most is-lands only one or two pairs nest.

In late May both oystercatchers stare fixedly at the nest, two tiny all gray-and-black chicks huddle together, while soft squeaks come from the other two partly pipped eggs. Within three hours all of the chicks have hatched, their ungainly bodies perched atop long black, wobbly legs and very large, sprawling feet. They blend with the speckled wrack, and I find them only because I know the nest's location. The family leaves the nest site almost immediately, but will usually remain nearby for several weeks. In a few days, the chicks will be graceful and hard to find.

Leaving them, we visit another island where the oystercatcher chicks are a week old. The family stands at the marsh edge, the parents probing for mussels, removing them from the mud, opening them, and delicately of-fering the tiny morsels to the chicks. Unlike most shorebirds, oystercatcher parents feed their young for several weeks while the chicks learn how to open mussels and other mollusks for themselves. Similarly, the foraging techniques of oystercatchers are very difficult to learn, and they must de-velop strong enough bills to pry open their prey. The parents lead the chicks to food, and pick up items and present them to the chicks.

On most islands we are greeted by a pair or two of oystercatchers, al-though their chicks are rarely visible. We walk toward the adults, they take to the air, and only a blur of motion running for the safety of the grass in-dicates that their chicks are safe. As the chicks grow larger, they move to the edge of the islands. The cordgrass is now green and lush; a foot tall, it will get no taller.

As we walk across the marsh a willet bursts from the grass at our feet, much as ducks will do when disturbed. As it flies from the nest, it hesitates, as if it will fall, and makes a few very exaggerated, deep wing beats. This usually succeeds in distracting the attention of the intruder, but we have watched them before, and so we stand our ground. Instead of disappearing, the willet circles around, calling loudly. The white wing patches glisten in the sun, and the willet dips closer and closer to us on each pass. After admiring the willet's attempts at distraction, we bend and begin to search the grass at our feet.

In most places the cordgrass is sparse and short, indicating a low level of tidal inundation, but to our right the grass is a bit taller, a bit denser, and seems to be twisted by the wind. Carefully we part this clump to reveal a nest with four large speckled eggs, each pointing toward the center. Although their eggs are cryptically colored, willets always hide their nests in the vegetation, and the eggs are not visible from any direction.

Willets seem to prefer dense clumps of grass, perhaps because these are on slightly higher ground. The nest, well constructed of dried cordgrass and salt hay, is woven into a nice cup. The grass was thicker here, but the incubating willets still pulled the grass over the nest as they incubated, making a closed canopy. When incubating, willets are impossible to locate except by nearly stepping on them. Only then will they burst from the nest. As we drive past an island, oystercatchers can be counted by scanning the marsh for their conspicuous brown body and red bill, but breeding Willets must be counted by painstakingly walking back and forth over the marsh.

Most of the salt-marsh islands in the inland waterways of New Jersey have resident willets and, depending upon the size of the island, may have three or four nesting pairs. They nest later than the oystercatchers, and their young hatch about the same time as the terns and skimmers. The young remain in the nest for a day or two, until all the chicks are dry and fluffy, and then the parents lead them from the nest. They do not go to the water or to the marsh edge, but stay hidden within the marsh grasses, where they feed on insects and invertebrates. The parents remain with their brood, although the chicks must find their own food.

The willets have a strategy for reproductive success that includes being spread out across the marsh, hiding their nests, and bursting to safety only when a predator is almost on top of the nest. The rapid departure usually startles a predator, and it either moves on or follows the adult willet. Although they sometimes nest on islands with terns, skimmers, or gulls, willets are often spread out on salt-marsh islands without them. In some places they nest in loose colonies, where adults are in vocal contact whenever a predator is near. Otherwise they cannot see each other when they are incubating or caring for chicks. When a predator approaches, they join together and fly about the predator, escorting it from the area.

Willets have always nested in the New Jersey marshes, and the earliest books of birds along the Jersey shore mention Willets. They decreased during market gunning, since they were one of the largest shorebirds. They

5.4. Pair of willets circling around a predator near their nest.

too festooned the hats of fashionable ladies, but their patterns of nesting solitarily over the marsh made it difficult to shoot large numbers of them.

Willets circle us calling loudly, "pill will et, pill will et," and as we move away from their nest, they land suddenly and disappear silently in the cord-grass (Figure 5.4). The silence soon is shattered by the mobbing calls of whirling common terns, circling a peregrine swooping over the colony. The oystercatcher adults take flight and circle low over the water, while the young sink to the ground and freeze, becoming invisible against the dark ooze and the green-and-brown grass stems. No willets are in the air, and they must still be in the grass with their chicks. Assaulted by the bold terns, the peregrine suddenly rolls over on its side, snatches one of the mobbing terns in its talons, and streaks off in the distance. The terns provided both early warning of the presence of the predator, as well as active defense, an advantage for nesting in the tern colony.

Several species of shorebirds that nest solitarily themselves often nest in colonies with terns or gulls, thus using the early warning system and active predator defense of the terns and gulls. Oystercatchers have few predatory defenses other than that their nests and young are cryptic and blend in with their nesting substrate. When actively pursued by a predator, oystercatcher young head for the water, dive in, and swim underwater for a few yards. Eventually they must surface, and are vulnerable to a persistent avian predator. Great black-backed gulls, for example, simply wait for the exhausted chick to surface, and then pounce and eat it in one gulp.

Besides succumbing to predators, some oystercatcher nests in Barnegat Bay fail because the nests are washed out by high tides. In years with exceptionally high tides, nearly all the nests are flooded out, but in most years only two or three of the thirty-five or so nests are washed away. When eggs are destroyed the pair usually relays, and young are often fledged from these second nests.

By early July most oystercatcher young are flying. Although they still obtain some food from their parents, they open most mussels themselves. Usually they stand in family groups at island edges, or on sandy spits with large flocks of terns and skimmers. The marsh grass is tall and lush, with no remnants of the brown and decaying stems of early April. The salt-and-pepper wrack remains, untouched by the summer's high tides. Hopefully it will weather the fierce winter storms and grinding ices, remaining intact for next year's oystercatchers, skimmers, and common terns.

6

The Spring Chorus: Fowler's Toads at Little Beach

Slowly the moon rises above the salt marsh at Little Beach Island, and the tops of the grass appear as dark shadows. It is a bit foggy, and the air is warm and wet. It is late spring, or early summer, depending on your mood. In the distance a foghorn sounds, tolling for small vessels still in the bay. Few boats should be out and about, for the fog has been thick for days. The Coast Guard has issued small-craft warnings.

Long, loud, high-pitched wails travel across the marsh. "Wa-wa-wa-a-a-a-a-a-a." "Wa-wa-wa-wa-a-a-a-a-a-a-." The chorus is soft and lilting from this distance, and it is difficult to pick out individual sounds. Like a magnet, the sounds draw me nearer, and I move silently across the marsh to identify the caller. The wails grow louder, until the sound is deafening. Now the "wa-wa-wa-wa-a-a-a-a-a" is nasal, and it sounds like bleating sheep. I find myself beside a small freshwater pond, merely a depression at the edge of the marsh, filled by the recent heavy rains.

Fowler's toads have gathered here by the dozens to engage in their courtship rituals. Toads are warty creatures, with granular undersides, horizontal pupils, prominent parotid glands behind the ear, and unwebbed toes. Each spot on the back of the Fowler's toad contains several warts, while those on the very similar American toad contain only one or two. Fowler's Toads are also slightly smaller than American Toads that are the familiar inhabitants of our gardens and lawns. Fowler's toads occur mainly along the coast from New England to the Gulf Coast, although they are generally absent from Florida. Toads are amphibians and are cold-blooded. Their behavior is related to air temperature, and they have waited for a warm evening before their whining chorus reaches full force. With their relatively long breeding season, these toads are opportunistic breeders that can breed from spring to fall, depending on freshwater conditions.

The males gather around the pond, singing loudly (Figure 6.1). They call nearly continuously, to establish their territories and to attract mates. Small

6.1. Male Fowler's toads gathered at a vernal pond to call to attract females on a warm, wet, foggy night at Little Beach Island.

fights break out now and again, but for the most part the males concentrate on their calls. The long, loud wails call females from the surrounding dunes.

In the darkness, females slowly make their way to the pond, drawn by the chorus and the warm, moist night, their bodies distended with eggs. They listen attentively to different calls, moving from place to place, listening again. Late in the night some females hop back into the surrounding vegetation. But others select a particular male and allow the male to grab them around the front of the body. This mating posture is called amplexus, and the firm grasp of the male literally forces the eggs from her body. The mating toads stay locked together for an hour or more.

During amplexus, female Fowler's toads can deposit between 4,000 and 8,000 eggs in long strings that look like gelatinous necklaces of tiny beads. As the eggs slowly pass from the female's body, the male deposits sperm on them. The thin strands wind around the vegetation like gossamer cobwebs.

With each passing night the chorus is louder as more males descend from the uplands. The calls are more irresistible, and females begin to arrive in droves. In the morning, there are more strands of gelatinous eggs strewn around the edges of the marsh, clinging to the inundated glasswort.

Once the adult toads have mated, they will leave the pond and remain in dry uplands the rest of the year. They stalk through the vegetation mainly at night to hunt great quantities of beetles, grubs, and other insects. Their dry, warty skin helps conserve moisture by preventing evaporative water loss, a

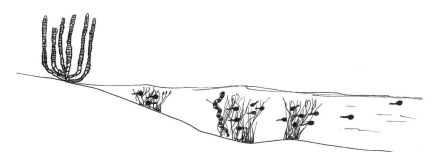

6.2. *Recently hatched Fowler's toad tadpoles hiding in vegetation. Glasswort grows along edge of pond.*

valuable trait in coastal environments where freshwater is in short supply, and they spend the hot, dry days buried in sand or at the base of vegetation.

Back in the pond, the warmth of the sun incubates the eggs. Slowly, the black dots turn to miniature BBs, and they develop tiny tails. The gelatin begins to melt away, and the strands break. A few eggs at the end that are just above the water dry out, turn white, and die. The others are healthy, and only hours from hatching.

The gelatin gradually disintegrates, releasing the tiny tadpoles, who make abortive swimming motions in the remaining jelly. Soon they are completely free and disappear in the flooded vegetation, where their dark shapes are less obvious to predators (Figure 6.2). The small larval toads, or tadpoles, feed on algae, diatoms, and other decaying microscopic plants. They remain in the pool while they grow—and it will take most of the summer for them to develop into small toads. Locked in a race with time, they must complete their metamorphosis before the pond dries in the late summer or early fall. This year the water is deep, and the pond may not dry up.

The pond here is relatively safe, for there are few predators. Since the toads lay eggs only in ponds that dry up, there are no fish, snapping turtles, or snakes. The toads' only worry is birds, which they can avoid by remaining hidden in the vegetation. Toads usually prefer to find these temporary ponds, but sometimes they have no other choice, and their tadpoles are left in water filled with predators.

The pond at Little Beach, now bordered by glasswort and by cordgrass, is of recent origin. It was once solid cordgrass. There was no break in the mass of green, no indication that this place was different. One winter snow geese used this area extensively. They rested here, they slept here, and they ate the grass roots. Their digging exposed other roots, which then were injured by the cold and ice that crept into the soil. The next spring the cordgrass grew only sporadically, and the rich black mud was exposed to the wind and rain. After each rain, water gathered in the holes left by the rotting roots and grass, and this created more holes. The grass never fully recovered, and now the area fills with water when the winter snows melt, or whenever there are heavy rains. It is a perfect place for Fowler's toads, for it is near the uplands.

Out on the barrier beach, Fowler's toads also breed in temporary ponds that are mere depressions in the white sand. Most of the temporary ponds on the beach were created by the relentless forces of high winter tides. The dark brown tadpoles are particularly obvious against the white bottom, and they have no place to hide. Young least terns sometimes spend many hours hover-dipping for these tiny tadpoles, practicing foraging skills they will later use when plunge-diving to catch fish in the bay.

According to Steve Garber and Robert Zappalorti, who have followed their numbers for years, many populations of Fowler's toads have succumbed owing to the vast DDT spraying schemes of the 1950s and 1960s. Once Fowler's toad lived everywhere from southern New Hampshire westward to southeastern Ohio, and southward to the Gulf Coast. It was very common along the coasts, but these areas suffered heavy spraying for mosquitoes. Sunbathers on beaches are particularly vocal about mosquitoes, and economic pressures dictated frequent spraying from trucks and airplanes. The toad populations on Little Beach Island survived because it is a wilderness area, there was no spraying, and few people were permitted on the island. Spraying cannot be the whole explanation, however, because toad populations continue to decline even though the wholesale use of pesticides has diminished.

The young tadpoles in the Little Beach pond must choose between remaining in the full sun, where they can soak up the warmth and actively search for food, or hiding in the vegetation to avoid avian predators. Sometimes least terns, or even gulls course over the pond, picking up the tiny black tadpoles. Fortunately, the black mud at the bottom of the pond allows some of the tadpoles to disappear from view. Their dark color helps them absorb the warmth of the sun, allowing them to grow that much faster. Some of the larger tadpoles eat the smaller ones, contributing to further differences in sizes. The ones that grow the fastest also metamorphose the fastest, and can leave the pools the quickest. Unlike most frogs, Fowler's toads metamorphose when they are relatively small, allowing them to leave the ponds quickly. This is another adaptation to life in temporary breeding ponds.

The Fowler's toads have only a few weeks to metamorphose before the ponds dry, and the process is rapid. Their tails grow smaller, their legs grow longer, and they find themselves sitting on the edge of the pond. Their digestive systems change also, from vegetarian to carnivore. They no longer are at home in the water; it is difficult to maneuver, and their legs are awkward. The land beyond seems foreign, and they wait lethargically.

In the late summer or early fall the small toads emerge from the Little Beach pond by the hundreds. They are barely the size of the smallest fingernail on my left hand, but they are just the shape of adults. They can fall prey to birds and small mammals such as raccoons, skunks, and even mice. I watch in the early morning as a few small toads sit around the edge of the pond.

Slowly a young garter snake slithers through the grass toward the pond and stops, its head raised ever so slightly above the mud. In the dark, its lateral yellowish stripe is barely visible. A row of keeled scales down the back form a slightly raised ridge, obvious only because I know it is there. Mud from the marsh grasses obscures the reptile's pattern, making it even less noticeable.

The snake watches and waits. Ever so carefully, moving only a bit at a time, the snake moves forward. Nearby the baby toads are completely oblivious, taking in the sun, warming up slowly. Closer and closer the snake inches, blending in almost perfectly with the muddy cordgrass stems strewn around the water's edge. One baby toad turns and hops toward the water, unsure whether emergence is really a good thing.

Little by little, the snake slithers forward, his head raised, his tongue darting in and out. The strike is so swift it is almost invisible, and in one swallow the small toad is eaten. Again the snake is still, and the other toads seem complacent, unaware of the danger (Figure 6.3). A minute later the snake starts another approach, slowly slithering inch by inch, using the few blades of grass as camouflage. Another strike, and another baby toad is no more.

Unlike many other snakes that suffered with encroachment of civilization, garter snakes seem to have prospered. Their populations declined during the era of extensive, indiscriminate pesticide use, but after the bans on some pesticides, garter snakes began to increase. They manage to live in the interstices of urban and suburban sprawl, largely because they bear live young and do not need to find safe egg-laying places. They do not require soft soil that has been untrampled by thousands of people, and they do not worry that the hordes of rodents which rule by night will eat their eggs.

The garter snakes on Little Beach Island no doubt became established when the sparse human population moved onto the island. In the late 1880s and first half of the 1900s there was a small village, centered around the Coast Guard Station. Although the station was once located beside the sea, it is now isolated in the center of the island, as the sea has formed a new, extensive sand spit to the north. There is quite a garter snake population still living among the ruins of the buildings, amid the broken beams and rubble.

Slowly, surely, silently, the garter snake I have been watching makes its

6.3. Garter snake capturing a Fowler's toad at the edge of a pond. The toad may escape because the snake is swallowing it hind-end first.

way around the edge of the pond, picking off an unwary toad here and there. The few who see him coming jump into the water. One tries to jump away in the grass but is quickly captured. In half an hour of feeding the snake manages to consume eleven baby toads. Then it disappears in the grass, in the direction of the uplands, no doubt to find a sunny spot to bask.

The snake leaves behind hundreds of toads still uneaten, and now they bask in the warming sun. Overhead a laughing gull circles and lands, its attention caught by the movement around the pond. It too feeds, picking up toad after toad until I wonder how any will make it to safety. Some make it and continue their journey to upland areas, where they will spend the next four months eating and growing. By October they must find a suitable winter hibernating place under an old log, in a mouse trail, or down between some roots.

7

Fiddler Crabs at Cheesequake

A creek meanders through an extensive salt marsh lying beside the Garden State Parkway. The marsh is still dressed in pale browns and yellows, and only a bit of new green growth indicates spring is here. The water rises against the cordgrass, for it is nearly high tide. The dark black mud beneath the cordgrass glistens in the sun. A clapper rail stands motionless, peering from the edge of the grass. Within minutes, the rail melts back into the vegetation, looking elsewhere for food.

On another nearby creek an old rowboat is half-buried in the mud, long forgotten. All that remains of a rickety dock is a group of water-logged poles and a few planks. The old fishing shack perched atop poles tilts slightly, shutters hang loose, and broken steps lead into the tidal water. The slanting shack has one main room, with a small toolshed behind. Piles of wire crab traps are tied to the walkway that leads to the shed, and old wooden floats lean against the side. Three old duck decoys hang from a nail beside the door to the shed, along with the flat outline of a pair of Canada geese, another type of decoy typical of the Jersey shore (Figure 7.1). Not far away another shack stands upright, its shutters neatly painted, its dock recently repaired. The crab traps here are neatly stacked in rows and are tied to the side of the house. But it too is empty, abandoned for the winter.

In front of the shacks the marsh extends seaward, its brown expanse broken only by creeks winding toward the sea. The tranquillity of the marsh contrasts with the high speeds of the cars careening along the Garden State Parkway only a few hundred meters away. The Cheesequake marsh is tucked between the sea and the parkway, a small salt-marsh jewel protected for the moment.

I am safe in the middle of the marsh, indifferent to the movements of the distant cars, and only the gently swaying grass catches my eye. I pole my boat into the cordgrass at the edge of a wide creek and wedge the oar in the mud to anchor the boat. It will be over an hour before the tide begins to drop, just enough time to take a bit of a nap. Using my light down

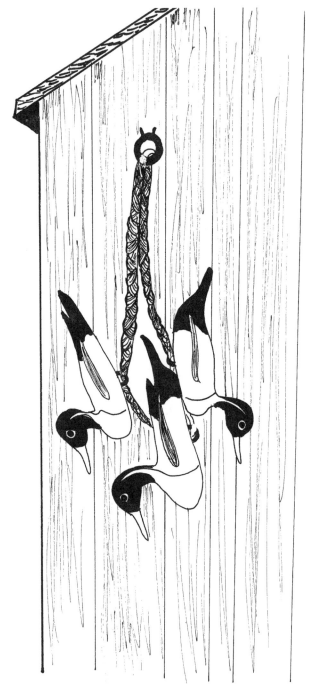

7.1. Duck decoys at a hunting shack at Cheesequake.

jacket as a pillow, I lie on the bottom of the boat and soak up the first rays of spring, waiting for the tide to drop. The air is still a bit chilly, but the sun's rays are warm in May. I begin to review my research plan in my head, but soon drift off to sleep for an hour.

Only the gentle tides lapping at the side of the boat, and the undulating roll, remind me that I am in the middle of the marsh. Soon the boat rocks no more, and the lapping stops. The boat has settled on the marsh, the tide is falling, and I am marooned. The waters have moved a third of the way out of the creek, and nearly three feet of mud are exposed.

I unfold my lawn chair and place it in the bottom of the boat, erect the canvas blind around the chair, and am ready to begin. I am here to observe the territorial behavior of fiddler crabs, and to determine how they use their burrows. With increasing pollution in many estuaries, I want to have baseline data on normal behavior of crabs in undisturbed, relatively pristine environments. The blind may not be necessary for fiddler crabs, but I want to eliminate any effect of human disturbance, and the blind provides some protection from the sun.

The bluish black mud, still unblemished and smooth, glistens in the sun. Within minutes, however, the tranquil surface of the mud is broken by holes that seem to implode from within. No piles of mud surround the holes; instead, they simply appear—one here, one there, and another until the mud is honeycombed with tiny holes smaller than a nickel.

Minutes pass, and finally the first fiddler crab emerges. It peers above the opening, its body half in and half out. There it remains for several minutes, while others also begin to peek out of their holes. With a jerking movement, one crawls out a few inches and begins to pick up bits of algae, bacteria, or decaying marsh grass in its claws, stuffing these rapidly into its mouth.

Within a few minutes, a female fiddler crab emerges and begins to feed. After twenty minutes she is covered with mud, and she cleans herself by submerging in her burrow. As the tidal waters recede, more and more holes appear, and within minutes fiddler crabs emerge from these holes. They too are watchful at first, but eventually they begin to walk away from the safety of their burrows. Others follow, and soon the mud is covered with fiddler crabs crawling slowly. They are all busy, for their feeding time is limited, and the next high tide will come soon enough.

A female fiddler crab near my boat faces me, frantically stuffing mud into her mouth (Figure 7.2). Suddenly she walks sideways, as is the normal pattern. She holds her body high and seems to prance. Stopping, she lowers her body and begins to eat anew. She has abandoned one burrow, and is now close to another. Slowly she moves over the tidal flat, stuffing in mud, oblivious to her increasing distance from any burrow. When a fish crow flies

7.2. Female fiddler crab feeding.

low over the marsh, she dashes to the left, then shifts directions and goes to the right. She continues this zig-zag movement until she is safely within a burrow. But the burrow is already occupied, and a brief scuffle ensues. She leaves, however, only when the crow has passed. Finding a burrow is her primary defense against predators or any sudden movement that bodes ill.

Down near the water's edge, a male is standing far from any burrow when the crow passes. He runs rapidly toward the water's edge and dives in; only his eyes peer above the water. Another merely rotates its body rapidly until it sinks below the mud surface. The oddest escape, however, occurs when a stranded fiddler crab begins rapidly digging a new burrow, tossing bits of mud in all directions. The crow, of course, is not interested in any of them.

Fiddler crabs resemble most shore crabs: they have a shell or carapace that is convex and smooth. The carapace usually has four to six sides, and on close examination, a variety of serrations, ridges, and furrows are seen on the sides of the carapace. The fiddlers have eight walking legs. The front legs are used as shovels to push into their mouth an endless stream of mud, from which they extract nutrients.

They feed by straining bits of organic matter from the surface of the mud. The front claws rhythmically bring pinches of mud to the mouth, where food is separated from the mineral matter and soil. Every few seconds the fiddler crab wipes its mouth, and the bits of soil drop to the ground, leaving a line of small pellets. Crabs usually stay near their burrow, or at least near the burrow where they spent the last high tide. Remaining near a burrow entrance ensures that they can escape predators such as clapper rails or black-crowned night herons.

At first the fiddler crabs all look alike (Figure 7.3). They are all small coffee-brown creatures with legs moving in all directions, and their shells seem similar in size. Gradually, differences appear. The crabs are not all the

7.3. Fiddler crabs near their burrows. Ones with the large claws are males, those with two claws the same size are females.

same size, and the front claws are larger on some. These are males. Each adult male has one of his front claws, or chelipeds, longer than his body, and when stimulated, he wields this vigorously in threat and courtship. Sometimes the large claw is used in contact combat, although usually the encounters are merely ceremonial. The male is handicapped by this large claw, for he has only one normal-sized claw to use for feeding. Females have two claws that are the same size, and they shovel food into their mouths with both claws alternating.

Fiddler crabs respond to high tides by going into their burrows, or feeding in very shallow water, always with their eyes above the water. Adaptations to differences in salinity are required, because most salt marshes can have salinities ranging from that of the nearby sea to nearly freshwater during a heavy rain. Even within the range of salinities they can tolerate, different fiddler crab species prefer a particular salinity.

The burrow is the center of the fiddler crab's activities. Even when the water is still far away, it can rise quickly. When startled or when driven by heat or dehydration, fiddler crabs rush down a hole and disappear. As the tide rises, fiddler crabs begin to repair their holes, flinging packets of earth in every direction. If a crab has wandered far from its burrow as the tide approaches, it must either steal one from a neighbor, or find an empty one.

Their burrowing activity is not simply selfish, for it is extremely important to the ecology of the salt marsh. In a year the population of fiddler crabs in a square yard of marsh, as many as forty or fifty crabs, can turn over nearly 20 percent of the mud in the upper six inches of soil. Burrows increase the surface area of the marsh, affecting the composition and chemistry of the salt-marsh sediments. The disappearance of fiddler crabs from the high marsh can decrease production of cordgrass by almost 50 percent, attesting to the importance of fiddler crabs to the marsh ecosystem.

Near the edge of the grass, a female fiddler crab has started to dig a new burrow. She begins to dig using the legs on one side, pulling mud away. Once she has a small hole, she enters the burrow sideways. She digs with the small legs, using them to curve around the sand, forming a basket with the setae. All material from the burrow is carried a short distance from the entrance and dropped. Now and then she tosses the mud to one side. The dirt is compressed into a ball by the rolling action required to remove it from the burrow. She works on and on, pulling more and more mud from the hole. For over ten minutes she works at the burrow, and then apparently tired, she begins to feed, rhythmically shoveling algae and small pieces of grass into her mouth.

After about fifteen minutes of feeding, she returns and begins to construct the burrow once again, flinging mud in every direction. Over the next hour she alternates feeding and building, paying little attention to nearby crabs. She will spend the next high tide in this burrow, and it must be deep enough.

Over the mudflat there is a bustle of activity. Most crabs are feeding, but some are digging burrows, fighting with neighbors, or engaged in courtship. Females devote almost no time to territorial defense, although the males are frequently aggressive. Instead, females seem oblivious to the territorial clashes of the males around them. Over the next few months, I am fascinated by the behavior of the crabs as they go about their daily activities. They can be active at all times of the day, but they are most active only at low tide, when the water recedes from their burrows. Fiddlers high on the marsh can stay active at high tide when there is only a thin film of water over the mud; they walk about with their eyes above water, stuffing food in their mouths. When it is still cool, most fiddler crabs are above ground. The crabs sometimes shun the heat of the day and will seek the shade of their burrows even at low tide. As night falls, they enter their burrows, pulling in a mud plug behind them. At dawn, or as soon thereafter as the tides allow, activity begins again. They emerge, feed, walk about the marsh, and defend their burrows.

Crabs have an odd sense of home: it is somewhat like our childhood game of musical chairs. Every fiddler crab needs a burrow when a predator arrives or when high tide approaches, so they must find the closest burrow. This means that the burrow any crab finds itself in was probably dug by some other crab. All burrows must be kept repaired, and the current resident takes this responsibility.

In the late afternoon, the tide is still low, kept down by strong offshore winds. The fiddler crabs continue to feed, walking sideways across the marsh, stuffing their faces with mud, and leaving tiny trails of mud pellets behind them. A black-crowned night heron flies in, causing mad dashes for burrows as everyone safely finds a hole. The heron walks to the edge of the grass, its dark shape blending into the shadows. Silently, it waits.

For ten minutes all is quiet, and the tiny holes appear empty. Then one fiddler crab, and then another, and then another, sticks its body half out of the hole. With one pair of legs still in the burrow, each crab emerges even more, and slowly begins to shovel in algae. As if on cue, crabs emerge from nearly every hole. They come out completely. They are a bit nervous, and the sudden movement of one crab sends them all scurrying back to their holes. But they stay near the surface, with only half of their bodies in their burrows. Gradually they emerge again and start to feed.

The heron remains motionless, staring fixedly at the crabs just out of its reach. The crabs move farther and farther away from their burrows, become more engrossed in feeding, and stop only to watch their neighbors. With one rapid step and a jab, the heron snatches a fiddler crab by the legs. They break off and the crustacean drops. But before it can scramble away, the heron grabs it back and gulps it down. Slowly the heron moves across the marsh, consuming dozens of fiddler crabs. Most escape, but careless crabs that are too far from burrows do not.

The rising tide prompts increased activity, and I watch as the crabs scurry about, searching for a burrow to hole up in while water covers the mud. Long before the water reaches the mudflat, each crab visits its burrow more often. When the bottom of the burrow is wet from the encroaching tide, the crab remains. It pulls in mud behind, packing the mud and sand into a plug. Finally the advancing tide water reaches the bottom of the burrow, and at the same time the water smooths over the surface above. The air remaining in the burrow is trapped, and the crab is safe in a small room packed with air. Crabs breathe air through their rudimentary lungs hidden beneath their shells. A thin film of water covers the mud, and no one would guess that a world of fiddler crabs is hidden beneath. For the next few hours they are safe from predators cruising in the water above their burrows.

Fiddler crabs are brachyuran crabs, part of the invertebrate phylum known as crustaceans. They are diurnal, active at low tide, and always gregarious. Adults live in the intertidal zones of sheltered bays and estuaries, digging and feeding in sandy mud and muddy sand. Fiddler crabs are distributed around the world from tropical to temperate regions. Since they are adapted to warm climates, their seasonal activity varies in different parts of the world. In the tropics they are active all year around, and breeding individuals may be found in all months. In the subtropics, breeding may be restricted to the dry season. In temperate regions like New Jersey, fiddler crabs are active from May until November, but reproduction occurs only in the warmer months.

There are over sixty species of fiddler crabs or *Uca* worldwide, although only three species live in New Jersey. These include: brackish-water fiddler, the sand fiddler, and the mud fiddler, which is found throughout the salt marsh. The distribution of the different kinds of fiddler crabs in New Jersey depends upon tidal conditions and salinity. The greater the tidal range and different salinity ranges in a marsh, the more different species of fiddler crabs will be present. Fiddler crabs, however, both as individuals and as species, are highly tolerant of both changes in salinity and changes in tidal state.

The three different species of fiddler crabs prefer slightly different areas of the marsh. The mud fiddler crab inhabits only the vegetated areas with dark, black mud. It ventures to the edge of creeks only where the vegetation is dense, and where there will be minimal exposure on the mud. Within the vegetation, however, it will sometimes stay above its burrow in shallow tidal waters for most of the day.

The brackish-water fiddler crab prefers a muddy substrate and brackish water, and can sometimes be found near the uplands, where freshwater enters the marsh. The mud fiddler crab can interfere with the ability of the brackish-water fiddler crab to defend burrows, and thus the brackish-water fiddler may be forced into the higher areas of the marshes. The sand fiddler crab is limited both by competition with the mud fiddler and by its preference for mud mixed with sand.

Returning another day at low tide, I drift slowly through the Cheesequake marshes in my boat. It is difficult to move through some of the creeks, and I push awkwardly with the pole. Finally I reach my observation site and settle in. The crabs initially dash underground at my approach, but within five minutes of silence, they begin to emerge, they have grown quite used to me by now. Mostly there are mud fiddlers, but here and there a large brackish-water fiddler scurries about. They begin to feed, fix burrows, and

7.4. Yellow-crowned night heron stalking fiddler crabs just emerging from their burrows.

move across the mud. Suddenly they dash for their burrows, and a clapper rail appears through the grass.

During the day avian predators along the Jersey shore include crows, gulls, willets, and clapper rails. Clapper rails specialize on fiddler crabs, and they skulk slowly through the marsh, blending with the grass, seizing dozens of crabs in the course of a day. I have sometimes located clapper rail nests by searching for small piles of crab legs hidden in the grass.

In the late afternoon and early morning black-crowned night herons prowl the marsh, looking for fiddler crabs. They often stand in the open along creeks, but they move so slowly that they are perceived only when it is too late. In a few places, yellow-crowned night herons also feed on fiddler crabs, they seem to prefer them over other foods (Figure 7.4). Yellow-crowned night herons are so rare in New Jersey that they are on the state's Endangered Species List.

At night raccoons prowl the marsh, and some specialize on fiddler crabs. The raccoons too blend with the night, and they can catch the few fiddler crabs that come out to feed during low tide. In the darkness, some careless fiddler crabs wander too far from a burrow.

When the warm breezes of summer sweep across the marsh, the fiddler

7.5. Two male fiddler crabs displaying to one another.

crab males begin to wave their giant chelipeds in courtship. Their displays increase in intensity with increasing temperature and as courtship advances. Males perform the waving display both to males and to females that wander by, either to repel or to attract them (Figure 7.5). The male rears up, tilts his carapace, and as courtship intensifies, each male waves his claw higher and higher in the air.

Eventually an interested female makes contact. The male slowly climbs the carapace of his intended, from the rear. The agreeable female indicates receptiveness by remaining horizontal, her legs bent and held close to her body. She is almost touching the ground. With his minor cheliped, the male taps or strokes her carapace. After several minutes of stroking her, the male turns her over and holds her to the ground. He inserts the tips of his gonopods into her gonopore, and they remain in contact for nearly an hour. The male passes sperm, in the form of spermatophores, into the genital opening of the female.

Nearby, another courting couple makes contact for about fifteen minutes, while a third couple makes contact for only a few minutes. This seems to be the range of mating times. Across the mudflat some males are displaying, and a number of different pairs are courting or copulating. Even so, most others feed, oblivious to the courtship around them. Females pay no attention to the combating males, or to copulating pairs.

The female carries the developing eggs, and just before they hatch, she makes her way to the water's edge. The young larvae float away with the currents, until they settle on a suitable marsh. Many young larvae perish before reaching such a marsh. Others are eaten by small fish. Since the larvae are carried passively by currents, they can move great distances, colonizing distant marshes.

Along the Jersey shore fiddler crabs are active only until November. They go into their burrows permanently when the winter winds sweep the marsh, and the temperatures drop below about 58 degrees F. Their burrows can be as deep as thirty-five inches, and as winter approaches they clean out the lower part of burrows, shore up the walls, and dig deeper if necessary. Below 58 degrees their activities decrease rapidly, and they must remain in the shelter of their burrows.

Most people who have the opportunity to see them are fascinated by fiddler crabs moving across the marsh, dashing sideways to reach a burrow, waving their large chelipeds in courtship, brandishing them in combat with a neighbor, or frantically shoveling food into their mouths. However, fiddler crabs are useful for a number of other reasons: They aerate the soil of the marsh by creating numerous holes in the mud, they are an important part of the food web, and they can serve as an early warning of environmental degradation.

Fiddler crabs are affected by environmental contamination, because they feed on the bacteria, algae, and decaying vegetation on the mud surface. Any contamination of this mud layer directly affects the crabs, making them particularly vulnerable to oil spills. They are often one of the organisms used to assess the damage from these spills, and information on the effects of oil on fiddler crabs comes from England, Europe, the Middle East, and the United States.

When oil spills occur in the spring or summer along coastal areas, there are always massive die-offs of invertebrates, birds, and marine mammals. Fiddler crabs that are oiled usually die. The crabs that survive show the effects of oil for many years. Following an oil spill in Falmouth, Massachusetts, fiddler crabs were still contaminated with oil for at least four years, and fiddler crab populations were depressed for at least seven years. Behavioral impairments also persisted for seven years, including reduced juvenile settlement, abnormal locomotion, decreased burrow construction, and heavy overwintering mortality. For many years, some fiddler crabs did not dig burrows that were deep enough to survive the winter.

When the oil spill in the Arthur Kill occurred on 2 January 1990, Mike Gochfeld, John Brzorad, and I rushed to the salt marshes, anxious to determine what creatures were affected. Several hours had passed before news of the spill became public, giving the oil time to be carried by tides to distant marshes, making it even more important for us immediately to assess the damage. We have been examining the foraging behavior and the prey base of herons in the Arthur Kill for a number of years. It is unusual to have baseline data from the exact area that experiences an oil spill, so the oil spill is providing a unique opportunity.

We find the marshes of the Arthur Kill resting for the winter, the cordgrass is broken and brown from winter storms. Although the air is warm, the marsh is dormant. During the winter months fiddler crabs in temperate regions normally reside in underground burrows that are steeply inclined or vertical. These burrows can be five to thirty-five inches deep, and the crabs position themselves within the burrows to maintain just the right temperature. In the early winter, the crabs pull a mud plug over the burrow entrance, which acts to reduce the flow of cold air. When the oil washed into the creeks, the fiddler crabs were safely underground.

The tides have receded now, leaving the marsh covered with a wet film of oil, and the oil is draining into cracks and crevices through the mud. Slowly the oil begins to seep into the fiddler crab burrows, moving through some plugs that are not sufficiently tight, or simply moving through the mud until it reaches burrows. Once in the burrows, the oil moves rapidly, until it touches the crabs.

Within hours of the spill the first fiddler crabs emerge on the surface at Old Place Creek, covered with oil. It is cold, and the crabs are sluggish. They lie in pools of oil, vulnerable to predators, cold stress, and eventually to desiccation. They remain on the surface, unable to find burrows or construct new ones. With each subsequent low tide, small pockets of water are tombs for fiddler crabs, covered in oil that glistens with a blue, red, and purple tinge.

Crabs continue to emerge from their underground burrows along J's Creek until early March. They are forced to leave the safety of their burrows by the oil, and once on the surface, are unable to survive the cold of winter. Differences in burrow structure or depth, soil properties, and oil exposure account for the differences in emergence times. They all die within a few days. Thousands upon thousands of fiddler crabs die following the oil spill, and the mud surface is littered with them. I expect that thousands more are dead in their underground burrows, for many may die before they reach the surface. Digging in the mud, I find the remains of crabs partway to the surface or at the bottom of their burrows in pools of oil. Unfortunately, the oil seems to affect the females more than the males, and a higher proportion of the emerged crabs are females.

It is not just the winter cold that is killing the fiddler crabs. When we compare the behavior of oiled crabs with that of crabs dug up from Cheesequake, the oiled crabs are clearly impaired by exposure to the oil. We bring the crabs into the laboratory, where they all have the warm temperatures they prefer, and wash off the oiled crabs before running the behavioral tests.

The oiled crabs take longer to right themselves, walk more slowly, cannot walk up an incline, are less aggressive, and do not defend themselves against healthy crabs. Oiled crabs are not performing any defensive behaviors; they simply stand there. The oiled crabs also do not feed, while the ones from Cheesequake do so even though it is winter. They become more active as they warm up and behave as if spring has arrived at Cheesequake.

The oiled crabs also do not perform appropriate burrow-digging behavior. When given a nice substrate, in their own little aquarium, they dig

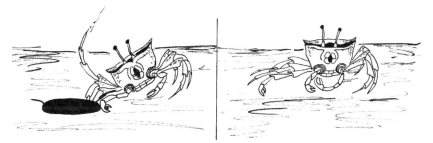

7.6. Divided aquarium where I tested the burrow-digging behavior of oiled (right) and control (left) fiddler crabs after the Arthur Kill oil spill of 1990.

a bit, but stop before they have constructed a burrow (Figure 7.6). They lie about on the surface, exposed. The other crabs, dug up rudely from their winter burrows in Cheesequake, quickly set about digging a proper burrow and soon disappear below the surface. It is not merely the cold temperatures that have injured the crabs, it is also the exposure to the oil.

The devastation to the fiddler crabs is greatest along the creeks that are closest to the oil spill, but fiddler crabs are affected throughout much of the Arthur Kill. A vast area of marsh used by a variety of species in the food web is affected, some marshes more than others. Over 20 percent of the cordgrass is killed by the oil, the 20 percent that borders the salt-marsh creeks.

Eventually, summer comes to the marsh around Old Place Creek. The fringe of cordgrass along J's Creek across from the site of the oil spill is dead, although the marsh beyond is lush and green. Here and there oil remains, on the mud and in the grass. The mud still has a blue and reddish sheen. Fiddler crabs are foraging along the mud banks, but there are fewer than there once were. The crabs spend more time standing around and less time feeding and displaying than do crabs at other creeks that are farther from the site of the spill. The fiddler crabs from the heavily oiled J's Creek also spend more time fighting than crabs from other places, and they build fewer burrows. When crows sail over the marsh these crabs are more vulnerable, for they are farther from burrows than they should be.

Snowy egrets, glossy ibis, and black-crowned night herons feed on the fiddler crabs along the oiled creeks. A snowy egret stands along the edge of the cordgrass, motionless, waiting for the crabs to emerge and feed. Without a breeze, even its feathers are still, and there is no motion on the marsh. Finally, one fiddler crab emerges and slowly moves away from its burrow, frantically shoveling food into its mouth. Another emerges, and then another. Within minutes the bank is covered with fiddler crabs, moving erratically along the mud, picking up small bits of algae.

The egret stabs quickly at one crab, then at another, and successfully captures both. This egret is nesting on nearby Prall's Island, along with hundreds of other snowy egrets, great egrets, night herons, cattle egrets, and glossy ibis. The heronries in the Arthur Kill are some of the largest in New York and New Jersey.

As the summer wears on, the parents build nests, lay eggs, and incubate. When the chicks hatch, the parents bring food to their waiting chicks, and snowy egrets and ibis bring back large numbers of fiddler crabs. Snowy egrets and glossy ibis experienced drastic declines in reproductive success that first summer following the oil spill. The parents lay normal clutches, and hatching success is normal. But few chicks fledge. These two species are the ones that primarily forage in the intertidal zone, the area hardest hit by the oil spill, the place where oil still remains. Other species of egrets and herons can escape the worst effects of the oil spill, because their diet is more varied, they feed in different places, and they often catch prey from the open waters of the Arthur Kill.

Reproductive success is lower again in 1991, and again in 1992 in the Arthur Kill heronries. Snowy egrets and glossy ibis fail to produce the usual number of young for three years following the oil spill. Only in 1993 does the reproductive success of snowy egrets and glossy ibis approach pre-spill levels. Fortunately, no large spills occur in the Arthur Kill from 1991 through 1995, and the ecosystem has a chance to recover. The cordgrass mostly is rejuvenated, although some areas are still bare. The fiddler crabs appear to be behaving normally now, and organisms higher on the food chain have recovered accordingly.

For the moment the fiddler crabs of the Arthur Kill and Cheesequake marshes behave similarly. In both places they maintain their burrows, feed on algae and decaying marsh vegetation, and the males wave their large chelipeds in courtship and aggression. The fiddler crabs are indicators of the health of our salt-marsh ecosystems. As they move about the mud, they are breaking up and aerating the soil, and contributing to the well-being of one of the most productive ecosystems in the world. They are important parts of the marsh's food web and wonderful creatures with whom to spend a warm summer afternoon.

8

Cattle Egrets on Islajo Island

Tiny whitecaps dance on the waves ahead of my boat, and blinding rays of light glance from them as I pass. The cool breeze is just enough to make it difficult to keep my fourteen-foot boat facing into the wind. The tiny distant salt-marsh islands are barely visible above the high tides that cover the lower stands of cordgrass. It is only three miles from my pier near Atlantic City to Islajo Island—but the trip takes nearly an hour across the unprotected, choppy bay and through the channel (Figure 8.1).

Ahead, near Islajo Island, a vibrant white snowy egret stands motionless along the shore, feathery plumes cascading down its neck (Figure 8.2). Suddenly its head darts downward, and in one swift motion it catches a tiny killifish. In one gulp it is gone, and the egret is again a statue. It is the only sign of the magic hidden among the reeds. I will visit Islajo twice a week during March, staying for two or three days at a time, searching for nesting cattle egrets. Then I will move on the island for the summer. I am here to study the interactions between cattle egrets and the native North American herons and egrets.

Islajo is a small salt-marsh island, with a high crown of dredge spoil dumped on the island years ago by the Army Corps of Engineers. It is one of the many islands of infinite shapes that dot the Jersey shore. A thin band of cordgrass grows on the leading edge, followed by salt hay and marsh elder bushes. The center of the island is dense *Phragmites* or reeds, with small cherry and Poison Ivy shrubs in the higher places. The very high winter storm tides seldom wash over the island.

When I first arrive in early March, the brown reeds seem inhospitable, and a cold breeze leaves frozen droplets on the stems. I tramp through the stiff, tall reeds left from last year, searching for the center of the colony of herons, egrets, and ibis. Although a few herons and egrets spend the winter in New Jersey, none are anywhere near the colony yet. The only indication that this will soon be an active heronry is the series of dead twigs and reed stems fashioned into nests that remain from last year. Herons and

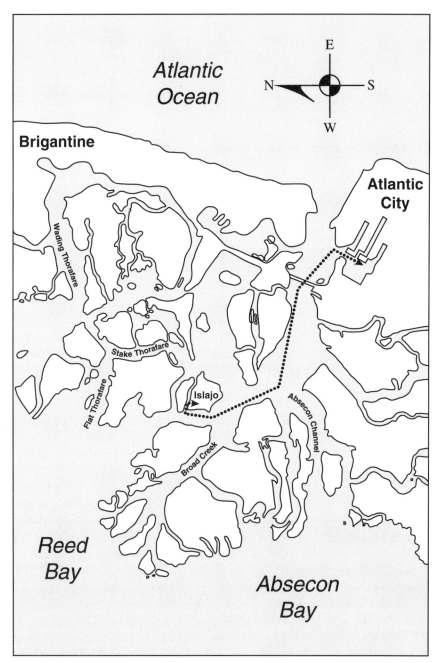

Atlantic
Ocean

Brigantine

Atlantic
City

Wading Thorafare

Stake Thorafare

Flat Thorafare

Islajo

Absecon Channel

Broad Creek

Reed
Bay

Absecon
Bay

8.1. *Map of Islajo Island near Atlantic City showing the path I take by boat to reach the island.*

8.2. Snowy egret feeding beside Islajo Island.

egrets usually use the nests that remain from the previous year, it saves them having to spend time searching for and collecting nest material.

I carry poles, wire, and canvas, and construct a blind in the middle of the greatest mass of old nests. Just for insurance I build a second in another area where there are fewer old nests, but these are smaller and higher in the reeds, perhaps indicative of cattle egrets. I camp on the island in a small canvas tent on the highest part of the island, nestled among the bushes and dense reeds. I wait that day, and the next, and the next, but no birds appear. Each night I snuggle in my sleeping bag, and huddle down against the March winds.

In late March a lone black-crowned night heron settles in the reeds a few yards from my blind, awaiting other night herons and the warm, bright sunlight. I watch, hour after hour, but only one black-crowned night heron stands atop the craggy cherry trees. Here in the middle of the island it is high enough for small cherry trees to grow, free from the threat of tidal inundation. The few trees are surrounded by poison ivy bushes; not the small vines we are used to, but proper trees, with strong trunks and branches. These small bushes provide enough support for the bulky heron nests, and because the bushes are short, the tall reeds protect them from strong winds.

Not far from the stand of cherry and poison ivy bushes is a small sand dune that rises a few feet above the floor of the heronry. It is high enough to avoid even the most violent winter storms, and a warren of tiny burrows near the edge indicate that a small colony of Norway rats live here. The burrows are maintained, as there are no leaves blocking the entrances, and the holes are round and smooth.

Two weeks pass before the breezes warm, tiny green shoots appear, and the first great egrets arrive. Some days are gems, with brilliant blue skies and warm breezes; others are raw and foggy. In early April I move onto Islajo for the summer, setting up my tent in the very edge of the marsh elder shrubs and reeds. It is still hidden from the view of boats passing the island, but is outside of the nesting colony. I will leave the island only to make a run for groceries and other supplies, for it is important to follow the nesting activities closely. I want to see the interactions, not just the results of competition.

Slowly great egrets, snowy egrets, glossy ibis, tricolored herons, and finally little blue herons arrive. Their numbers swell over the next week to some twelve hundred pairs bustling in the marsh, fighting over the old nests, defending new nest sites, collecting nest material, and soliciting mates. The cacophony of sounds is deafening in the early morning hours.

By late April the first new nest platforms are completed, and they sway gently in the bushes. Lone birds chase all intruders while waiting patiently for their mates, who are off foraging in the nearby bay. Courtship and mating take place on the nest platforms, often interrupted by aggressive advances of neighboring birds. Eggs appear in the night heron nests in late April. Soon great egrets begin egg-laying, and the smaller species follow suit. But still there are no cattle egrets.

It is now early May, and as I approach the island after being away for two days, I am anxious to see if the cattle egrets have arrived. This is one of the largest heronries in all of New Jersey, surely there will be cattle egrets. Cattle egrets never nest by themselves, but always join colonies of the native egrets and herons.

Cattle egrets are not native to New Jersey, nor are they native to North America or the Western Hemisphere. Rather they are indigenous to East Africa, where they forage on insects in grass and shrub fields. Insects, however, often remain hidden in the safety of the vegetation and emerge only when disturbed. A cattle egret walking through the grass is simply not heavy enough to startle or stir up insects. Cattle egrets in Africa were successful by relying on other, heavier animals to stir up the insects for them. They followed the large wild ungulates such as wildebeest and buffalo. The egrets had to walk quickly to keep up with the moving buffalo, but each animal step startled grasshoppers or other creatures, which the egrets deftly snatched (Figure 8.3). This method was more successful than walking alone. And so, over time, the egrets that moved with the wild African herds were more successful and prospered. This led to a stronger dependence on ungulate herds.

8.3. Cattle egret foraging behind a buffalo on African plain.

In the noonday sun, when the wild African animals rest under shade trees, the egrets also rest and preen while waiting for the animals to begin foraging again. Although adapted to feeding with wild animals, cattle egrets did not increase in numbers because they were limited by the amount of grassland for feeding. Tropical rain forests and deserts provided impenetrable barriers to their spread in any direction. Wherever the herds of ungulates fed, the egrets followed.

Then the Europeans invaded Africa, clearing land, planting crops and pastures, and raising cattle. The wild animals were displaced, shot for food, ivory, or skins. Some ungulates died from diseases brought by the European cattle. The great herds of African ungulates dwindled with the shrinking savannah, and were often viewed as competitors of the cows that were cherished so by the Europeans. The Europeans provided more grassland for foraging egrets, but they all but eliminated the native animals that the egrets depended on as beaters.

However, to a cattle egret in search of a wild ungulate, a cow is a fine substitute. Cows plow slowly through the grass, munching, changing locations, startling up insects just as the original wild African animals did. Egrets soon adapted completely to the cows brought by the Europeans and followed any that were moving. Without habitat barriers such as rain forests or deserts, cattle egrets easily spread throughout the rest of Africa and moved into Europe. Their spread was swift, for without vegetation barriers, they could follow cows everywhere.

Some time in the last century, cattle egrets must have crossed the relatively narrow ocean gap between West Africa and Brazil. The first cattle egrets to colonize Surinam in South America were documented to have arrived by the 1880s. No doubt cattle egrets had reached the shores of South America now and then over the eons of time, but the thick tropical forests

8.4. Cattle egrets in breeding colony in cattails in North Dakota.

made it impossible for them to forage or flourish. By the 1880s, however, European settlers had arrived, and there were cleared pastures and cows ready and waiting. The few birds that arrived in the 1880s bred and slowly expanded south into Brazil, while others moved northward.

A few cattle egrets appeared in Florida in the 1940s, where the small, white, elegant egrets with the buffy crowns and plumes were exotics to be searched for eagerly. In 1953, a pair built a nest at Lake Okeechobee, and the first North American cattle egret chicks climbed among the branches. Since then they have spread along the Gulf Coast, up the Atlantic coast, and into Canada. They have spread west, where they nest in dense cattails in gull colonies (Figure 8.4). In the forty years since this first successful nest in the United States, they have become the most common heron or egret along the coast of the Gulf of Mexico. Along the Atlantic coast they are third in number of breeding pairs, only to white ibis and snowy egrets. Their amazing spread has been attributed to their use of a new niche not occupied by native species.

Unlike all our native herons and egrets, which feed primarily on fish, cattle egrets feed on insects in fields. They are very adaptable, and I have watched them feed ferociously on insects scared up by lawn mowers, tractors, and bulldozers at garbage dumps. Where large bulldozers roam over the surface of garbage dumps, mashing and redistributing the garbage, the egrets have learned to follow close by the wheels, as if they were simply giant feet, exposing fresh food with each step. In this they are more adaptable than the gulls that maintain a respectable distance from the large, noisy machines. Gulls that get too close are crushed, unable to stumble out of the way; but the egrets have had eons of time to learn to avoid the crushing feet of massive buffalo or elephants

Their adaptation for feeding on garbage is impressive, and throughout New Jersey they feed on any active garbage dumps. Although New Jersey has closed some of the 240 active dumps we once had, they served to provide the egrets with an abundant food supply while they were expanding within the state. Landfills provided just the impetus the cattle egrets needed to become established in breeding colonies and to learn the other local foraging sites.

In the early 1970s when cattle egrets were invading New Jersey, they were eagerly searched for by birdwatchers. Conservationists and ornithologists, concerned for our native herons and egrets, began to study competition between cattle egrets and the native species. In the Gulf region and in Florida, where the first cattle egrets bred in large numbers, they often nested several months later than our native species. Since they also fed on different foods in a different habitat, early reports claimed that cattle egrets did not compete with our native species for food and nest sites.

However, heronries once filled with snowy egrets, tricolored herons and little blue herons in the southern United States were dominated by more and more cattle egrets. Heronries that once contained only little blue herons now are filled with only cattle egrets. Alarm has spread rapidly through the conservation community—despite early complacency, there is cause for great concern.

In the mid-1970s I began to examine the nesting dispersion of herons and egrets in many colonies throughout the United States, Mexico, and in Argentina. A pattern gradually emerged: the largest bodied herons and egrets usually arrive first at breeding colonies, and they establish territories where they please. When the smaller species arrive, they are forced to select nest sites from the remaining, available places. The larger species usually select the highest places that are farther from ground predators and that afford them the best view of approaching avian predators. Thus they are in the best position to determine whether they can protect their eggs by merely sitting on them, or should abandon the nest to save themselves. They have the earliest warning of impending danger.

The smaller species are forced to nest lower in the vegetation, exposing them to any ground predators and preventing them from the earliest views of approaching hawks. This pattern applies to all the native American species, whether they nest in New Jersey, New York, Texas, Mexico, or Argentina. Everywhere the pattern is the same. Great blue herons and great egrets nest on top, and snowy egrets and glossy ibis nest at the bottom.

Only the cattle egret is different: it nests higher than its size would predict. Instead of nesting at the very bottom, because it is the smallest heron or egret in North America, it nests just below great egrets, and some nest at the same level as the great egrets. This suggests that either the cattle egrets can insert themselves among the already nesting, larger species; or that they actually displace some of the larger, native species. I am living on Islajo Island to observe how the cattle egrets interact with the native North American herons and egrets; and to see if they aggressively out-compete the other species, or whether the process is passive. I can answer this question only if the cattle egrets come.

In the bright sunshine of early May, the young green shoots of the salt hay are vibrant, and the marsh elder bushes have finally leafed out. My boat, hidden within the bushes, is not visible from the channel. Indeed to a passerby, Islajo Island looks deserted, and there are no outward signs of either the heronry or my two blinds hidden within. The strong green stems of the fresh reeds reach my chin when I walk through them. I am glad my path is well trod, for it would be difficult to forge a path through the old and new reeds now, and impossible to be silent. I must reach my blind without disturbing the incubating birds.

I creep slowly through the reeds, along the cramped tunnel of burlap that hides my final approach, and enter the first blind. I sit silently for three hours, watching the snowy egrets and tricolored herons go about their daily routine. There are no unoccupied stick nests from last year; they have all been claimed, probably by last year's owners. Some birds incubate, some stand and preen, some coo softly to mates, touching bills and facing gently away. Every hour or two they exchange incubation duties, and the departing mate brings a twig or two to add to the nest. There are no cattle egrets here, and there are few interactions between neighbors.

Discouraged, I leave, creeping silently through my tunnel and out to the edge of the colony. It feels good to stretch a bit before going into the other blind, where I will remain for the rest of the day and will sleep overnight. The wind has died down, the sun is bright and warm, and the water at the edge of the island is smooth as new-formed ice. A lone snowy egret feeds at the edge of the island, and a fish crow standing on the bleached remains of an abandoned boat bends to eat a pale blue egg. It must be either a tricolored or a little blue heron, for it is too light for a glossy ibis, and a shade big for a snowy egret (Figure 8.5). Fish crows often appropriate just such a piece of wood for a feeding station, and they usually bring eggs and other food here to eat at their leisure. I have watched crows bring clapper rail

8.5. Fish crow with common tern eggs near cache.

and common tern eggs here before. Sometimes they merely cache egg, and do not eat them for days, but usually they eat them immediately. Dozens of shell fragments lie scattered about, some blue from the heronry, others a speckled brown from the gullery.

I begin to move slowly back through the tunnel of reeds, into the burlap entranceway, and into my second blind. It is spacious and roomy, large enough for me to spread my sleeping bag on the ground and still have space to put my gear alongside. I settle myself, get out my notebooks, and wait a few minutes before opening the peephole. Finally I open the tiny front panel and peer out.

I am astonished to see six cattle egrets standing about on branches and reeds, their reddish-orange topknots glistening in the sun, and crests of orange plumes lying along their necks. An orange tinge washes their breasts, made brighter by the stark white of the rest of their plumage. They are smaller than their neighbors, but their feathers are puffed up in an attempt to appear larger.

They are not standing low in the cherry trees or poison ivy bushes, as their size would predict, but are scrambling higher and higher in the stunted trees and poison ivy, until they are almost as high as the great egrets. They do not seem to be hunting for their own nest sites, nor are they trying to fit between the territories of the other species. Instead they have moved into the dense part of the heronry, just outside my peephole. One cattle egret

stands not far from a tricolored heron, another two are near little blue
herons, and two stand close to snowy egrets. The last cattle egret is on the
nest only a foot from my peephole, a nest that only a few days ago belonged
to a snowy egret with five eggs. The nest is empty now and seems to be a
bit less sturdy. A few twigs that were once part of the nest hang lower in the
poison ivy bush, evidence of a struggle. On the ground below are two pale
blue eggs and bits of broken eggshells. This too is evidence of a struggle
rather than predation, as predators would have taken the eggs away or eaten
all of them. Although wind can cause this kind of damage, eggs are not missing from any other nests, and no other eggs are strewn on the ground.

A cattle egret to my right begins to approach aggressively a tricolored
nest, but the owner threatens, and the egret stops. After a few moments,
the cattle egret stalks still closer, bends, and grabs a twig, but the tricolored
stands firm and pecks aggressively at the smaller egret. The egret backs up,
drops the twig, and waits. The tug begins again, with the egret moving
closer, the tricolored jabbing menacingly, and the egret grabbing for twigs.
All afternoon the territory clashes continue, but the tricolored heron stands
its ground. In the process, one of its eggs tumbles to the ground, reducing
the clutch to three.

Slowly a cattle egret sidles even closer to the little blue heron incubating
quietly. With a quick jab, the egret pulls twigs from the heron's nest and steps
back out of reach. The heron turns to face the cattle egret, but continues
to incubate. Minutes pass, and then the egret walks closer and pulls another
twig. The heron rises, jabs at the egret, but the egret stands his ground. The
cattle egret eventually retreats, but every few minutes it moves in again. Finally the egret pulls a big twig free, dislodging two eggs, and forcing the little blue off the nest. With two quick steps the cattle egret is on the nest,
tossing the remaining eggs to the ground. In only two hours the cattle egret
succeeded in forcing the little blue heron to abandon its nest.

Another cattle egret standing on a dense poison ivy bush slowly moves
toward a snowy egret that is peacefully incubating in the full sun. The
snowy shifts incubation positions to face the cattle egret directly, a posture
that usually wards off snowy egret intruders. The cattle egret ignores the
subtle message, moving closer, and closer, and closer, until it is close enough
to grab a twig and pull, amid the pecks and wing-flapping of the snowy
egret. Eggs fly in every direction, but the snowy egret refuses to budge. All
afternoon the battle continues, until the nest is half dismantled, and only
one egg remains caught in the nest twigs. It is no longer in a position
where the parents can effectively incubate it.

By nightfall, it is a standoff for the cattle egret competing with the tricolored heron, but the snowy egret has already lost all its eggs and a third
of its nest to another cattle egret. Three other cattle egrets have been agi-

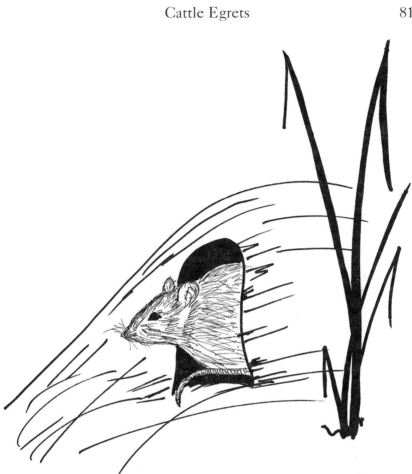

8.6. Norway rat in burrow on Islajo Island.

tating other snowy egrets and tricolored herons farther away. One of the little blue herons has lost its nest and eggs to a cattle egret. The cattle egrets initially try to usurp an entire nest, but if this fails, they settle for stealing the material to construct their own nest. These disruptions interrupt normal incubation, eliminate normal pair-maintenance activities, and halt any further nest building or nest maintenance of the resident birds.

The colony is silent at night, except for a minor squabble or two between a cattle egret and little blue heron. As the moon slowly rises, it encases the small flower heads of the reeds in a golden glow. A faint rustling in the dead leaves below the heronry may well be Norway rats, scurrying to devour the remains of the eggs that fell from the nests. This part of the heronry is not far from the sandy knoll, with its warren of rat burrows (Figure 8.6).

I slip lower in my sleeping bag, happy that I buried the canvas sides of my blind beneath the soil. There is still the door, with its gaping hole. Unable to sleep with thoughts of a rat rummaging around just outside, I use my camera and equipment bag to hold down the flap of the blind. I wedge my chair in the corner, closing the remaining hole. This helps with the mosquito problem as well, and gradually their buzzing quiets down. Rats are not really dangerous to me, but they can damage equipment and destroy my food. It must have worked, for the night passes without incident.

With the first rays of dawn I find that the cattle egret closest to my blind has laid one egg in the nest she usurped from the snowy egret. She sits quietly on the edge of the nest, and her mate returns within minutes with a particularly nice twig I suspect he stole from someone else. After tucking it gently in the nest, he leaves in search of another.

In the early dawn the second snowy egret finally loses its nest completely to the cattle egret. Forced from its nest for the tenth time in an hour, the snowy egret moves lower and lower in the poison ivy bushes and settles on the very lowest possible place. When its mate returns, they both gather sticks from the ground, sticks that belonged to their original nest. They start to construct another nest. Without the distraction of the cattle egrets, they engage in pair-bonding displays and begin the courtship rituals once again.

Above them, the cattle egret pair is busily repairing the nest they partly dismantled. One egret moves twigs around from place to place, while the other flies off to gather other sticks. They do not leave the nest unguarded, for an unguarded nest is fair game for other cattle egrets standing nearby. They too engage in courtship activities, but they seem much more intent on repairing the nest and fending off intruders.

Two other pairs, a snowy egret and a little blue heron, unaccustomed to the aggressive behavior of the cattle egrets, eventually abandon their sturdy nest and move to the edge of the colony, where they nest in small, unstable bushes exposed to the full coastal breezes. Other snowy egrets and little blue herons simply move lower in the vegetation or build nests on the ground, eventually losing eggs to the rats, which find low nests an easy source of food. By this time the safest nest sites are all claimed by other herons and egrets, the snowy egrets and little blue herons must settle for places that are more vulnerable to strong winds as well as to predators.

Some cattle egrets are not successful at stealing nests, so they steal nest material. Some particularly bold cattle egrets even remove sticks from beneath incubating snowy egrets, little blue herons, and even tricolored herons—usually with only a jab from the rightful owner. During the next heavy rain and windstorm, some of these weakened nests fall or collapse, while in others the eggs tumble between twigs and smash on the ground. Many egret nests are rather fragile affairs, and eggs can fall through the holes in the nest in a good stiff wind.

The native herons and egrets had spent weeks establishing territories, working out the borders with neighbors, courting, building and repairing nests, and finally settling down to lay eggs. The cattle egrets swarmed in, took over as many nests as they could within a few days, and immediately laid eggs. Meanwhile they continued to steal nest material from the other herons and egrets rather than search for their own.

They never really constructed proper, strong nests, but continued to add a twig now and then when the nest seemed too flimsy for the soft breezes. One cattle egret builds a nest a few inches from my side window and seems unaware of my comings and goings. I grow quite used to his calm stare and occasional pecks at the string that ties my blind to the swaying branches.

In only a few days twenty-five pairs of cattle egrets have inserted themselves in the small area visible from my blind, taking over many of the high, choice places by sheer will and overt aggression. For the most part they ignore the much larger great egrets, but all other species are fair game. These intruders are more gutsy than the native species, and far more persistent.

At the end of my week of observation, I motor through the choppy bay to the pier at Atlantic City and drive off to the local grocery store for food. I have grown used to the confines of my small blind and find the wide-open spaces of the channel and bay distressing. The grocery store is even worse, with its bustling, loud, raucous crowds. A trip to K-Mart is required to stock up on string, mosquito netting for the windows of my blind, and other field supplies (Figure 8.7). I browse slowly through the store, picking up items that will make life in the blind more pleasant.

I have spent too long in K-Mart, for when I reach the pier a strong wind has blown up. The aluminum boat is light, and with only a nine-horsepower motor, it will take longer to travel the three miles against the wind. Still, I must go now, for it could get worse. I load the boat quickly, putting the heavier items in front to hold it down, and start across the open water. I can see the channel ahead, but the tide is coming in and combines with the wind to make the passage nearly impossible. I am blown to the far shore, farther away than when I started. The boat has taken water, and some of the supplies are wet. I am really scared, for the boat nearly tipped over out in the bay. I am torn between prudence and my strong desire to get to the colony during this critical period. Missing even a day could disrupt the entire study. I must go on.

After bailing out what I can, I start out again, this time heading directly into the wind, even though it will put me a ways from the opening to the salt-marsh channel. When the bow veers only a tiny bit to one side, the boat begins to ride up on the whitecaps, but I succeed in getting it back on course. It takes over an hour to negotiate the open water that I can usually

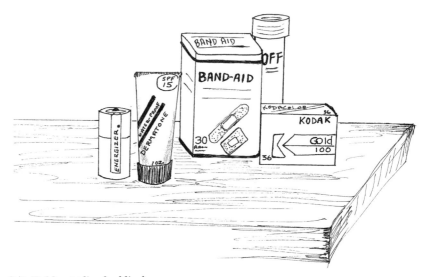

8.7. Field supplies for blind.

cross in ten minutes, and I still must motor up the channel. I am exhausted from sheer worry—but once in the relative safety of the channel the going is easier. Soon my docking area looms ahead, and I can drag the boat to the safety of its hiding place in the dense bushes.

No herons or egrets are visible above the vegetation, yet they must be there. I throw the gear and food into a backpack and, carrying the rest, head through the reed tunnel to the safety of my blind. Many of the cattle egrets stand at the tops of reeds, waiting. I allow the birds a few minutes to adjust to my presence and then open my peephole. Most of the birds have settled down to incubation, and only a few cattle egrets are still in the egg-laying stage.

And so it goes, with my recording aggressive interactions and documenting the direct competition between cattle egrets and the native species. Every day I wake at dawn to the soft sounds of the herons and egrets exchanging incubation duties for the day. I spend the days recording all interactions of the birds that are visible from my blind. Twice during the hatching phase I make the rounds of the nests in front of my blinds, banding the newly hatched chicks with Fish and Wildlife Service and color bands, so I can identify the chicks from each nest. Otherwise, I never go out into the heronry, for I want to minimize my disturbance.

By late May the new green shoots completely hide me as I pass quietly beside nests to enter my blind. All around me egret and heron eggs are hatching, and the soft cheeping calls from the pipping eggs give way to the loud, insistent, begging demands of hungry chicks. Still the cattle egrets harass the snowy egrets by continued pilfering of twigs. The breezes are now warm, and the gentle swaying of the reeds provides soothing music.

The chicks creep slowly into the vegetation in the heat of the day, safe from the glaring sun and the gleaming eyes of avian predators who might glide overhead. Each chick claims a favorite hiding place and predictably plunges there at the least sign of danger. Usually marsh hawks are the only real danger, and I can watch their approach low over the colony.

One day a ground predator enters the colony, for I can hear the disturbed calls of the young birds at its edge. Adults fly from the colony and disappear out of view. Slowly the disturbance moves through the colony. The raucous departure of adults and the loud clamor of chicks frantically climbing branches and plunging to the ground suggest that the intruder is a threat to both adults and young. The birds in front of my blind eventually react and scatter in all directions. A baseball cap appears through the reeds fifty feet from my blind. I creep through my tunnel, out to the path, and quickly confront the thoughtless bander moving through the colony. Unaware of my presence, he was simply herding the young herons to the far edge of the colony, where he would band them. This is a particularly bad time to do this, as chicks are small enough to get lost and might be unable to find the way back to their nests. The bander leaves quickly, after apologizing profusely, and the colony slowly settles down. Little by little the banded young return to their nests, and everyone is accounted for.

The constant chatter of chicks begging for food accompanies rustling as they climb around in the leaves. When a parent returns with food, the chicks scramble up branches beneath the nest. Clamoring for the first food, the young chicks peck frantically at their parent's bill, stepping on the backs of their siblings to reach the top. As soon as the parents leave, they become silent.

The pattern repeats itself hour after hour, day after day. The competition for food is particularly strong in the cattle egret broods, the clamoring louder, and the fighting more vicious than in their neighbors' nests. No one seems to notice when the smallest chick, the last to hatch, perishes beneath the nest, leaving more food for the older young squabbling above. In some nests, the youngest does not perish gracefully, and an older sibling actually pushes it out of the nest. This small, already weakened chick falls to the ground, unable to climb back up. Although at first this seems an accident, "siblicide" is well known in herons and egrets, and it seems to function to reduce competition for food when food resources may be tight. As long as food is abundant, the parents can return quickly and offer a bountiful meal of semidigested fish, enough for all chicks to feed contentedly. Siblicide happens more in years when food is limited, and less in years when there is abundance.

With the passing weeks, the young grow strong and clamber about more deftly amid the branches. Down is slowly replaced by feathers. All around me young herons and egrets flap their wings, eager to fly. Few parents remain in the colony; mostly they are shuttling back and forth, in search of feeding grounds, or carrying food for the ravenous young.

It is early July, and breeding is almost over. Near my blind, many snowy egrets were forced by the cattle egrets to nest lower in the vegetation. Elsewhere in the colony, the snowy egrets nested high in the vegetation, well off the ground and away from the hungry, hunting rats. Here, where cattle egrets nest among them, the snowy egrets raised only two young per nest; while in areas devoid of cattle egrets, the snowy egrets raised three young per nest. Little blue herons have suffered the same fate. The cattle egrets have claimed their toll, and the snowy egrets and little blue herons have suffered.

The din of the colony reaches a peak as in nest after nest the parents return with food for the young. At the first sight of their parents, egret and heron young rush to intercept them before they reach the nest, before siblings get there. Flapping furiously, blundering from bush to bush, other young egrets make their first flights. Branches bend and bows break under the weight of a young cattle egret that tumbles through, unable to land gracefully. He is unharmed and climbs back up.

The sun is directly overhead, hot rays slice through the leaves, making it impossible for chicks to find any shade or hide among the reeds. No breeze intrudes, no clouds cast shadows. The three cattle egret chicks who live so close to my blind return only sporadically to wait for parents that never seem to come soon enough. Somehow above the clatter they recognize their approaching parents, and they each begin to climb to the top branches. Feeding takes only a few seconds now, and the parents quickly depart.

A few days later, these same cattle egret chicks sit and wait, but no parent returns. And still they wait. Finally, facing their desertion, the chicks fly with surprising grace to nearby branches, then to distant bushes, before disappearing in the far reeds. The reeds have grown so tall that only a small circle of sky peers through. And I wait also, for minutes, for hours, and then for days. The hoarse clamor of my cattle egret chicks has ceased: they come no more to peer into my hide. The silence I had long waited for is deafening, and I am alone.

It has been a long field season, but I am still saddened by the silence, by the skeletons beneath the shrubs, and by the lack of bustling activity. None of the eggshells remain beneath the nests, for they were consumed by a number of organisms as a source of calcium. I can walk around the colony to measure internest distances, and I place permanent markers beneath each nest. I take down the blind, pack up my supplies, and fold up my tent.

After one long, wistful glance back at the gently waving reeds where hundreds of young herons and egrets recently fledged, I turn and face the clear, calm, blue channel. As I pass a shallow mudflat, I see one young snowy egret foraging, darting here and there to pick up small fish. There are no young little blues feeding in the creeks, only adults. And only I know that last year three young snowy egrets, and two young little blue herons, foraged in that same mudflat.

Even as I contemplate their competitive edge here in New Jersey, I begin to wonder what happens in Africa where cattle egrets are native? Do the cattle egrets nest where they should, based on their size? Or are they able to out-compete the other species?

I wait many years to answer this question, but eventually I travel to South Africa and Kenya to study the nesting pattern. My anticipation is overwhelming. It is not easy to work in the heronries in Africa, and I must brave the dangers of marshes to measure the pattern. Beneath the dark, warm waters lurks Bilharzia, otherwise known as a blood fluke that develops in a flat snail. Once an organism is infected, the fluke is nearly impossible to eliminate. But I have come so far, and I must know. I plod through the mud, the water nearing the top of my waders, waders that are several sizes too large, making it difficult to walk. My field companion is over six feet tall, and his waders are well above the danger line, but I must hold mine up to avoid water pouring in.

Impatient to see how the data comes out before I can return to the United States, I sit up all night, adding and subtracting, figuring out just where the cattle egrets nest relative to the other native species. Here in Africa, cattle egrets are just one of the many native herons, egrets, and ibis. They are not intruders.

As I had predicted so many years ago when I sat in the blind on Islajo Island, cattle egrets in Africa nest where they should, based on their size. In most heronries in Africa they are forced to nest low in the vegetation, and most other species nest above them. There is another difference: they nest at the same time as the other herons and egrets, so they must compete with all the other species at once. Here in Africa they are less aggressive and do not challenge the larger native species.

Away from the colony, out on the African plain, they walk among the wildebeest, buffalo, and zebra, hurrying to catch up, bending to pick up an insect or two (Figure 8.8). When the pace quickens, they fly up to land on the zebra's back and cling as the herd moves faster. Clouds of dust obscure the white hitchhikers, but still the herd moves across the plains. Eventually

8.8. Zebra in Africa with foraging cattle egrets.

the herd slows, and the animals bend to graze, slowly plowing through the deep lush grass beside the waterhole. The cattle egrets swoop down to the grass and take up positions beside a zebra's head, beside its front feet, and just behind its back legs. Each egret moves in tiny circles around the animal, picking up insects, using the elegant zebra as a "beater." When the zebra stop and sit beneath a giant baobab tree on the African plains, the cattle egrets rest also, waiting for the herd to move again, as it has for so many eons.

9

Killifish Move In

As the weather warms in the spring, the marshes turn a rich green, glasswort buds peak above the mud, poison ivy sprouts deep red and glossy leaves, shorebirds gather in dense flocks on their way north, and resident birds set up territories and begin to breed. Other less obvious changes occur as well—changes that are equally important to the ecosystems along the Jersey shore because they form the basis of the food chain.

In the bays and estuaries phytoplankton, other algae, and other aquatic vegetation grow. Widgeon grass flourishes in the shallow water, and beds of eelgrass choke the deeper water. They provide food for a variety of invertebrates, shellfish, and fish that live in the calm bay waters, in creeks and channels, and in the pools on the salt marshes. Estuaries have some of the highest productivity rates in the world and serve as nurseries for many of the organisms that live in the open oceans. Their productivity even rivals agriculture.

Wandering along the beaches, boating through the inland waterways, or jet-skiing over the bays, visitors to the shore may easily forget that the basis for the food chain is hidden in the bays and tidal creeks. Long and complicated food webs exist entirely within the estuaries or weave their way out through the inlets to the ocean beyond. Phytoplankton, other algae, and plants convert sunlight into energy usable by zooplankton, invertebrates, and vertebrates. Invertebrates and small fish form the next step in a food web that leads to bigger and bigger fish, which are eventually eaten by bluefish and other large predatory fish.

Vegetation and invertebrates are eaten by ducks and geese. Invertebrates serve as the prey base for shorebirds that feed on the marshes, along the creeks, and in the surf. The small shellfish and finfish of the creeks and inlets provide food for the terns, skimmers, and gulls that nest in abundance on the salt-marsh islands and sandy beaches. Larger fish and invertebrates are the prey for herons, egrets, and ibis that nest in *Phragmites*, shrubs, and trees along the coasts. Still larger fish are taken by ospreys. Lastly, the fish and shellfish of the bays and estuaries are an important human food source, and were exploited first by Native Americans, then by the early settlers, and now by both sport fisherman and commercial interests. People fish from boats, from piers, or they wade chest deep in the shallow bays. Some species of fish are in danger from overexploitation by recreational fisherman, and the depletion of fish stocks by commercial fisherman are legendary. Most people are interested in the food chain below the bay waters because it provides food or recreation for ourselves or for birds, although more and more marine ecologists are interested in understanding the whole estuarine ecosystem. The narrow, low-salinity tidal creeks and channels that wind through the marshes provide safe nursery grounds for a variety of fish that migrate into the estuaries to breed. They also harbor young fish of species that breed just off our coasts: these young fish come into the bays to find food and safety from predators and the force of the tides. Even the shallow ponds and pools on the salt marsh provide habitat for small fish and shrimp, which make their way here during the high tides when the marshes are flooded, and are then marooned when the tides drop. Abundant algae and widgeon grass provide the small fish with food and places to hide from birds. There is spatial and temporal separation in how fish use the bays and estuaries, just as there is in how the birds use the adjacent terrestrial habitats. Some fish species live primarily in the creeks and on the marsh surface, some live in the creeks and in the bays, and some live and move between the bays and the ocean.

Fish have different annual cycles. Like birds, some species are resident, but most are migratory. A few fish spend their whole lives moving within the bays and estuaries. There are two different migratory patterns in coastal fish: Some migrant fish come to our estuaries in the summer from warmer waters farther south, while others come in the winter from colder waters farther north.

Barnegat Bay, centrally located along our 143-mile Atlantic coastline, has over one hundred species of fish in nearly sixty families. Only twenty species, however, are year-round residents. The rest are migrants. Some 65 percent of the fish are warm-water migrants that come into the Jersey bays and estuaries from April to November. Many of these are here only as young, and they use the estuaries as nurseries, leaving once they mature. Only about 3 percent of our fish are cold-water migrants that come to the Jersey shore from November through April. These migrants are mostly young herring and cod.

This pattern is like that of our birds, for most of the birds that breed along the Jersey shore migrate to southern climes in the fall as well. Very few are truly resident, remaining in New Jersey during the winter. Species such as the fish crow, belted kingfisher, and Canada goose remain along our shores

9.1. Canada goose with brood.

all year. Canada geese are recent residents, having bred in New Jersey for only thirty-five or forty years. Before this they were migrants that nested farther north in Canada. People were so enamored with the geese that they pinioned some, forcing them to stay and breed in New Jersey rather than migrating to their breeding grounds farther north (Figure 9.1). As a result, we now have a huge and growing permanent population of geese. Many communities and corporate headquarters are disenchanted with the geese that have taken up residence on their expansive lawns, but we brought it on ourselves.

Other bird species that are present all year, like the herring and great black-backed gulls, are actually migrants. The herring and great black-backed gulls that breed along our shores migrate farther south in the winter, some going as far as Florida. The gulls we see along our shore in the winter have come south from New York, Massachusetts, and Maine. The other birds that we associate with the shore all migrate to the southern United States or South America: Piping plovers and least terns go to the Caribbean, skimmers go to the Gulf Coast and the northern Caribbean, herons and egrets go to Florida and the Caribbean, Forster's terns go to Florida and the Greater Antilles, and common terns go to South America.

Just as the kinds of fish in the bays and estuaries vary with the season, so do the numbers of fish. The seasonal changes in abundance that are so evident in the birds that nest along the shore are also prominent in the fish; we just cannot see them as easily below the murky waters. As with birds, populations of fish are highest immediately following breeding, when the adult populations are swelled with the vast number of young produced.

Sampling fish is a challenge, because the kinds of nets or traps used influence what fish are caught, as any good angler knows. This makes it very difficult to find out whether overall fish numbers have decreased or increased. It is particularly problematic to determine long-term trends. If a fish seems scarce this year, it could either reflect a mere blip, a real downward trend, or merely a slight shift in migratory pattern or timing. Fisherman and fishery biologists do not always agree on whether a population is in jeopardy.

Nonetheless, in the short run, it is clear that there are six to fifteen times more fish in the bays and estuaries in the late summer than in the dead of winter. The greatest numbers of fish are present in our estuaries in October, when both warm-water and cold-water fishes are present, and when young fish of several species abound. The bay anchovy and Atlantic silverside are the most common species, and these species are caught extensively by colonial nesting birds. In years when sand lance are abundant, these are the mainstay of several birds, since even a tiny chick can swallow the slender, tapered fish. Even species such as silversides that are so common along the Jersey shore fluctuate dramatically during the year. These changes in the number of fish are very important, because they form part of the food web base for the nesting terns and skimmers, as well as for the larger fish that osprey and fisherman catch, such as bluefish.

Years ago, Dary Bennett stimulated my interest in the phenology of fish movements. Now Ken Able and I have embarked on a project to understand the relationship between fish populations and nesting birds in Barnegat Bay. Over the years, the birds have consistently nested on some islands, suggesting that fish resources may be abundant and available nearby. We are comparing the avian and fish populations at the southern end of the bay, near the Rutgers Tuckerton Field Station, with those in the middle and north end of the bay. For twenty years the northern part of the bay has harbored a healthy population of common terns. Although they have shifted from island to island, depending upon the location of the nesting herring gulls that prey on them, the population remains healthy and reproduction is always high. This suggests food resources are good, despite the distance from an inlet.

Late spring or summer is the main spawning time for the salt-marsh minnows, such as killifish or mummichogs, sheepshead minnows, and sticklebacks, but killifish larvae can even appear in the salt-marsh pools as early as late April. They generally spawn on the spring tides. As the season for spawning approaches, the normally dull males begin to change colors. Stickleback get darker, almost black on their backs, and their bellies turn yellow; the mummichogs turn steel blue along their sides; and the sheepshead minnows' backs turn blue and their bellies and fins turn yellow to orange edged with black.

Mummichog males take up territories in the marsh creeks and display to females (Figure 9.2). The brightest, biggest, or otherwise most "attractive" males get the females. While the male grasps the female with his fins,

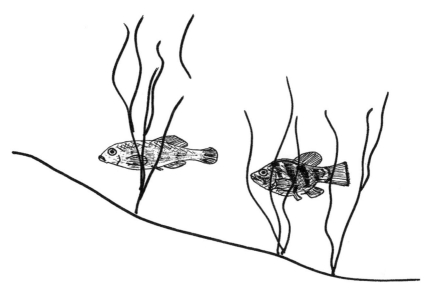

9.2. Mummichog and sheepshead minnow (on right) in salt marsh pool.

she lays her eggs in shallow water, and he fertilizes them with milt. The fish sweep the water vigorously with their tails, "blowing" the sticky eggs toward the cordgrass stems at the water's edge. There the eggs adhere while they develop. After two weeks, the minute fry hatch and then depart with the next very high tide.

Most mummichogs live only one year, although some live for two or three years. During the winter the mummichogs may move farther out along the creeks, into slightly warmer water in the deeper creeks or bays. Two- and three-year-old Mummichogs, though scarce, are important to the food web, because they provide more energy to their predators than do the smaller fish.

Unlike the mummichogs, sticklebacks do not leave their eggs so much to chance. The males build nests of small pieces of plants and mucous, and display from them. Following spawning, the males pick up any stray eggs in their mouths and place them in the nests. The males remain with the nests, guarding the eggs until they hatch. The adults guard the fry for a time after they hatch, until they swim off on their own. Silversides live along the shores of creeks and estuaries, but during the winter they migrate to deeper waters in the estuaries or nearby Atlantic Ocean. In May the silversides spawn, attaching their eggs to vegetation such as eelgrass or widgeon grass growing in the shallow bays. The young hatch within a few days and grow rapidly. Most silversides spawn the first year and then die, although some live to spawn a second year.

Reproduction for these small minnows that breed on the Jersey salt marshes peaks in June and July, although the breeding season extends from May until September. Juveniles usually have microhabitat preferences that are similar to those of fry. High-marsh tidal pools, nontidal pools, and ditches that dot the marsh surface may be more important habitats for breeding fish than previously thought.

Many young fish, called larvae, stay in the wide channels or the shallow creeks that meander through the marsh, but some move onto the marsh itself during spring tides when the marsh floods. After the waters recede, many larval fish remain in the marsh ponds, marooned until the next spring tide. These pools are important habitats, however, for they often have lush algal carpets and profuse widgeon grass for food and shelter. Although only a few species of larval fish use these ponds, numbers can be great. Grass shrimp also abound in the luxuriant vegetation, providing food for foraging shorebirds and waders.

With each spring tide there are changes in the ponds, as some fish move from pond to pond or out to the creeks and channels. When the waters cover the marsh, only the tips of the cordgrass hint that a lush marsh lurks beneath the waters. Flocks of laughing gulls converge on the marsh and float about the surface, picking up shrimp and fish. Some gulls and shorebirds swim in tight circles, rapidly picking up shrimp as water flows off the marsh. The birds look like giant tops that are wound too tightly and cannot stop pecking. Herons descend in large groups, moving across the marsh, stabbing at every killifish that passes by. When the waters recede in their wake, few small fish remain in the ponds.

Some of the fish that were floating across the marsh make it back to the creeks and channels. Although only nine or ten different species of fish occur in the salt-marsh ponds, nearly ten times as many live in nearby tidal creeks. The mummichogs and sheepshead minnows that are so common on the marsh ponds abound in the tidal flats.

These small, short-lived fish occur mostly on the salt marshes and in the creeks and channels, but other fish move between the estuaries and the ocean. The life cycle of fish that live for many years, such as bluefish, differs dramatically from that of the short-lived fish such as mummichogs or silversides. Bluefish are migratory and come into our waters from April through November. One of the most abundant sport and commercial fishes in the Mid-Atlantic region, they are eagerly sought by fisherman along the Jersey shore. Bluefish use the Jersey bays and estuaries as nurseries, and most bluefish in the bays are less than three years old.

Unlike silversides, bluefish spawn in the ocean, and the young fish then move into the bays to feed and escape predators (Figure 9.3). When the estuarine waters begin to cool, the bluefish head offshore to warmer waters.

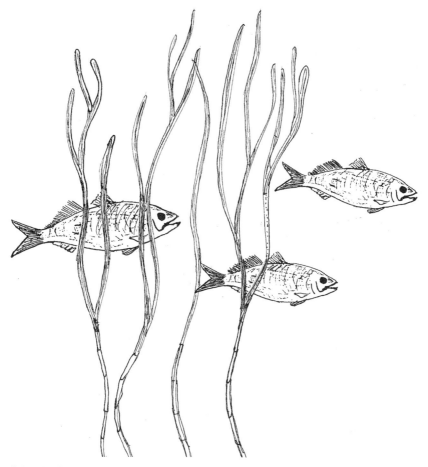

9.3. Bluefish young in salt marsh creek.

The older, adult bluefish remain offshore during the summer, and anglers must brave the near-shore ocean waters to catch the ten- to twenty-pound blues. Bluefish migrate to warmer, southern waters in the winter.

The individual life cycles, like those of the killifish and the silversides discussed above, are of interest mainly because they affect the food web. The food web within the bays and estuaries is complex; it includes plankton feeders such as mummichogs, silversides, sheepshead minnows, and bay anchovies. These species are often called baitfish, because they are used as bait by fisherman. They are also called prey fish because they are the main prey of terns, skimmers, herons, and egrets. Populations of prey fish directly affect population levels and reproduction of the birds.

Killifish are important predators in salt marshes, feeding on benthic (or

9.4. Summer flounder, a fish with both eyes on the same side to permit bottom-dwelling lifestyle.

bottom-dwelling) invertebrates. Large killifish even prey on grass shrimp, which are themselves predators on benthic animals. Killifish can thus have both a direct effect on benthic invertebrates because they eat them, as well as an indirect effect when they eat the grass shrimp.

A number of bottom-feeding fish prey mainly on bottom-dwelling organisms such as crabs, lobsters, shrimps, clams, oysters, mussels, and worms. Benthic fish include Atlantic sturgeon, white perch, black drum, tautog (also known as blackfish), and winter flounder. Most of these are eagerly sought by fisherman along our shores. Winter flounders are unusual fish in that they have a compressed oval body, and they swim with one side pressed to the bottom. Both their eyes are on top of the body. They spend most of the year in river mouths and estuaries, and spawn from February through March. When the waters warm in the spring, winter flounders move to cooler offshore waters.

Weakfish move into the estuaries at about the same time as bluefish in the late spring, when many are about to spawn. They also spend the summer inshore, but migrate south to Virginia and the Carolinas in the winter. They get the name from their weak mouth, which tears easily when hooked.

Summer flounders, or fluke, also visit the estuaries in the summer (Fig. 9.4). They are also flatfish that change color according to the bottom where they lie. Larger than winter flounders they can reach nearly three feet long. In the summer they move inland, and in the winter they move offshore to spawn. They feed on small fish as well as crabs, shrimp, and worms.

Over the last decade or two, many of these species have suffered serious declines in New Jersey and along the rest of the Atlantic coast. Several species of sturgeon are endangered, winter flounder have experienced long-term declines, and tautog have been seriously depleted recently by the Japanese fleet. Conservation organizations are just beginning to include fish as an important conservation issue; and the National Audubon Society has initiated a Marine Conservation Program, under the direction of Carl Safina, that is addressing these conservation issues.

The large predatory fish at the top of the food web are perhaps the most interesting, for they run up and down the Atlantic in large schools, coming into the bays and estuaries to spawn. Such predators include bluefish, weakfish, summer flounder, and striped bass. The young of many predators spend the first year or two in bays. These predatory fish are also favorites among fisherman, who spend a great deal of time searching for "runs." Runs of various species are dependent on water temperature in the bays, and in many shore communities water temperatures are regularly given on weather forecasts.

The bluefish is one of the first predators to move into the local estuaries in the spring or early summer. It is sea-green with a silvery belly and can grow to about three and a half feet long. Migrating north and inshore in the spring from warmer, southern waters, bluefish travel in massive schools of hundreds or thousands of fish. They summer in inshore waters, feeding on any kind of fish they can catch. The bluefish is a destructive and ferocious predator, running through dense schools of smaller fish, leaving mangled bits of fish in its wake. In the late summer bluefish spawn over the western half of the continental shelf off the Jersey shore, and the hatched larvae return to the safety of the estuaries. Large adults remain off the Jersey shore, but smaller adults may enter the bays and estuaries.

Predatory fish, such as bluefish, are eagerly sought by foraging terns, for schools of baitfish are concentrated and forced near the surface. When a school of bluefish is after a school of small herring or silversides, the blues force the smaller fish toward the surface, where they fall easy prey to terns hovering overhead. For a few minutes the frenzy of activity over a school of bluefish is incredible: the water boils with baitfish leaping out of the water to escape the large bluefish rising from below. Above, dense flocks of up to a thousand terns hover, picking off fish after fish from the white froth. Within only a few minutes the bluefish school moves, and the baitfish scatter below the surface, out of reach of the terns. The terns remain in the area, searching for the bluefish school, locating it a few hundred yards away, and hovering over the new site.

For many years Carl Safina and I studied the foraging behavior of common terns along the Atlantic coast, trying to understand the relationship between the abundance and behavior of prey fish and tern foraging. We used sonar to assess how many small baitfish were in the zone just below the water surface, where terns could catch them. Although baitfish sometimes come close to the surface, this event is infrequent, and the terns have a difficult time finding them over the vast open water along the coast. Terns have better luck finding baitfish near shoals or in the shallow bay waters. However, terns can find dense schools of baitfish when they are forced to the surface by predatory fish. Bluefish or other predatory fish feed from underneath the school of baitfish, while the terns feed from above. The terns thus search for predatory fish or marine mammals as a signal of the availability of baitfish. Without the bluefish or other predatory fish, most small prey fish in the open sea would be unavailable to the terns, because they remain too far below the surface.

We also found that prey-fish numbers built through May, peaked in June, and declined thereafter. Their decline was coincident with the arrival of the predatory bluefish. Bluefish abundance and feeding behavior correlated inversely with prey-fish abundance and depth: the more bluefish, the fewer prey fish. The more feeding bluefish, the shallower were the prey fish. We concluded that bluefish were driving the seasonal patterns of prey-fish abundance through direct predation and by causing the prey to flee.

The movement patterns of the fish along the Jersey shore are varied, and a whole world of different life-cycle strategies lies just below the water surface. It is much more difficult to follow the movements of all the age classes of all the fish that live in even one estuary than it is to follow the movements of all the birds that live above the estuary. Yet the information is necessary to understand the complicated food web of the estuaries, the population cycles of the birds that depend on the fish, or the potential for sport or commercial fisheries.

The distribution of fish form a mosaic of patterns that relate to where they live, when they spawn, what water temperatures they prefer, what they eat, who eats them, and whether they travel in large schools or skulk in the marshes or on the floor of the bays and estuaries. When spring arrives and the bay waters warm up, many plankton feeders move in, followed by the predatory fish. The small killifish and other prey fish drift into the creeks and ponds on the marsh, where they can escape predation by the larger and more voracious fish. The run of bluefish into inshore waters can predict the coming of spring and summer just as easily as the arrival of killdeer on the Rutgers campus or the first black-crowned night heron on Islajo Island.

10

Horseshoe Crabs on Delaware Bay

A sea of dark brown shapes agitates the shallow water, giving the impression of intense fermentation, a massive pot of coffee coming to a boil. In some places the horseshoe crabs are a layer or two deep, while in others, they are piled high, radiating from a central point. The odd brown domes seem to come in different sizes, but all are about the same color. Each one looks like a squashed helmet with a long spike at one end. It is difficult to recognize the shapes as individual animals, involved in one of the most ancient mating rituals. Horseshoe crabs have come by the thousands and thousands to breed along Delaware Bay.

Even on the beach, the deep brown shells of horseshoe crabs are strewn about. Half buried in the wet sand, the same shapes are motionless. These seem to be broken in two, with a long spike coming out of one end (Figure 10.1). Trails that look like treads on a miniature bulldozer lead from the sea to the half-buried females. Many of the shells are isolated, while others seem to be attached to one another, with two bulldozer trails leading from the sea. The second shell is smaller than the first. Still others are obviously upside down, with claws and legs nestled in the shell, the long spikes cocked upward at an awkward angle. The beach looks like a disaster zone, with thousands of shells strewn about, scattered as far as I can see, like victims of some unseen war. Some of these creatures will swim out when the next high tide covers their bodies, but others will be stranded in the hot sun and will perish before the tide returns. As long as they are right-side up, horseshoe crabs can withstand up to eighteen hours of drying in the sun and can still make their way safely back to the sea with the next tide. They find their way to the water more by moving down slopes than by receiving visual cues. In some years nearly 10 percent of the adult horseshoe crab population along Delaware Bay dies of stranding.

It is a warm and balmy afternoon on Delaware Bay, the sun is high overhead, and the rays are warm. Waves gently lap against the wet sand ten yards from the high-tide line, and a flock of shorebirds moves rhythmically with

10.1. Horseshoe crabs on beach.

the waves. Farther out, laughing gulls feed in a dense flock, their noisy cries audible at a long distance. Despite all the bird activity, it is impossible to look at anything besides the mass of horseshoe crabs.

This incredible scene is repeated along most of the beaches of Delaware Bay and along some other parts of the Atlantic coast, although in fewer numbers. Thousands of horseshoe crabs breed on the bay each year, and this is one of the truly unique natural-history sights of New Jersey. It ranks with the dramatic breeding colonies of gulls, terns, and skimmers along our coasts in June, the spectacular hawk and songbird migration at Cape May each fall, the elegant flight of migrating monarch butterflies in Cape May in September, and the massive flocks of snow geese at Brigantine in the winter. Although the large flocks of shorebirds that gather on Delaware Bay in the spring to feed on the horseshoe crab eggs are spectacular, so too are the many thousands of horseshoe crabs that converge on the beaches when a full moon and high tides coincide.

It is mid-May on Delaware Bay, not quite the peak of breeding for the horseshoe crabs. That peak will come in a few days, with the spring tides. Egg-laying always peaks at the end of May, although some horseshoe crabs breed from April through September. Horseshoe crabs are limited to the warm temperate oceans, and only four species remain of the many that roamed the seas millions of years ago. Indeed, they are often referred to as living fossils, because they have remained on Earth unchanged for 200 million years. Three of the species are found in the Far East from Japan through India, but ours is found from Maine southward along the Atlantic coast to Yucatan. Delaware Bay is the center of the Atlantic coast population.

Horseshoe crabs are arthropods, along with insects, spiders, scorpions, and crabs. However, they are not true crabs, for they lack the crab characteristics of two pairs of antennae and a pair of mandibles or jaws. Most edible crabs have five pairs of legs, whereas horseshoe crabs have seven pairs

10.2. Female horseshoe crab with three male suitors.

under their shell, known as a carapace. Their closest relatives are spiders and scorpions. Despite their menacing appearance, horseshoe crabs are not dangerous as long as you do not stab yourself with their sharp tail. Indeed, they have been used for food and medicine.

The horseshoe crabs gather along the Atlantic shores in the millions. After the breeding season they walk on the bottom muds of Delaware Bay to reach the ocean and swim languidly as far out as the edge of the continental shelf. During the winter, horseshoe crabs lie half buried in the mud in the sediments below the shallow seas. This "hibernation" allows them to slow down their metabolic processes even further, and to avoid predators. Recent information from divers, however, indicates that some may remain active throughout the winter, although at a lower level.

With the lengthening days of spring, the crabs begin to stir and to move toward the beaches. First the males arrive, and a week or two later the females appear. The females are some 30 percent larger than males and weigh four to six pounds, while the males weigh only two to three pounds. Females can produce up to 20,000 or more eggs at a time, and their larger size is an adaptation to their prolific egg production.

To attract a male, females release a pheromone, or natural chemical, into the water. Males patrol the waters, searching for females. When a male finds a female, he clasps her "abdomen" with his first pair of legs. She swims toward the beach, pulling the male to the tide line. The sex ratio of crabs along Delaware Bay is about three males to every female. The competition for females is great, and it is not unusual to see eight or ten males trying to grasp one female (Figure 10.2). The male that arrives first, however, gets the female, and large males are no more successful than smaller males.

Eventually the female **drags her** male, or two or three, to the sandy beach. She scoops out a shallow nest at the wet tide line and deposits over 20,000 lime-green eggs in the eight-inch hole, while moving slowly forward. The eggs are like little bits of tapioca and are nearly opaque. The male fertilizes the newly laid eggs as the female moves forward. Following egg-laying, the crabs return to the water. When the tides recede too quickly, the crabs get stranded above the tide line and must wait for the next tide. If they are upright, they can survive the wait; but if turned over by an animal or a thoughtless person, they may dry out and die before the next tide rescues them. As long as the beach has a slope, the crabs can find their way to the water. Many will die if they have emerged on nearly flat beaches, because they have no clues to orient themselves toward the water.

Females may lay eggs more than once during the season and can lay up to 80,000 eggs each spring. Hatching rate for those that remain buried within the sand is high. Despite the large number of eggs that are laid by over a million females along Delaware Bay, only about 130,000 of these eggs will develop into adult crabs.

The thousands of tiny eggs in a nest, only one-sixteenth of an inch across, double in size over the next few days and become transparent. The moisture supplied by the bay and the warmth of the sun incubates the eggs, for the female departs immediately after egg-laying. Females time their egg-laying for the new and full moons, when the tides are the highest. The eggs take about thirty days to hatch, so they hatch during the next high tide that can carry them safely out to sea.

The small larvae are vulnerable to predation by birds, mammals and, later, by fish. A very small percentage of the larvae remain in the soil for the entire summer and through the winter and emerge in the spring. Larvae that spend the winter beneath the sand face possible injury from winter storms, but they avoid avian predation by emerging when few birds are around.

The young larvae, called trilobite larvae, dig their way out of the sand about two weeks after hatching. They look just like adult crabs, but they are only one-eighth inch across. Shortly after emerging, they will molt into juvenile crabs. Like newly hatched birds and reptiles, they can live on their yolk sacs for a few days, until their digestive systems mature. When the yolk sac is gone, they begin to search for minute worms and clams to eat, pushing their way along the bottom of the bay. They search for prey by plowing through the bottom sediments, feeling with their front legs. Once they find prey, they use their legs to crush the worm or clam and stuff it into their mouths. Without jaws, the crabs must crush with the base of the legs.

All along Delaware Bay this scene is played out countless millions of times, as the tiny horseshoe crabs grow larger and larger. The crab periodically molts its shell or carapace, as it outgrows the old one. It sheds the carapace by simply walking out through a split that develops in the front where the upper and lower shells are joined.

Usually the discarded shells languish in the mud or disintegrate in the seas, but occasionally conditions are just right, and thousands of tiny shells are left on the wrack line by high tides (Figure 10.3). It looks as if there was

10.3. Shed shells of young horseshoe crabs.

a massive die-off of young crabs, because the shells are complete with seven pairs of legs and a tail, or telson. But the pale beige shells are empty, and the young crabs are safe in the bay, growing new shells.

During the first few years, the young horseshoe crabs molt frequently, but thereafter they usually molt only once a year. After a crab sheds its shell, it pumps in water to expand the new soft shell by 25 to 30 percent, so the shell is bigger than the crab's current body. Then the shell hardens within twenty-four hours, leaving room for the crab to grow. The shell must harden quickly, for the young crab is vulnerable to predators while it is soft.

Males reach sexual maturity when they are nine years old, but females require ten years. Although the exact lifespan of horseshoe crabs is unknown, they live for at least thirty years. This contrasts sharply with true crabs, such as the blue crab found along our shores, which has a usual lifespan of one and a half years. The reproductive strategy of a species that does not breed until it is ten years old must be different from one that lives only a year or two, for there is high mortality at every point. Of the millions of eggs that hatch along Delaware Bay each year, only a small percentage of the young will survive to breed.

As I walk along the beach, I watch one large female lying on her back trying to right herself using her tail. Digging the tip of her tail in the wet sand, she pushes, elevating her shell sideways until it is high enough to tip over by its own weight. She burrows down a bit in the wet sand, taking advantage of the moisture, waiting for the next high tide only a few hours away. Once awash by the surf, she will trundle back to the sea. She is shiny, a rich chocolate brown with a few coffee-colored highlights. Not far away is a large female with three barnacles growing on her shell, and another has a blue mussel attached to the rear. Once these organisms have attached themselves, they are there until the crab molts.

Several species hitchhike on horseshoe crabs, including barnacles, blue mussels, slipper shells, bryozoans, sponges, flatworms, and even bacteria. Most of these cling to the shell and cause no harm. Since adult horseshoe crabs shuffle slowly along the bottom, they hardly notice the extra weight. The flatworms glide around the top and ventral surface of the crab, and pick up food scraps around the claws. The flatworms deposit their eggs in the gills of the horseshoe crabs, and the cement used to attach them may eventually abrade the shell, allowing bacteria to move in. The bacteria eat away at cracks in the shell and can eventually cause death.

Although adult horseshoe crabs do not have many natural enemies, they are exploited for a variety of purposes by humanity. The indigenous peoples of North America ate them, used the shell to bail water from their dugout canoes, and fashioned the tips of the tails into fishing spear tips. Indians also used horseshoe crabs for fertilizer, and this practice was immediately adopted by the early European settlers. Horseshoe crab flesh is high in nitrogen, and a thriving fertilizer industry lasted until the 1950s in south Jersey. Even today some farmers in Cape May deposit dead horseshoe crabs in their fields. Crabs were used for over two centuries to feed chickens and hogs. This practice was discontinued because people did not like their chickens to taste like the sea. Nonetheless, between the 1800s and the 1930s some 1.8 million horseshoe crabs were harvested annually.

Horseshoe crabs are effective bait for catching eels and conch. They have been used for bait for as long as there have been fisherman in Cape May, and the few that any one local fisherman took did not harm the population. As bait became harder to get along the east coast, truckers from nearby states converged on Delaware Bay. They arrived first with small trucks and then with larger trucks. Eventually they came with large tractor trailers that they filled with thousands of dead, dying, and even vibrant, female horseshoe crabs. The females are preferred because they contain eggs, used to attract eels. Great masses of people began combing the beaches to pick up the hapless crabs and put them in barrels for loading onto the trucks. They cleaned up entire beaches, disturbed the large flocks of migrating shorebirds, and removed the entire breeding population of crabs from some areas. The devastation in their wake was immense. Moore's Beach once contained a thriving population of breeding crabs, but on my last visit, only about a dozen were along the shore.

The wholesale removal of horseshoe crabs was finally reduced by setting catch regulations. It was made illegal to pick up the crabs during the day to reduce disturbance to migrant shorebirds that must feed before their long northward migration. And it became illegal to pick up the crabs on consecutive nights. This stopped the interstate trucks, because it was impossible to fill a tractor trailer in one night, and they could not keep the crabs for days before returning to their destination.

These regulations do not hurt the fisherman of Cape May County, because they can still get enough crabs for their needs in only an hour or two at night. The overexploitation of horseshoe crabs on the beach ceased, at least for the moment. However, the populations were still depleted from two centuries of overuse for fertilizer, chicken feed, and fish bait.

Fishermen, however, can change as fast as the regulations. With the restrictions on picking up crabs from the beach, they have switched to harvesting them from the water using toothless dredges or bottom drags. Although only 128 to 140 permits have been issued to collect horseshoe crabs, fishermen managed to harvest nearly a quarter of a million crabs in 1993, and 307 thousand in 1994. Each crab can bring up to a dollar. The population of horseshoe crabs is only about 4 million along the east coast, and with the quarter million that die each year because they are stranded on the shore, the take may be too high to sustain the population. There is even some indication that the selective harvesting of females has changed the sex ratio. The Endangered and Nongame Species Program is working hard with the Fisheries Division to devise regulations to preserve the horseshoe crab populations.

Horseshoe crabs have been very important to medicine. They are model animals for the study of eyes, because they have large compound eyes that have a simple construction, with an accessible optic nerve. They are easy to work with in the laboratory. The chitin shell of the crabs has also been used to make chitin filament for suturing wounds, and chitin-coated suture material enhances healing time by 35 to 50 percent.

One of the most important medical discoveries, made by Frederick Bang in the early 1950s, was that the copper-based blood of horseshoe crabs contains a clotting agent that attaches to bacterial toxins, the poisons produced by infectious bacteria. This clotting agent, called Limulus Amoebocyte Lysate (LAL), is produced by many companies, including Limulus Labs (once called Marine Biologicals, Inc.) that operates near Cape May.

To obtain blood for LAL, female horseshoe crabs are collected from Delaware Bay and brought to the laboratory. They are bled with a stainless-steel tube that is inserted directly into the circulatory system. The females are held for a few hours and then returned to Delaware Bay. It appears that the females are not harmed by this process.

Horseshoe crabs may have other problems in Delaware Bay. The Delaware Bay estuary is one of the most heavily used systems in the nation: it harbors one of the world's greatest concentrations of heavy industry. About 70 percent of the oil arriving at the east coast of the United States comes through this estuary. It may be a time bomb waiting to happen; planning for the possibility of a massive oil spill is essential. Should an oil spill occur, it will in all likelihood happen when the winds are strong, the possibility for containment small, and the maneuverability of oil skimmers diminished. The ecosystem is fragile even though it is ancient.

For now, the mass movement of horseshoe crabs to Delaware Bay goes on as it has in bays since the Paleozoic, with over a million of them arriving each May to lay their eggs beneath the intertidal sands. The sand is littered with shells, with their plowlike trails leading to the bay. Shorebirds gather in the thousands, blackening the sand, darkening the sky when they are disturbed from their feeding. Out on the sandbars laughing gulls squabble over horseshoe crab eggs, trying to gather as many eggs as possible before the bar is covered by the rising tide.

11

Shorebirds along Delaware Bay

The narrow strip of white sand at Reed's Beach is alive with thousands of shorebirds that form dark ribbons undulating at the water's edge. As the tide recedes, the birds follow, some standing on wet sand while others are knee deep in the foam. Their bodies nearly touch one another, and the whole mass moves as one great amoeba, ebbing with the tide. The tapestry of black, buff, brown, rufous, and white is made up of over 12,000 shorebirds. It is the end of May, and the peak of both the spawning of a million horseshoe crabs and the migration of over twenty species of shorebirds.

For centuries hordes of shorebirds converged on Delaware Bay each spring to feed on the bountiful horseshoe crab eggs. As wave after wave of crabs came ashore, they dislodged the eggs of countless females before them, creating a surplus for the birds. Between late April and early June well over a million shorebirds pause here to feed on the eggs. Some estimates run as high as one and a half million. Some shorebirds will travel more than 8,000 miles from their wintering in South America to their Arctic breeding grounds. They fly at 12,000 to 18,000 feet, according to radar observations, at speeds of 35 to 60 MPH. Many of those arriving in Delaware Bay have already migrated 4,000 miles from South America and may have flown nonstop for sixty or seventy hours. Still they are only halfway. They will have depleted all the fat reserves used to fuel their long migration, and many have lost half of their body weight. They stop here for days to refuel and to lay down enough fat resources to complete their northward journey. Most stay for a week or two, in which time they double their body weight. In their brief stay in Delaware Bay, the shorebirds may consume over one hundred tons of horseshoe crab eggs. Females must arrive on their tundra breeding grounds with enough resources to lay a clutch of eggs, for they will have little time to forage before they lay eggs. The breeding season in the high Arctic is short, and they have no time to lose.

Shorebirds nesting in the Western Hemisphere undertake lengthy migrations from coastal beaches and wetlands in South America to northern

11.1. Red knots on wrack line resting near horseshoe crab shell.

Canadian breeding grounds. They have only a few intermediate stopover points along the route to feed, and these places are called "staging areas." Staging areas provide abundant food, enabling the shorebirds to regain weight quickly and be on their way. Few staging areas are as strategically placed as Delaware Bay.

During spring migration Delaware Bay hosts the largest concentration of shorebirds in eastern North America and the second largest concentration in all of North America. Biologists from New Jersey's Endangered and Nongame Species Program have observed as many as 350,000 shorebirds in a single two-hour survey of the beaches along the bay. This does not count the birds in the salt marshes or in the upper salt marsh creeks. Over twenty different shorebird species and over a million shorebirds move through the bay. Each spring, over 80 percent of the shorebirds in eastern North America pause on Delaware Bay. That makes it important habitat for shorebirds overall and a critical staging area for some species.

The most abundant shorebirds migrating through Delaware Bay, accounting for well over 95 percent of the birds, are semipalmated sandpiper, ruddy turnstone, red knot, and sanderling. Counts for these species are the highest for the hemisphere, attesting to the importance of Delaware Bay. Most of the species are present in peak numbers from mid-May to early June. Nearly a third of the world's red knot population moves through Delaware Bay in the spring (Figure 11.1). Because Delaware Bay is so important to the well-being of migrant shorebirds in the Western Hemisphere, it is critical to understand trends in populations. Each spring since 1986 the Endangered and Nongame Species Program takes a census of the shorebirds once a week from early May until mid June, circling the large flocks in an airplane to estimate total numbers and species composition. Rich Kane usually leads these surveys, providing consistency among the years. The populations of most species have varied over the years, but sanderlings and semipalmated sandpipers have decreased precipitously. Sanderlings have declined from 35,000 in 1986 to about 10,000; and semipalmated sandpipers have declined from over 250,000 to about 50,000 in 1994. Although these differences may represent usual cycles for shorebirds, there is cause for alarm.

Delaware Bay is particularly attractive to the mass of migrants, because it is directly in the center of their ancestral migration route, and the horseshoe crabs are laying eggs just when the shorebirds are moving through. The food supply is unending, since more horseshoe crabs lay eggs with each tide. On a warm spring day the beach is littered with horseshoe crabs stranded on the sand, while hundreds of others thrash about in the wash, often several layers thick. Where the waves lap gently against the shore a band of shorebirds moves slowly out with the tide, picking up the eggs washed from nests by wave action. The light green eggs are easy to pick out from the white grains of sand.

Horseshoe crabs lay their eggs in nests that are eight or ten inches deep, but the constant digging of hundreds upon hundreds of females disrupts the nests of other females, releasing masses of eggs into the surf. The surf sparkles with a green tinge as sunlight strikes the thousands of eggs boiling in the wash.

The band of shore where horseshoe crab eggs are available is narrow, and so the shorebirds crowd in. Usually touching one another, they move in unison with the tide. Often they form groups of all one species, but sometimes the flocks are mixed. The shorebirds are so thick that they darken the sand.

For the most part, their bodies rub without interactions, they are so intent on foraging. They must maximize their intake of eggs, and they feed continuously. Occasionally squabbles break out in the mixed-species flocks. The smallest species and the largest species are least aggressive, but for different reasons. The small semipalmated sandpipers initiate few interactions because they usually lose: most species are larger than they. The largest species that win encounters, such as turnstones and dowitchers, are not very aggressive, because the other species do not challenge them. Intermediate-sized species, such as sanderlings, are the most aggressive, because they are not large enough to bluff, but are just large enough to win some of their fights.

As the rising tide covers their foraging space, the shorebirds move higher on the beach and stand about in dense flocks (Figure 11.2). When the tide advances even higher, they are forced to fly to high ground on adjacent salt marshes. Formerly the shorebirds could just move higher along the shore to rest, but now there are no dunes or uplands next to the beach; instead, houses and shacks line the shore.

A flock of over 10,000 semipalmated sandpipers and other peeps (the

11.2. Semipalmated sandpipers on beach.

name for small sandpipers) is huddled on the remnant of beach, waiting for the tide to fall. A photographer moves down toward the birds, trying to get closer, hoping to get that perfect shot. As I watch, the birds become restless, they move a bit, they stretch their wings, they give every indication of preparing for flight. Still the photographer advances.

Signs all around say "Do not disturb the birds." There is an observation tower to accommodate birdwatchers and photographers. The birds are far from the platform. Looking furtively around, the photographer moves slowly down the beach, ever closer. In unison the entire flock takes wing, a huge swirling mass of birds; it circles around and lands at the other end of Reed's Beach. For the moment the birds remain alert, no bird tucks its head, and no bird stands on one leg. They watch, and wait.

The photographer ambles back up the beach, shrugs, and continues toward the flock of birds, his bags and cameras swinging in all directions. I suggest to him, mildly, that the shorebirds should not be disturbed; but after a nasty reply, he moves on toward the flock. Again he ignores their obvious intention movements, the raising of their wings, the restless shuffling. Once again the birds take wing, and circle back to their original spot. The process is repeated two more times before the shorebirds fly out across the bay, searching for another beach, one that may be deserted.

The shorebirds along Delaware Bay have faced this intense human disturbance for only the last ten years. From 1928 to 1938 Charles Urner, founder of the Urner Ornithological Club in Northern New Jersey, counted shorebirds in New Jersey and failed to make any mention of Delaware Bay. The masses of shorebirds that used Delaware Bay as a migratory stopover area went largely unnoticed until the late 1980s. It was then that we conducted, in conjunction with the Endangered and Nongame Species Program, the first aerial surveys of shorebirds along Delaware and Raritan Bays. Delaware Bay was a safe place to count birds, but one of my assistants returned from counting the birds along Raritan Bay to find his Volkswagen turned upside down—proof that I was wise to use only males there. These censuses were our first inkling of the incredible numbers of shorebirds passing through Delaware Bay.

We assume that these large masses of shorebirds have used Delaware Bay for thousands of years. However, it is just possible that heavy use by both horseshoe crabs and shorebirds fluctuates over the years, depending upon human exploitation of the crabs. As previously noted, horseshoe crabs were harvested extensively in the 1800s and early 1900s for fertilizer, and it is likely that their populations were so low that shorebird use was low as well. The shorebird populations moving through Delaware Bay may have built back up along with the horseshoe crabs since the 1950s, after the extensive exploitation of the crabs ceased. Although ornithologists might have missed the massive flocks of shorebirds, and clearly they did so for many years in the 1900s, it is unlikely that the market gunners would have missed them in the 1800s. It is also curious that there are no local records, lore, or shorebird decoys connected with shorebirds along Delaware Bay.

Whatever the past fortunes of the shorebirds on Delaware Bay, the discovery in the late 1980s attracted the attention of birdwatchers, and they arrived in droves to see the massive flocks. Most stayed back at a safe distance, awed by the spectacle. Most were content to watch with binoculars and telescopes. Unfortunately, some wanted to get uncomfortably close, as if they could look over every bird, to find one rare one. Some deliberately flushed them to see the spectacle of a flock darkening the sky. Others wanted to get close enough to take the perfect photograph.

The birdwatchers were followed by professional photographers, who felt that they had a right to pursue their profession to the best of their ability. Some found it impossible to resist putting the birds all in the air at once, again and again, as they tried to get dramatic flight shots. While one birdwatcher or photographer approaching too closely is not a problem, large numbers approaching repeatedly day after day are. Over and over, the shorebird flocks rose from the beach.

Forcing the flocks into the air stresses the birds: they expend energy to fly, they must find another suitable place to rest or feed, and the process may unnecessarily expose them to predators. The birdwatchers and photographers also annoy the local people who own houses along Reed's Beach. The residents come to view the birds as a nuisance because they attract the crowds who wander their beaches, bringing dogs and trash.

The shorebirds clearly prefer beaches toward the lower end of Delaware Bay, where the greatest number of horseshoe crabs lay eggs. Both horseshoe crab eggs and shorebirds increase along the bay shore from Higbee's Beach near Cape May Point to Moore's Beach. In some places, the density of horseshoe crab eggs in the top two inches of sand exceeds 100,000 per square yard.

Shorebirds concentrate at the leading edge of waves, where eggs literally boil up in masses. The densest flocks feed near jetties and salt-marsh creeks, where passively drifting horseshoe crab eggs concentrate. When legions of people arrive on these same beaches, they force the shorebirds to less optimal beaches, where there is less food.

The mass of shorebirds that crowd along the tide line is awe-inspiring, their sheer numbers nearly uncountable. For years, the dramatic display was blinding, and we wondered only what beaches they visited when they flew from the advancing tides, from dogs or other predators, or from human spectators. After years of walking the beaches, I have failed to discover where the many thousands of birds disappear to with each high tide.

When the birds are pressed between rising tides and the shallow dunes or houses, they fly inland and disappear into the vast tidal salt marshes that dot the landscape in southern New Jersey. These vast marshes were largely ignored, thought of as waste land, managed only for mosquito control, but for the shorebirds they are important resting places that are safe from predators. Here the shorebirds rest, standing silently on one leg, waiting for the next high tide, waiting to return to the beach.

Over the last twenty years, ecologists have grown to appreciate the importance of examining habitat use over large regions or landscapes. No small patch of shore, no matter how prime, truly is independent. Instead, the small habitat patches combine with others, forming a mosaic of habitats. On the Cape May peninsula there is a mosaic of sandy beaches, salt-marsh creeks, salt-marsh islands, mainland marshes, upland edges, and human developments. The sandy beaches vary in their attractiveness to horseshoe crabs and to shorebirds. Some creeks are small, others are wide, others have shallow beaches where the horseshoe crabs gather by the hundreds. Eggs linger in the slow-moving waters. Salt marshes range in elevation from those that are frequently flooded to those that seldom flood: some marshes have numerous pools teeming with mosquito larvae and other invertebrates.

The importance of marshes to shorebirds needed to be examined before we could understand why the birds are attracted to Delaware Bay. Kathy Clark, Larry Niles, and I wanted to find out what they did on the marshes, and whether they merely rested as most biologists thought. We watched shorebirds on the marshes for many hours to answer these questions.

Large flocks of shorebirds move along the pools, searching for food. Although some rest, most are actively foraging. Depending upon the marsh, nearly 60 percent of the shorebirds are probing for invertebrates. Shorebirds are adding both biomass and nutrients to their diet of horseshoe crab eggs garnered from the beaches. Shorebirds cannot survive on horseshoe crab eggs alone, but must also eat insects and other invertebrates that contain nutrients not present in horseshoe crab eggs. Only by eating invertebrates with the crab eggs will they gain weight.

Although many shorebirds rest on the salt marshes, and most sleep there at night, the marshes provide additional foraging sites. The marshes are more important for some species than for others. When they are on marshes, dunlin and dowitchers spend over 60 percent of the time feeding, whereas ruddy turnstones spend only 40percent of the time foraging. Even sanderlings, once thought to feed exclusively on sandy beaches exposed to the pounding surf, spend half of the time foraging when they are on marshes.

The shorebirds on Delaware Bay spend their time moving between the sandy beaches, tidal creek, and marshes. They can feed along the sandy beaches only around low tide, but they can forage on the marshes throughout the day. Avian and mammalian predators have easy access to the birds lingering along the tide line, but shorebirds on the marsh are free from mammalian predators. Shorebirds can maximize their foraging time, and supplement the energy derived from crab eggs, by moving from habitat to habitat.

For many years the focus of attention has been on the massive food resource provided by the spawning horseshoe crabs. Yet the mosaic of habitat patches on Cape May peninsula is essential to the maintenance of the large migrant shorebird populations. We no longer believe that we can preserve the shorebirds by preserving only the sandy beaches bordering Delaware Bay, although these are essential. We must preserve a variety of habitats, for the full range of habitats are used by different species of shorebirds.

As the tides begin to rise, the frenzy of courting horseshoe crabs along Reed's Beach intensifies. Male crabs line the beach, waiting in the shallow water. A female moves through and is followed by one male, then another, until she is attacked by a dozen males of all sizes. As she digs her nest and deposits her eggs, she releases eggs deposited earlier by other females, and they float free. Dozens of shorebirds feed all around the water's edge, picking up the loose eggs.

The flocks of small shorebirds are not the only ones exploiting the eggs of the horseshoe crabs, for they are joined by laughing gulls (Figure 11.3). On a single census in mid-May nearly 45,000 gulls can be counted feeding on crab eggs from Cape May Canal to the Maurice River, including 8,000 herring gulls and great black-backed gulls. Young herring gulls sometimes feed on crab eggs, but they prefer larger prey. Surprisingly, small flocks of laughing gulls are unable to displace the shorebirds, because it is difficult for small numbers of large birds to penetrate the mass of sandpipers. Instead, the gulls feed on the edge or fly out to small exposed sandbars. There they feed, squabbling for the best places, packed side by side, unaware that Debbie Gochfeld and I are watching their every move.

11.3. Laughing gulls feeding on horseshoe crab eggs.

The gulls are all intent on foraging, and their bills move up and down with the rate and rhythmicity of a high-speed sewing machine. They barely raise their heads. As they feed they call softly to one another, and their calls carry across the water. Now and then one of the gulls feeding on the edge of the flock glances up, watching for predators or other danger. It soon returns to foraging. Even though they are foraging in dense flocks they still must be vigilant for predators such as dogs, cats, or hawks.

The gulls feeding on the edge of the flock spend more time watching for predators, and less time feeding, than gulls that are not on the edge. Vigilance time detracts from feeding, and the edge birds take fewer pecks and obtain fewer eggs. The gulls push and shove, crowding in as the rising tide slowly covers their sandbar. They leave in twos and threes, until only a handful remains on the slender bar. Then they are gone.

Some of the laughing gulls stay only long enough to fill their stomachs, and then they fly to breeding colonies at Stone Harbor. Here they nest in the cordgrass, and incubation is well underway. In only a few days the young will hatch, and these same parents will gather horseshoe crab eggs to feed their chicks. Unlike terns that carry food in their bills, gulls swallow their food and later regurgitate it to their young. Many of the laughing gulls nesting at Stone Harbor feed their chicks horseshoe crab eggs, but they always mix in fish, fiddler crabs, and other invertebrates. Crab eggs are not sufficiently nourishing to sustain the chicks. Laura Wagner and I have experimented with this diet in the laboratory, and both adult and young laughing gulls cannot maintain their weight on horseshoe crab eggs alone. No matter how many eggs are available, they require other foods. Yet as inefficient as these waxy eggs are as a source of food, they are the mainstay of the diet of some chicks. Chicks fed only a diet of crab eggs die within a few days. Shorebirds also cannot gain weight on horseshoe crab eggs alone.

When the tide begins to fall again, the gulls will return to Delaware Bay to feast on crab eggs on the sandbars. The shorebirds on the nearby beach are still pressed into dense, tight flocks along the tideline. Almost no wet sand is exposed above the high tide, and many birds are resting up near the houses. Laughing gulls fringe the flock, facing into the wind. It is still early morning, and the tide will begin to fall in another few hours, exposing more horseshoe crab eggs. They wait, huddled together in a tight flock.

While the laughing gulls and shorebirds are roosting on the beach in dense flocks, great black-backed gulls and herring gulls are wandering the beach amid the overturned horseshoe crabs. They viciously attack the live crabs before the crabs can use their tails to turn over. Gulls usually go straight for the respiratory structure, called book gills, tearing the gills viciously from the undersurface. Although crabs try to protect themselves with their tails, the gulls continue, pulling out the gills, and removing the legs. Predatory gulls may kill over 7,000 crabs a year, a relatively new threat since the first herring gull nested in New Jersey in 1948, and great black-backed gulls moved during the 1970s.

Day after day, the cycle continues. Shorebirds feed along the shore, following the frenzied activity of the horseshoe crabs. As the tides advance, the shorebirds move higher on the beach. Eventually they fly to the large creeks, and then the creeks too are covered. They fly to the back salt marshes, seeking the pools where insects abound. When the tides recede, the flocks again converge on Delaware Bay. Laughing gulls feed here also, moving back and forth between the bay and their breeding colonies, where they courtship-feed their mates with the eggs, or feed them to the chicks.

Then one day in early June, the shorebirds are gone, only a few horseshoe crabs swim for the beaches, most are scuttling back toward the sea to rest again in the bottom muds, hidden from danger. Only the laughing gulls from Stone Harbor continue to come, searching for the few remaining eggs.

The Delaware Bay ecosystem is fragile, and the shorebirds and horseshoe crabs are exposed to threats from over-harvesting of the horseshoe crabs, direct development, human disturbance, and toxic chemicals. Now horseshoe crabs can be harvested along the shore only every other night, but these regulations could be challenged, and fisherman have started to harvest them from the open water just out from the beaches. Human disturbance is a serious problem, as birds are frequently displaced by birdwatchers, photographers, other naturalists, and by some of the beach residents who see the shorebirds as a threat to property rights.

On any day in May or early June, when the crabs and shorebirds are in full force, there are up to eighteen oil-tanker passages, moving in and out of ports in the upper bay. An oilspill prior to or during the spawning or migration period would kill the horseshoe crab eggs, make food unavailable, would poison some birds, and might cause other birds to suspend migration. Or the birds might move immediately on, dying before they reach the tundra, or arriving half-starved, unable to survive or produce eggs. Any further loss of habitat will surely reduce feeding and roosting sites.

Delaware and New Jersey have joined to make Delaware Bay one of the charter sites in the Western Hemisphere Shorebird Reserve Network, which is encouraging the protection of shorebirds and their wetlands. This step was critical, but the next steps are equally important. We must have habitat protection, horseshoe crab protection and management, toxic chemical and oil containment, and reduced human disturbance for the shorebird migration to go on as it always has.

The shorebirds have migrated through Delaware Bay unnoticed for thousands of years, following the age-old spawning cycle of the horseshoe crabs. Each spring the horseshoe crabs swim slowly along the bottom, moving toward the bay, toward the calm waters of the sandy beaches, where they can join the frenzy of other crabs. It is a delicate balance, based on a healthy environment for both the crabs and the shorebirds. It is up to us to preserve this balance, for we have the power to tip the scales forever.

Summer Scenes

12

Laughing Gulls at Stone Harbor Marshes

Dried goldenrods stiffly balk against the whispering winds that bend the delicate beach grass, twirling it, making soft circles in the sand. The beach is narrow, the dunes abrupt, and a lone buckeye butterfly disappears over the dunes. Bright sunlight sparkles off the wet sand, as the tide waters recede. Below, the rippling waves are set aboil by an undulating wall of large brown horseshoe crabs, each female pursued by up to a dozen males competing to fertilize her eggs. Although she digs herself in to deposit her eggs below the sand, the surging surf and the next wave of females will dislodge some. Well into summer, some horseshoe crabs come ashore. Horseshoe crabs have remained unchanged for millions of years; and untold millions of crabs have amassed in the surf of Delaware Bay and along the Atlantic coast since the last ice age receded. All along the tideline the crabs are stacked two and three animals deep, extending out from the shallows to beyond my view. The surf is pink and pale green with millions of tiny gelatinous eggs, often hidden from view by masses of shorebirds too dense to count. Not far away the waves brush a sandbar, and over five hundred laughing gulls busily feed on the horseshoe crab eggs. The birds almost touch one another, and their heads move rhythmically up and down as they peck at the tiny eggs.

Every May the shores of south Jersey are alive with a million shorebirds that stop on their northward migration, and with thousands of laughing gulls that will breed on coastal marshes of New Jersey. Horseshoe crabs breed all along our coasts, and laughing gulls can be found wherever there is this abundance of eggs. I have watched them at Corson's Inlet, near Brigantine, and in Barnegat Bay, but never in the dense concentrations found along Delaware Bay, where ribbons of gulls fringe every beach and sand bar. Although most feed continuously, those on the edge occasionally look up, searching for predators. A gull on the edge of such a flock is more vulnerable than one within the dense milling group. Most aerial predators would not enter such a compact flock but might try for a bird on the edge. They are separated from the mainland by open water, but with the tide receding, ground predators can soon approach.

In the sheltered bays near Stone Harbor the horseshoe crabs breed in smaller numbers, and the gulls concentrate in dense flocks to feed on the eggs. Once satiated, some gulls leave in small flocks, flying to coastal salt marshes. In early May the *Spartina* is only just beginning to grow, and last year's brown stems still protrude from the rich, black mud. Here and there mats of *Spartina* grass and eelgrass lie in ribbons along the high-tide line. The mats, strewn here by the highest winter storm tides, are indicators of places safe from summer tides, since higher tides reach this high only during hurricanes.

Laughing gulls migrate back to New Jersey in early to mid-April from wintering grounds in Florida and Mexico. In the Northeast they nest in colonies on salt-marsh islands, though in Florida and Texas they nest on sand or spoil islands. The Stone Harbor marshes are surrounded by signs of civilization, and the gulls are forced to nest on salt marshes rather than the open beaches near the ocean.

In early May the gulls settle on the Stone Harbor marsh, behind the Wetlands Institute, where they seek mates and establish territories. On each small mat of *Spartina* a lone male laughing gull stands, watching the sky. When a laughing gull lands at the far edge of the mat two to three yards away, the male charges forward, giving loud long-calls, forcing the male intruder to leave. Another gull lands, quickly turning its head delicately away, making its black hood less visible, and the male gives a soft head toss before slowly walking toward the female. He moves too fast, and the female flies away. A few minutes later another female lands and again faces away. The male moves forward, and again the female flies, but she returns, and finally the female stands her ground for a few moments (Figure 12.1).

Over many days the male displays to the female, but each time she leaves after a few moments, only to circle back and land again. Finally she remains, allowing him to approach and stand beside her. After many bouts of mutual head-tossing, he leaves her to guard the territory, while he goes off to fish. Returning, he lands softly beside her. As she walks back and forth in front of him, giving low cooing noises and exaggerated head tosses, she pecks lightly at his beak. He bends down and regurgitates fish for her, which she gobbles up. This courtship-feeding ritual will go on for a week or two. Not only does courtship feeding cement the pair bond, but it provides additional food for the female to aid in egg production. Courtship feeding is often followed by mating, and the white inner wing-linings can be seen far across the marsh (Figure 12.2)

Females whose mates do not feed as much or as often are likely to lay smaller eggs. Smaller chicks hatch from smaller eggs, leading to lower survival

12.1. Female approaching male laughing gull during pair formation.

rates. Or a female may throw up her wings in despair and find another mate. Failure to courtship- feed is grounds for divorce.

With time the pair move off the mat, standing about for hours in several different places within their territory. All over the marsh other pairs are also shifting around their territories, standing at one place and then another. They mostly shift sites after particularly high tides, abandoning wet spots and seeking the higher spots. For almost a month they assess potential nest sites, selecting the highest spots free from tidal inundation. Here they construct strong, bulky nests of *Spartina* grass.

On this island the laughing gulls are alone, no other gulls compete for these sites. Laughing gulls have been displaced from some nesting islands by herring gulls. Herring gulls are not native to New Jersey, but first nested here in 1948. Since then, they have increased quickly, taking over island after island. Some remain near the colony through much of the winter, and others arrive two to three months before the native laughing gulls. They have well established territories before the laughing gulls even arrive, and they have laid eggs, and in some years their chicks have hatched. When the laughing gulls return to their colonies in the spring, the herring gulls have claimed all the best places, high on the marsh where no flood tides will reach. The laughing gulls are forced to move to lower places or to other islands. Those that remain near herring gulls run the risk that the larger gulls will steal their eggs, or eat their chicks. Faced with intense predation

12.2. Copulating laughing gulls.

from gulls that are three times their size, laughing gulls often abandon their traditional colony sites and move to less optimal places.

Like other species of marsh-nesting gulls, laughing gulls construct large nests that may be two to three feet across and a foot high. Such bulky nests are protection against high tides, for if the tides are not too high these nests will float and resettle on the marsh when the tide recedes. In exceptionally high tides even these nests are dislodged, often floating over the marsh with an agitated parent flying overhead. Sometimes nests come to rest intact on the marsh, and the parent settles to incubate. Other less lucky parents see their eggs or chicks float away on surging tidal waters.

As tides rise, laughing gulls with vulnerable nests frantically add nest

12.3. Laughing gull rebuilding nest after I simulated a flood by putting a cup filled with water in some nests (on right), while others had an empty cup (on left).

material, building the nest higher and higher. Such makeshift efforts often succeed in keeping the eggs above the tide. Their intense nest-building is stimulated by wet feet. When I put small plastic saucers in their nests and filled them with water the gulls all began adding more grass stems until their feet (and their eggs) were no longer wet (Figure 12.3). They did so even though it was sunny and the ground around their nests was dry. Gulls with cups in their nests, but no water, did not add more grass to their nests. Their eggs will still hatch if the eggs are covered by salt water for a few hours, but after that, submergence kills the developing embryos.

Laughing gulls lay eggs in late May; each female usually lays three eggs unless food is particularly scarce. The eggs are dark olive brown with darker speckles and scrawls that render them hard to see by a predatory crow or gull flying over. The colony is quieter now because most birds have found mates, and pairs have established territories and are incubating. The pairs are scattered widely over the marsh and are not as dense as in other colonies of gulls. Their scattered nesting pattern is a result of the low elevation of the marsh habitat: Only a few scattered spots are high enough to escape flooding. Since most nests are not close together, territorial defense is minimal, and the gulls often doze while incubating.

The gulls incubate quietly for about twenty-four days, each parent incubating in shifts of three or four hours. Off-duty parents fly away to fish or to feed on crabs on nearby mudflats at low tide, or they cross the peninsula to feed on the few remaining horseshoe crab eggs along Delaware Bay. There are fewer crab eggs as June wears on, but some gulls have a fondness for

12.4. Incubating laughing gull, with mate standing nearby.

them, and still search for them. When not away foraging, the off-duty parent usually stands nearby (Figure 12.4).

In mid-June the first chick hatches, a wet ball of beige fluff with dark brown spots on the head and back. Like the eggs, the chicks are cryptically colored, blending in with their nests and the marsh. When only a few hours old they can wobble to the edge of the nest and hide in the cordgrass, blending into the shadows.

Standing on wobbly legs, a three-hour-old chick pecks at its parent's red bill, and the parent gently regurgitates partially digested fish into the chick's bill. Both parents feed the chick, one always standing guard while the other goes off to forage. Only two hours later the second chick hatches, and within hours, they are dry and fluffy, and vigorously beg for food. The third chick hatches over a day later and now must compete with its older and slightly larger siblings for food. Food is abundant this year, however, and all three chicks grow quickly. In other years, when food is scarce, the third chick often starves to death, ensuring that the older two chicks obtain enough food to grow adequately. Ultimately, reproductive success is higher if parents fledge only one or two heavy, healthy chicks rather than three very light, emaciated chicks that will not survive long after fledging.

At a week of age the fluffy chicks sleep quietly on the nest while the female stands guard nearby. For the first week or so, females usually stand guard, and the males do most of the provisioning. A sudden, raucous alarm call from a neighbor breaks the silence, and all adults take wing, flying in wide circles and giving alarm calls. Far across the marsh a female marsh hawk sails low over the ground and lands amid the grass. The gulls hover overhead, diving down toward the hawk and calling loudly. Within seconds the hawk flies up with a chick dangling from its talons and disappears across the marsh, followed by a mob of loud, agitated gulls.

The nests around my blind which moments ago were filled with chicks are now all empty. The chicks scrambled over the nest edge and into the grass at the first alarm calls. Gradually the gulls settle, each landing at its nest, crooning softly for their chicks to return. This chick call sounds like mooing and is termed mewing. The chicks climb haltingly up on the nests and settle beside their parents, tucking their bills in their down to sleep in the warm sun.

Although islands are relatively free from mammalian predators, laughing gulls nesting on salt marsh-islands are vulnerable to aerial predators such as crows, hawks, and owls. Even herring gulls will eat laughing gull eggs and chicks when it is convenient. Crows eat only eggs, returning on successive days until the whole clutch is gone. Hawks and owls normally eat only chicks, although they can take adults incubating on nests.

One year, two or three chicks disappeared each night, and an adult was killed, its partially eaten, decapitated body lying forlornly on a nest. This predation is typical of great horned owls. Over about two weeks the owl ate chicks or adults in over twenty nests, and the small colony eventually was abandoned by the gulls.

This colony has escaped heavy predation, and the gulls are generally quiet. Here and there an adult flies directly to its nest, relieving its mate, feeding its chicks. I hardly hear the soft long-call from above that causes the chicks to jump up and down, calling loudly. But the long-call was enough to send the guarding parent off on a foraging trip, and the caller lands to begin feeding its chicks.

As the days pass the chicks gain weight, begin to lose their fluffy down, and acquire pin feathers and the awkwardness of gangling youth. They wander off a bit now and again, but mostly they sit quietly on the nest. Their parents have stopped adding new material to the nest, which is becoming obliterated, the nest cup less obvious, the nest flatter and less well-defined. A firm, tall nest is no longer essential, because the chicks can withstand short periods of high tides by moving to high ground, remaining on floating nests, or swimming to the safety of thick mats.

When they begin to wander about the nest, the chicks are attuned to the calls of their parents. At only six or seven days old, the young can distinguish their parents' calls from those of neighbors and can recognize the calls of their siblings at about the same age. This allows the chicks to find their parents or nest if they wander too far away, and they can eject foreign chicks from their nests.

Parental recognition in gulls and terns usually develops at about the age when chicks begin to walk away from their nests. Chicks of gulls that nest on cliff ledges or on floating nests in marshes, where they usually remain on the ledge or platform throughout the chick phase, have delayed parental recognition. Chicks abandoned by their parents often wander about the colony, seeking adoption. They are unsuccessful unless they can find a nest where the chicks are less than a week old. Otherwise, they are severely attacked by the resident chicks and driven from the nest.

As their wings grow and primary feathers develop, the chicks spend more time jumping up and down and flapping their wings. Such exercise no doubt strengthens flight muscles. Finally the flapping lifts them slightly off the ground. Their parents still guard them most of the time, continuing to bring back fish, horseshoe crab eggs, insects, and other foods to regurgitate for them. They are now nearly full grown, large enough to protect themselves from neighbors and predators. Their parents must spend nearly all their time foraging. By early July the young are learning to fly, making erratic flights from their nests to crash-land in nearby *Spartina*. The parents continue to feed them at the nest, and the young make short flights around the nesting territory. The flights gradually lengthen until the fledglings negotiate their first landing at the edge of a tidal creek and discover the presence of food.

Time passes, and more and more young leave the colony, followed by anxious parents still willing to feed them. The family becomes a mobile unit, but one parent usually remains with the chicks. Once they are able to fly well, however, the chicks are not vulnerable to flood tides and are less vulnerable to predators. The biggest problem they face is starvation, and both they and their parents work at remaining together while the feeding continues. Fledglings must learn food types, how and where to forage, and how to open difficult foods such as clams or crabs. The period immediately after fledging is the most dangerous for young gulls, and more young will die in the few weeks after fledging than at any other time over the next year.

Within days the marsh is deserted, the gulls spreading up and down the coast in bays and estuaries. Most learn to forage on natural foods such as fish, crabs, clams, and other invertebrates, but others discover garbage dumps, feeding largely on junk food and meat scraps. The young gulls are not as efficient as adults at finding food on the dumps, but with enough time they can find sufficient food to sustain them. At garbage dumps, both adults and young sit on the edge of the dump for much of the day, flying in to search the dumping face only when the trucks that carry food waste come in mid-morning. During August and September flocks of adults and chocolate brown young sit on sand bars at high tide and feed on mud flats at low tide, storing fat for the long migration to Florida and points south. On moonlit nights, both adults and young can be found foraging along the shore. The adults have lost their bright red bill and jet black head, and their sporadic long-calls are raucous and hoarse. Here and there a chick still begs from an adult, who reluctantly regurgitates a mass of fish, indicating a tenuous bond. Mostly they stand about, facing into the wind, waiting for the long journey south. By December, laughing gull numbers have dwindled along the Jersey shore, and we find them in abundance in Florida and along the Gulf Coast. Many have migrated farther south, to Mexico and beyond.

13

Civilized Mallards at Manahawkin

On the salt-marsh islands in Barnegat Bay, mallards, gadwall, and an occasional black duck nest, hidden in the grasses. In mid-May we wander across Harvey Sedge, while counting herring gull nests. Outside the gull colony, the marsh is quiet, and the cordgrass glistens in the bright sun. As we walk through the grass a seaside sparrow flushes ahead of us, flying so low over the grass it almost seems like a small mouse. Here and there scattered over the marsh are others, mostly males setting up territories. There are few perches in a salt marsh, so the birds stand on a bit of grass that is just an inch or two taller than the rest. Seaside sparrows that survive the winter usually return to the same bit of marsh to set up housekeeping the following spring.

As we continue, the sparrows fly from the grass, land only a few feet away, and disappear in the sea of stems. They are small enough to scuttle through tiny trails in the grass to escape approaching danger. Suddenly one bursts from a thick tuft of grass, flies a few feet at shoulder height, and drops like a stone. We part the grass at our feet to expose a nest. On our rounds of the salt-marsh islands, we are always on the lookout for sparrow nests, but usually they have eluded us.

This nest contains three heavily speckled eggs in a deep cup woven of marsh grass. The elegant structure is raised slightly above the mud, buoyed up by dense grasses and suspended by others. The terminal blades of grass arch over the nest, obscuring it from view. We walked by this spot only a few days ago, unaware of the nest, watching the male displaying on a perch not far away. The marsh was dotted with males then, each displaying to unseen females lurking in the grass. Their songs not only attracted the females, but also defined their territories for other males. Pulling the blades carefully back over the nest, we move on (Figure 13.1).

We pass a flattened patch of salt hay, the delicate stems forming a mat of swirls. The marsh must be slightly higher here, for otherwise cordgrass would grow. The salt hay is a lighter green than the cordgrass and is much

13.1. Seaside sparrow incubating on nest in salt marsh.

finer and softer. A duck bursts from the ground, momentarily startling us into turning and following her departure with our eyes. It is a female mallard. Had we been quicker, we could have caught her with our bare hands. Her flurry of activity has obscured exactly where she came from, still we search for the nest among the swirls of grass.

We spread the grass and see a carefully woven nest of dead cordgrass and salt hay stems. The nest is over a foot across, with a nice tidy rim that holds the eleven immaculate white eggs. They were not visible until we parted the grass and removed the soft gray down, but once exposed, they glisten in the sun. Down feathers tucked around the edges partly obscure some eggs, but the female did not have time enough to cover the eggs completely before she left.

Like most ducks, this female is alone, incubating the eggs by herself. Typically, the male mallard's role is completed when he mates. Although he is quite attentive when he is courting, this ceases with mating. Males must devote time to courting, because if they leave the female only for a few minutes, another male may move in and mate with her. Some or all of the female's eggs might then be fertilized by the intruder. All the effort and time the male devoted to his mate would be wasted.

This mate-guarding is quite common in birds, a cost the males of many species must incur if they want to ensure that they have the exclusive opportunity to mate with their female. Mate-guarding is particularly strong in birds that have biparental care, where both parents incubate the eggs and care for the young until they fledge. It is doubly important to ensure paternity for males that will stay to incubate the eggs and care for the chicks. In these species the male may follow the female everywhere and even forego feeding for a few days. The female is always assured that the eggs in her nest are hers, but this is not so for the male. Males can never be positive the eggs are theirs, but they can improve the chances by staying with the female every minute.

Considering how common mallards are today, it is hard to believe that when I was growing up, mallards were still rare along the Atlantic coast. Even though the image of a mallard is what comes to mind when most people think of a wild duck, few easterners had actually seen one, for the mallard occurred mainly in the prairie states. Beginning in the 1950s, it spread eastward rapidly, claiming freshwater and estuarine wetlands. Today, the mallard is abundant and has largely replaced the black duck as a coastal breeding bird.

The female mallard has chosen her nest site well: it is high enough on the marsh to avoid most tidal flooding, and in dense grass that obscures the nest from predators. The male had no part in her selection of the nest site; he had already flown off in search of another potential mate on another island in the bay. The nest is at the edge of the salt-hay patch, which will provide a nice smooth lawn, easy for the young to traverse when they first hatch.

We leave the nest, noting its exact location relative to the patch of salt hay, and move on to the gull colony. The gull colony is centered on the higher part of the island, where marsh elder bushes grow. Only slight changes in elevation result in different flooding patterns, and the vegetation reflects these differences. With the gulls swirling above our heads, we begin to search slowly for their nests, checking to see how many have hatched and how old the chicks are.

Tiny, well-worn paths from the open salt hay lead through dense bushes to the nests, often at the base of marsh elders. Flooding three weeks ago has desynchronized the nesting pattern, for nests that survived the floods have young chicks, while in others the eggs were flooded from the nests and lie a few inches away, smelling fouler than most rotten eggs. In some, the herring gulls have relaid a fresh clutch, and they are about a week into incubating these second clutches.

An hour later with our census completed, we head for the boat and check the seaside sparrow nest on our way. Now there are four speckled eggs, and the clutch is complete. We must have disturbed her before, just as she was ready to lay. It is the duck we are after, and we sneak toward the duck nest. We are expecting the exploding female. When she comes, Fred is ready, and he reaches unerringly—plucking the female from mid-air. She carries on her right leg a numbered metal band—one we had placed on her when she nested on this very same island two years ago.

Since she was banded as an adult, we no doubt caught her the same way before. There was no way for her to avoid being captured again, however, for it is part of her defense to burst rapidly from the nest when approached by a predator. The strategy of many ground-nesting birds is to stay hidden until the last minute, fully expecting not to be detected. Usually it works. When a potential predator gets too close, a female needs to take evasive action to save herself. Such evasive action usually succeeds in startling the predator into following her, rather than searching for her nest.

When her eggs hatch, over the course of a day, she will lead the young to the water after they have dried off. They will then remain at the edge of the island, where they can plunge into the water to avoid land predators, or head into the grass to avoid aquatic predators. The female alone has the task of protecting her young until they are able to fend for themselves.

This pattern of female incubation and parental care in mallards plays out all along the Jersey shore, on salt-marsh islands, on deserted barrier beaches, and on abandoned fields and open meadows. The domestic scene is different on the barrier beaches, where houses crowd together, and masses of people invade the island in June. On islands such as Manahawkin the male mallards are more responsible citizens.

Mallards adapt readily to living among people, as long as they can avoid dogs and cats. Mallards have increased everywhere along the barrier islands, for they have adjusted to the houses and roads, and live in the spaces between them. People of all ages, from tiny children to seniors, love to feed birds, and ducks are excellent candidates because they are large, tame down quickly, are happy with bread or other easily obtained foods, and there is no danger that overzealous ducks will bite your hand.

I often pause to watch a flock of twelve to twenty mallards being fed by children at the public pier in Manahawkin where we launch our boat. Salt marshes lie just out in the bay, where other mallards carry on as they always have. But here, the mallards travel in large flocks and hang out in groups on the fishing piers and docks, waiting for a handout. They compete with gulls and with one another for the bits and pieces of food dispensed by people launching their boats for a day fishing on the bay. There is a steady stream of people putting their boats in the water, or dragging them out

13.2. Female mallard incubating under steps, with male guarding her nearby.

again at the end of the day. Most of them have extra food they are only too willing to part with; food that is soggy from the salt spray, crumbled from the jostling, or melted by the hot sun.

When May comes to Manahawkin, and these half-tame mallards begin to think of courtship and breeding, their activities occur in groups, rather than the lone pairs courting on the marshes. Several males may be courting the same female at the same time. It is more difficult for a male to get his female alone, and he has to work hard to isolate her from the group. Sometimes a female is beset by three or four males, all trying to mate with her at once, and such females are lucky to escape alive. Gangs of ten or twelve males all trying to mate with one female can suffocate or crush her.

Once pairs form, the males guard their females throughout the day, sticking close. They wander from the group, where they can court in private. Only when loud squabbling indicates that someone is tossing out food do the mallards rush to join the main group. The females on Manahawkin are also responsible for finding a nest site. The limited choices usually include hiding the nest under a porch steps, behind the hydrangea bushes, or in the tangle of rose bushes beside the old abandoned wooden boat (Figure 13.2). As the female searches for her nest site, the male tags along, still guarding the female from other males.

When she begins laying her eggs, the male still remains, escorting her to and from the nest as she searches for food. Once incubation starts, the male stands nearby, often the only visible sign that a female may be nesting close by. He seems to be guarding her from predators or other dangers, or is merely able to warn her if danger approaches. Many dangers lurk amid the houses: Cats and dogs are about, rats sometimes abound, and small children rush to investigate anything new. Unlike the truly wild mallards out in the marshes, the male remains with the female throughout incubation.

He carries on his attentive vigil until the chicks hatch, and then both parents accompany the chicks to the water. Like the salt-marsh mallards, the brood remains near the shoreline, where the chicks can seek shelter either on land or in the water, depending upon the predator. At other times, the broods parade in line, with a parent at each end.

Manahawkin is a dangerous place for ducklings, even though it is such a nice place to panhandle for food. The young chicks are small, and the neighborhood has many cats and dogs. It takes the efforts of both parents to protect the ducklings from these foes. Within only a few days most broods are down to one or two chicks. Only a few pairs succeed in fledging any ducklings. When the ducklings finally reach adult size, they are large enough to avoid being eaten by rats and are able to fly from other predators such as dogs or cats.

The cycle continues, with the salt-marsh mallards behaving as they have for eons; the males deserting the females following mating and the females assuming all the incubation and parental-care activities. The Manahawkin mallards have slowly developed male parental care, and both parents travel with the young. I have seen this pattern in many barrier-beach communities. It seems to be a function of high population densities of mallards, high predation pressures, and the difficulties of living amid houses rather than the wilds of marshes, meadows, or fields.

14

Common Terns
and Skimmers at
Barnegat Bay

A thick fog blankets Barnegat Bay, and the silence is broken by a foghorn bleating every minute. It comes from Barnegat Lighthouse, and we can use it to gauge our location. It has served as a beacon since 1858, although the original one built in 1834 was untenable because of sea encroachment. Almost no one will venture out in weather like this, and the bay is deserted. At least we assume so as we head blindly across the bay toward a tiny island. The small spoil island lies directly in our path from the mouth of Tom's River to Barnegat Lighthouse, and we throttle up the engine to head for it. As the foghorn grows louder, we slightly correct our course.

Barnegat Bay is dotted with over 250 small islands of all shapes and sizes, ranging in elevation from low cordgrass islands that are almost completely covered by most high tides, to those with well-defined uplands with reeds or small bushes. Many of these islands were created over three thousand years ago, when sea-level rise slowed enough for islands to form from the buildup of peat, which enabled the grasses to take hold.

There are also other islands, much more recent, that were created just this century by the Army Corps of Engineers, intent on keeping the Intercoastal Waterway open through periodic dredging. Barnegat Bay is part of the great Intercoastal Waterway that stretches from Massachusetts to Florida. Guided by channel markers, boats can travel most of the way protected by barrier islands. Keeping the waterway open requires constant dredging, and the spoil must be deposited somewhere. Once the dredgers dumped it anywhere, but now they must examine the alternatives and file environmental-impact statements.

The several spoil islands in Barnegat Bay are usually higher than the surrounding natural islands. Most are circular and domed-shaped. Whenever fresh spoil is added to these domes it provides ideal places for beach-nesting birds that can no longer find safe havens on the crowded sandy beaches along the ocean. The spoil islands are really artificial beaches, wide-open stretches of sand that allow birds to watch for predators in all directions. The high elevations ensure that their nests will be above high tide. Piping plovers are often the first to move onto the fresh spoil, followed by least terns, and then black skimmers.

Least terns form relatively dense colonies, for there are no mammalian predators to search the sand for their eggs. Black skimmers move in among the least terns, settling in small groups of ten to twenty pairs. These species live in relative harmony, defending territories, incubating eggs, and finally feeding chicks with fish caught in the surrounding waters. By late July most young have fledged, and the islands are again deserted.

With time, seeds blow in from other nearby islands, and vegetation gains a foothold. Within only a few years beach grass grows on the berms, gradually getting denser. Eventually reeds colonize and spread rapidly through underground rhizomes. Vegetation succession occurs rather quickly on the fresh spoil, and the birds nesting there shift as the habitat changes. After three or four years the least terns, piping plover, and skimmers are relegated to the top and windward sides of the island that are still relatively free from vegetation.

I am drawn from my thoughts suddenly by the appearance of land. Out of the fog looms Barnegat Island, but we do not slow the boat until we can drift onto the shore. From the edge of the island we count over 200 pairs of nesting least terns, and 65 pairs of black skimmers visible through the mist. The skimmers are in a tight group, clustered between the terns and the beach grass. It is early June, and most are still incubating. There is no need to disturb them. Two piping plovers and their chicks feed along the shore, walking slowly along the wet sand, probing, watching, probing again.

We push the boat out through the shallow water and start out again, passing Pelican Dredge Island on our way. This is another dredge-spoil island, but it is a bit older, and its succession is several years advanced. Dense reeds grow on one side, thick forbs on the other. Herring gulls nest in the vegetation, and many fly up to circle the island as we pass. Hidden in the top of the island, where there is still bare sand, a large flock of brown pelicans stands guard. They are mostly young birds, and the nests they have constructed are rudimentary (Figure 14.1). This is only the second year flocks have been seen in New Jersey; we expect that these prospecting young birds will someday breed here. They have set up housekeeping, but it may be several years before they nest. This prospecting of colony sites is common in pelicans. They sit about the island, practicing, defending territories, building nests, but never really getting around to laying eggs.

The fog lifts briefly as we start for other salt-marsh islands farther south. Unerringly, Fred threads his way through unmarked channels to West Vol, West Carvel, and then Pettit. As we sail through the creek beside Loveladies, we notice that the houses are deserted still; it is not quite warm enough for

14.1. Young brown pelican sitting on nest.

the summer people. We find only a few common terns nesting on Vol Sedge, and there are no skimmers. Vol Sedge is close to the barrier beach, and dogs, cats, and people have prevented most birds from nesting here. However, they have not discouraged the few nesting herring gulls that have settled here, and it is a wonderful island for little boys to explore. Here too, the herring gulls nest on the higher places, near the bushes that will protect chicks from the hot sun.

West Carvel also has few common terns, for this has been a herring gull stronghold for many years. Only about fifteen pairs of terns nest together on the wrack on the tip of the island. Over the last five years the few bushes have grown dense, and the gulls have increased. Three pairs of great black-backed gulls have moved in as well, and the smaller terns cannot compete and will almost certainly abandon this island before long. Discouraged, we head into the fog once again.

Next is Pettit, a tiny salt-marsh island just north of Manahawkin bridge. By dead-reckoning, Fred aims across the bay, for the fog has settled in again. Mornings like this with intermittent fog are common in the spring and early summer. If fog lasts for several days in a row, it is much harder for the terns to find fish. Soon Fred cuts the engine and noses the boat toward the peat at the edge of Pettit. I am always amazed that we arrive at the right place through the thick fog. Pettit is a low salt-marsh island with only cordgrass, but it has a nice thick mat of eelgrass left by the high storm tides of winter. The thick mat, which rings the edge of the island, is six yards wide in some places. It provides high quality nesting sites for terns and skimmers because these are the last places to flood. When flood waters seep under the mat, threatening to wash out the nests, the mat rises slowly, carrying the nests securely above the water.

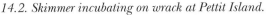

14.2. Skimmer incubating on wrack at Pettit Island.

As we sit at the edge of the island with our motor turned off, only a few terns fly overhead. Otherwise it looks deserted. The boat nudges the mudbank and we sit quietly, counting the birds in the air. About thirty yards away are fifteen pairs of skimmers, silently incubating (Figure 14.2). To be sure, their heads are raised in the air as they peer at us, their wings jutting out from their bodies as if they are ready to fly. One or two stand, giving their hoarse barking calls. Gradually all of the skimmers start to bark. As we prepare to leave the boat the skimmers all stand and take off in unison, wheeling slowly over the bay. They circle around us, closely at first, giving loud barks before flying out into the fog, their barking call disembodied and ghostlike. Pettit is so small that the skimmers will not land while we are still on the island.

The terns respond to the skimmers, and within seconds the air is filled with fifteen hundred pairs of common terns, circling, calling, diving, mobbing, making a real ruckus. Just as suddenly, many descend, landing everywhere on the mat, in the cordgrass, on the wooden duck blind, and on the edge of the mudbanks. We return to the boat and sit quietly. Gradually the noise abates, although two common terns signal their suspicions by diving repeatedly and uttering menacing "kek kek kek kek" calls. A few minutes later the skimmers return, flapping slowly out of the fog, to land on the mat and resume incubation.

For twenty years Fred Lesser and I have surveyed the common tern and skimmer colonies in Barnegat Bay, traveling from the Lavalette Islands in the north to Tow Island at the mouth of Great Bay. We sail our sea, in all kinds of weather, using tiny rowboats or seventeen-foot Boston Whalers. Sometimes it seems as if we are on the high seas, for stiff winds, high waves, and whitecaps can rule Barnegat Bay. At other times it is calm and peaceful, though never like glass. Each spring, when the warm winds blow and the terns and skimmers return to Barnegat, we are like slaves, unable to resist the mysterious pull of the Bay. We start out once again to run the forty-six miles from Lavalette to Holgate, looking for the tern colonies.

Barnegat Bay is dotted with over 250 islands, if you count every piece of land surrounded by water as an island. Yet, each year there are only between 14 and 24 colonies of common terns nesting on the salt-marsh islands, and black skimmers nest with the terns on only 7 to 15 of these islands. At first glance, it seems likely that the terns and skimmers have plenty of space to breed, and there is little conservation concern for any given island.

Yet year after year, we find that the terns nest on the same islands, and when a traditional island becomes overgrown with bushes and overrun with gulls, terns simply move to a nearby island. In all our years of traveling the bay, terns have nested only on 37 of the 259 islands in the bay. Although seabirds often nest in the same traditional places every year, salt marshes are inherently unstable, because they change over the years, and with slight changes in elevation, the vegetation shifts. When high-marsh plants and shrubs move in, so do the predators.

We spent one whole winter working on this problem: Are all salt marsh islands alike, or do the terns see something we do not? Using high-resolution maps and aerial photographs, we measured the size of the islands, determined their acreage, measured the distance from each island to the mainland and barrier beach, described their vegetation, and noted their exposure to open water. When we did this, back in the mid-1970s, we traced the outline of each island using a device called a polar planimeter, which cleverly computed the area of irregular outlines. Today, of course, we would simply scan the maps into a computer and hours of painstaking work would be completed in seconds.

We then examined the characteristics of the 34 islands where terns had nested, and of the 222 islands where they had never nested. We were looking for characteristics that distinguished between these two groups of islands, used and unused. We used the characteristics of the 34 occupied islands to define the limits of an acceptable habitat, and applied these to the 222 unused islands.

To our great surprise, when we eliminated the islands that were too large, too small, too narrow, too close to other islands of the mainland, too far from the barrier beaches, not exposed to open water, or were in shallow water, there were only eleven suitable, unused islands left. When we then imposed the vegetation preference of the terns for islands that were over half covered with *Spartina*, we were left with only three unused islands in all of Barnegat Bay that fit the overall pattern of habitat features used by colonies of common terns. We were amazed: Out of all those islands, few were truly suitable for nesting. The terns had told us, in their own way, that suitable nesting habitat was quite limited in the bay. If they lost any more colony sites, there was virtually nowhere else they could colonize.

We have followed the breeding colonies of terns over the years since then, and the terns eventually nested at least once on all three of these islands, but they have not nested on any of the other islands. For many years we have waited, but they still nest on the same islands, year after year. They shift among these islands, abandoning gull-infested ones, but they do not venture onto new ones.

Their choice is determined by two main constraints: flooding and predators. If the terns nest on high islands with bushes, shrubs, or reeds, then they are exposed to predators such as rats and herring gulls. Rats cannot live on islands that have winter washovers because they will drown, and herring gulls will not nest on islands where their nests can get washed out by spring high tides. Islands too close to the mainland are shunned, presumably because terrestrial predators would have easy access.

On the contrary, the terns cannot nest on islands that are too low or their nests will be washed out by high tides. They balance these two problems by selecting those islands that are high enough to avoid summer high tides, but low enough so that there are no rats and nesting herring gulls. This is a very narrow zone, and there are few islands that meet these requirements. The terns also can lower their chances of being washed out by high tides if they find islands with large, stable mats.

The eelgrass mats have been washed up and stranded on the islands by winter storm tides. In summer, waves seldom reach these highest mats and they persist when lower ones have washed away. By choosing mats that are white and bleached by the sun, the terns can be assured that the mats have even survived the high tides of the past winter. Skimmers will nest only on these high wracks, and in years when there is no appreciable wrack on any Barnegat Bay islands, the skimmers do not nest on the salt marshes.

During a few years in the middle 1980s when there were no severe winter storms, the tern islands lacked wrack. The ever-present eelgrass in Barnegat Bay always comes to rest on some islands. In these years the wrack rested on islands that were too low for tern nesting. Fearing that the skimmers would have no place to nest, we built them artificial wracks. In late February and March we commandeered several boats, and with a crew of volunteers, we hauled boatload after boatload of eelgrass from low-lying islands to West Carvel, Pettit, and other islands. Fred, Mike, and I used old driftwood to make frames.With the added help of Jim Jones, David Gochfeld, Debbie Gochfeld, Gaylord Inman, and several other volunteers, we piled the eelgrass between the boards.

It was a great success, and in some years, all the skimmers on salt-marsh islands nested on artificial wrack. No other wrack was available. Our wrack served as a magnet for the tern colonies as well, and thousands of tern and skimmer chicks fledged from Barnegat Bay in those years. It was such a success that the *Sandpiper* and other shore newspapers carried pictures of us hauling boatloads of eelgrass, and of the skimmers nesting contentedly.

Soon I received a letter from the New Jersey Department of Environmental Protection, demanding to know if I had a "proper building permit."

I answered, showing pictures of our operation, of the wrack, and of the nesting birds. I explained that we gathered all the eelgrass from nearby islands, that we used only driftwood to build our frame, that the wrack and frames washed away the following winter, and that no permanent structures were built on the marsh. Months passed with no reply. Finally, we received a nicely written response stating that since we used driftwood and erected no permanent wracks, we could continue. Within a few years, the period of low winter storms ceased, and we no longer had to build wracks. Now, in the mid-1990s, we seem to be reentering a period of low wrack availability; once again, we must consider building some.

The terns also prefer islands with some exposure to open water and prevailing winds, because these islands have nice, large mats that are blown high on the land. Islands surrounded by other islands, or protected from the winds, never have nice mats, and they never have nesting terns and skimmers.

All salt-marsh islands are not alike for another reason: Their placement in the bay influences their exposure to tides as well as to winds. Tidal waters can enter Barnegat Bay from the south through Great Egg Harbor, or from the middle through Barnegat Inlet. Salt-marsh islands located in the north end of Barnegat Bay have the least range in tides. It simply takes so long for the water to flow in through Barnegat Inlet and up to the north end that by the time it gets there the tide has turned and is already flowing back out of the inlet.

For the terns, this means that the Lavalette Islands seldom experience really high tides. Only when there is a gale force nor'easter do these islands have the potential to flood. The terns know this full well, for the largest colonies have consistently been on the Lavalette Islands. From 600 to over 2,100 pairs of common terns have nested on these four islands at the northern tip of Barnegat Bay, and the birds raise young every year. They are never completely flooded out.

In the meantime, herring gulls increased on the bay. Historically, terns did not always have to contend with competition from the herring gulls, for the first herring gull nested in New Jersey in 1948. As herring gulls have increased in number, common terns have been forced from some of their traditional breeding sites. Not only do the gulls compete with the terns for nest sites, but they also eat their eggs and chicks (Figure 14.3). The terns respond by shifting colony sites, often to lower islands that may render them vulnerable to flooding.

Herring gulls have gradually moved onto the Lavalette Islands. In the early 1980s only a few juvenile herring gulls stood about the very tip of one of the islands, resting between foraging trips out into the bay. The terns

14.3. Herring gull about to steal egg of common tern.

continued to nest in full force in the cordgrass throughout the island. In time the gull numbers increased, until nearly a hundred young herring gulls loafed on the island. They ignored the terns, for they were more interested in eating crabs, clams, and fish from the bay.

In the mid 1980s the first herring gulls began to nest on the northwestern tip of North Lavalette. Three pairs nested that first year, all subadult birds with black tail bands and bits of dark feathers on their heads. They failed, for they could not work out their incubation rhythms, and their eggs did not hatch. The next year there were thirteen nests, and with the benefit of prior experience, some of the pairs raised young.

The colony grew rapidly as the young gulls that loafed on the island matured and developed an interest in the opposite sex. Soon there were fifty pairs nesting, and they occupied most of the north end of Lavalette. With more experience, many pairs raised two or three young, and these birds took up residence, loafing at the edges of the colony.

When the terns arrived in late May, the herring gulls were already incubating eggs. The gulls now owned the island, and the terns were forced to the south end. Small groups of terns tried to establish nest sites, but were constantly harassed by the gulls. Some terns persisted and hunkered down in the thick cordgrass. They laid eggs and incubated quietly.

Young gulls began to maraud the tern colony, eating eggs and disturbing the peace. By 1990 only seven hundred pairs of terns nested on the four islands, down from over two thousand. The situation has worsened with every passing year, until almost no terns nest on the Lavalette Islands today. They were forced out by space competition with the herring gulls, and by the continual harassment and predatory behavior of the much larger gulls. A common tern weighs less than four ounces, whereas a herring gull weighs over two pounds. There is no contest.

The terns from Lavalette shifted to other islands, but these islands are not as well placed, and they take the brunt of storm tides. Some moved to Little Mike's Island, just north of the Seaside bridge, where they were sheltered from storm tides. Many others moved to Pettit Island, which is high enough to withstand daily high tides but not the worst storms.

This year there have been no excessively high tides, and the six hundred pairs on Pettit are courting or incubating serenely. Some of the terns have not laid eggs; here and there a male brings back a silverside to courtship-feed his female.

Once the terns are paired, the female stands about the territory, guarding it from intruders. The male spends his day flying back and forth, bringing the female fish after fish. Although she does some fishing on her own, he provides her with a substantial amount of food. This allows her to assess the quality of her mate, and whether he will be able to provision her chicks. By providing abundant food, he also allows her to lay larger eggs, which assures a higher rate of survival for her chicks. Every now and then he pauses to court and copulate, but mostly he flies immediately away.

The skimmers occupy the mat in pairs, one incubating, the other standing quietly nearby. It is easy to identify males, for they are nearly a third larger than females, unusual for seabirds, whose sexes tend to be similar in size. Since males are larger, they usually perform much of the territorial defense, always chasing other males. Females sometimes chase females, but often they merely stand by unless there are two or three intruders. Then they jump in with wings flapping.

Skimmers are partly nocturnal and perform much of their courtship displays, courtship feeding, and territory defense at night. A male occasionally flies out in search of a nice fat killifish to feed his female during the day, but usually he just stands around, waiting for nightfall.

As the sunset reddens the sky behind the Manahawkin bridge, the last terns pour into Pettit marsh, and the population nearly doubles with returning mates. Many skimmers are just leaving to feed. They follow the salt-marsh creeks, skimming the surface, searching for fish. With their bodies barely above the water, they fly with their lower, vibrant red mandibles slicing the water's surface (Figure 14.4). When the bird feels a fish, his bill snaps closed, and he rises majestically from the still waters to fly directly back to the colony.

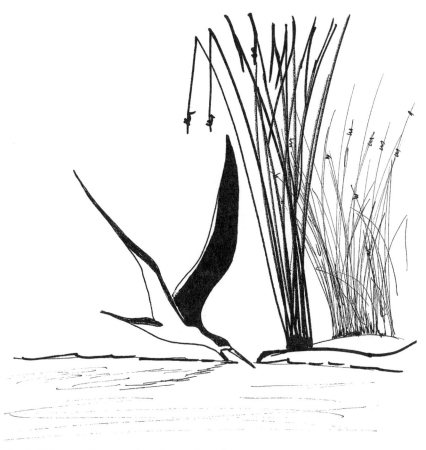

14.4. Skimmer skimming in salt-marsh creek.

Across the bay on nearby Holgate, where a large colony nests on sand among the dunes, skimmers are returning with fish for their mates. Some miles away at Corson's Inlet and at Hereford Inlet, other congregations of terns and skimmers are also in the midst of nesting. As night falls, the terns quiet down, and the skimmers begin to skim the meandering creeks. After an hour or two of fishing, the skimmers exchange incubation duties, and their mates go off to forage.

At Holgate, Corson's Inlet, and Hereford Inlet the skimmers and terns nest on the open beach, nestled between dunes, protected from the wind and surf (Figure 14.5). In nearby New York and Massachusetts they nest on sand, although Ian Nisbet has found them nesting in dense vegetation, and Jeff Spendelow and Helen Hays study colonies where the terns nest amid rocks or beach grass. Champagne Island guards Hereford Inlet, as it has

14.5. Common tern and skimmer colony at Holgate. Top: laughing gulls displaying; middle: skimmer; bottom: common terns displaying and incubating.

done for all of this century. Witmer Stone extolled the virtues of Champagne Island over seventy years ago, and it still remains one of the loveliest islands in New Jersey. It has remained vital while other sandy islands have disappeared or been developed. Here skimmers and terns battle time and the tides to raise their young. Skimmers from other breeding colonies gather here as well. In the late summer thousands of shorebirds feed and linger during spring and fall migration.

On the sandy beaches skimmers nest near beach grass that will provide some protection for their young chicks. The skimmer eggs, a pale gray-white with black or brown splotches, are nearly invisible on the white sand. The females commonly lay four or five eggs, and they begin incubation with the laying of the first or second egg.

Although the first two eggs usually hatch within a few hours of one another, the rest of the eggs hatch a day apart. The young skimmers remain in the nest, waiting for the other chicks to hatch. By the time the full brood has hatched, the first chick is quite large; the young chicks look ill-matched. They remain near their nests and settle down in the sand so they are nearly level with the surface and cast no shadows. They freeze whenever they hear the alarm calls of their parents or the nearby terns, and can easily go unnoticed by predators and people alike.

Within only a few days most of the tern and skimmer parents have chicks to feed. The rush to bring back fish continues unabated. One parent at each tern nest is almost always out on a foraging trip, and even the skimmers take up fishing during the day. So many birds returning with fish in their bills makes piracy a temptation. Some terns and a few skimmers prefer to steal fish rather than forage on their own. On sandy beach colonies, where visibility is high and there are no annoying vegetation barriers, pirates may take up to 15 percent of the fish brought back to chicks. They pirate fish to feed their own chicks.

Since the skimmers are larger, the tern pirates generally ignore them in favor of other terns. Now and then a skimmer chases another skimmer to steal a fat, long fish. Terns standing about the colony watch, and if neighboring chicks have trouble swallowing particularly large fish, the marauders make a pass and abscond with the uneaten fish. Parent terns are under a lot of pressure to bring back just the right size fish, so it will be swallowed immediately instead of pirated.

As the tern chicks grow, parents bring back larger and larger fish. Terns carrying large fish are more attractive to pirates, and so parents must balance the benefits of bringing a large fish to their chicks against the potential costs of piracy. The threat of piracy never ends, but parents can reduce it by bringing in slightly smaller fish that will be less tempting to pirates. They can also lower the risk of piracy by flying low over the colony, making it difficult for pirates to maneuver around them.

The skimmers have little to fear from the terns. The terns cannot outcompete them for space, the terns do not harm them in territorial encounters, and the terns do not eat their eggs or chicks. The skimmers derive advantages from nesting with the aggressive terns, for the skimmers are far less persistent at defending their nests and chicks from predators. When a predator enters a skimmer colony, the skimmers usually leave en masse, flying away from the danger. The terns, however, aggressively mob most predators, often driving them from the colony. The skimmers also derive early warning from the terns, whose noisy cries at the approach of danger can be heard above the normal din of the colony.

Skimmers may occasionally give an elaborate, injury-feigning distraction display. They dip to the ground, flop their wings, and drag their feet. It looks as if the birds are injured, but should a predator come too close the skimmers fly away easily. Distraction displays are relatively rare in salt marshes, for there is no smooth sand for skimmers to flop over. Here on the sandy island at Hereford Inlet, nearly a hundred skimmers give distraction displays as we approach.

The young skimmer chicks are mostly white, but slowly their plumage changes to salt and pepper, and finally to a mottled brown and black above. They blend with the sand and are very hard to see when they freeze. On the salt marshes they melt into the bleached eelgrass, where they can go unnoticed except by the most experienced predator or observer.

As the chicks near fledging, the parents of both common terns and skimmers increasingly leave the chicks alone. They are large enough to protect themselves, and they have learned hiding places. The young terns stand under the beach grass, waiting for the return of their parents, and the skimmers lie nestled in the sand. When the sand is very hot, the skimmers make deeper scrapes by kicking vigorously with their feet, snuggling their bodies from side to side until they reach cooler sand. There they wait motionless for their parents.

In the late afternoon the young birds jump up and down, flapping their wings vigorously, strengthening their muscles in flight practice. Soon they make short flights, landing awkwardly in neighboring territories and running through the sand or grass to reach home. Everywhere, as young terns and skimmers career carelessly to and fro, displaced birds are ignored for the most part.

Back in Barnegat Bay the terns have fledged from Pettit Island, leaving only a few young skimmers who linger. Nearly a thousand young terns have taken wing, and most are moderately heavy, indicating that the fishing was good this year. Each pair of skimmers has flying chicks.Only the youngest one from each brood is still practicing. Skimmers stand beside their chicks, waiting for nightfall, when they will skim the salt-marsh creeks, bringing back the last few meals to their chicks. The flying young can be seen practice-skimming in the waters around the colony. By late August or early September, the birds have left the colony to join others at important staging areas like Champagne Island. The marsh will be silent for another year, until the skimmers return in May to join the courting common terns.

15

Piping Plovers at Corson's Inlet

A flock of sanderlings lingers quietly on the wrack line; with feathers lightly ruffled, they face into the wind. The tide is high, limiting the foraging space along the surf. Only a narrow edge of wet sand is exposed, and few invertebrates lurk beneath the dry sand above the waves. The sanderlings wait for the tide to drop, and as the band of wet sand widens, they run to the edge and begin to follow the waves in and out. They forage in a tight flock even though there is plenty of space, and the beach is otherwise deserted.

A hundred yards down the beach, two piping plovers feed at the interface of the wet and dry sand, seemingly ignoring each other. As one works its way down the beach, the other follows. Their movements are coordinated, and they take turns watching for people or for predators. It is late March. Theses are among the first piping plovers to return to New Jersey. Piping plovers are small, pale shorebirds that nest solitarily along the sandy beaches of the Atlantic coast. Inland populations nest on riverine sandbars and alkaline flats.

These birds are cryptically colored, with white underparts and light beige backs and crowns. Their white rumps, black tails, and black-and-brown breastbands provide a two-toned pattern that breaks up the outline of the body. The bird blends with the sandy beach. Both of the pair have bright orange legs and bills. One bird has a completely black breastband, the other only a partial collar. These identify the couple as a breeding pair. Although the male and female are similar in size, it is possible to separate the sexes, because the male's breastband is wider and complete. In the fall the orange bill will fade to mostly black, the legs to a pale yellow, and the black breast and brow bars fade and almost disappear. It is not possible to determine the age of the plovers; they can breed at one year of age.

In only a few weeks Corson's Inlet will have at least six or eight pairs of plovers. There should be more, many more. Fifty years ago pairs of piping plovers nested every few hundred yards along the Jersey shore, and the population in the state may well have exceeded 1,000 breeding pairs, accord-

ing to Dave Jenkins, who surveys them each year for the Endangered and
Nongame Species Program. Now the breeding population is down to only
135 breeding pairs. Since the early 1980s I have been studying piping
plovers along the Jersey shore to try and determine the factors that caused
the decline: Only by understanding the needs of the plovers can we hope
to protect our remaining population.

The same drastic decline in piping plover populations has happened all
along the Atlantic coast and in the interior regions of North America. The
species is currently endangered in Canada and the United States Great
Lakes, and threatened elsewhere in the United States. Declines were a result of direct harassment of nests and birds by people, dogs, and vehicles,
destruction of beach habitat, changes in water levels that engulfed nesting
habitats, and increased predation due to human presence in otherwise pristine beach habitats. When they were placed on the threatened list in 1986,
only 800 pairs of plovers remained along the Atlantic coast from New-
foundland to North Carolina.

Piping plovers breed in the Northern Great Plains from southeastern Al-
berta southward to Nebraska and Iowa; and along the eastern coast from the
Maritime Provinces to North Carolina. In the winter they are found along
the Atlantic coast from North Carolina to Mexico and on the Caribbean Islands. They seek out similar habitats both while breeding and wintering.

Effective management of piping plover populations requires that we
know the total population size of the species, its distribution pattern, and
habitat requirements. In 1991 the International Piping Plover Census, involving over a thousand biologists and volunteers from ten nations, col-
laborated to carry out a census over 2,000 sites, yielding a breeding
population of over 5,000 adults. Even if this represents 5,000 pairs, the population still is severely depleted. More likely, the number of breeding pairs
is around 2,800 in all of North America, with the total United States Atlantic
coast population being fewer than 900. Thus, the 135 pairs in New Jersey
are a critical component of the East Coast population.

New Jersey is a typical model for the problems the plovers face all along
the Atlantic coast. When the first Europeans arrived in North America, they
avoided the beaches and marshes, because the hordes of mosquitoes were
unbearable. With the control of mosquitoes following the First World War,
beaches became prime real estate for marinas, hotels, restaurants, and private homes. Except for state and federal lands, there are no undisturbed
Atlantic coast beaches left in New Jersey. When people invaded the barrier
beaches, they brought cats and dogs, which were only too happy to chase
small shorebirds and eat their eggs and chicks.

When masses of people moved onto the barrier beaches, they inadver-
tently encouraged other predators to follow. Bridges were built, allowing

15.1. Piping plovers on wrack line at Corson's Inlet with skate egg cases and broken spider crab shells.

foxes, raccoons, and skunks to cross from the mainland. Permanent human habitation provided a predictable year-round source of food in the form of garbage and other trappings of towns and cities. Without the threat from their own predators, such as wolves and cougars, the small predators increased. Rats also moved in, living among the houses and marinas, and eventually colonizing the higher salt marsh islands.

The beach at Corson's Inlet is one of the few remaining habitats that is still suitable for nesting piping plovers (Figure 15.1). Since it is a state park, there are no houses or other buildings on the dunes. The beach is wide and long, and the gentle slope ensures that the wrack line is well away from the waves. The debris, vegetation, and dead sea creatures left by the high tides provide shelter for the plovers from the onshore winds or places to look for insects and other small invertebrates. The gently rolling dunes are covered with beach grass that can hide and protect nests, eggs, and chicks.

Corson's Inlet is an ideal nesting area for piping plovers for another reason: Least terns and black skimmers also nest here. Piping plovers can take advantage of the terns and skimmers to warn them of potential predators. Piping plovers nest solitarily and remain on the ground most of the time. Their view of approaching predators is limited, especially if they nest near vegetation. In contrast, there are nearly always terns flying above a nesting colony, and from this vantage point, the terns can spot predators long before they come near a colony. Using other species to provide early warning is called social parasitism (Figure 15.2).

The terns also provide defense: whenever a predator flies over or enters a tern colony, the terns mob them by flying around and dive-bombing them. This is sufficiently annoying to predators that they often leave the tern colony and search elsewhere for suitable prey.

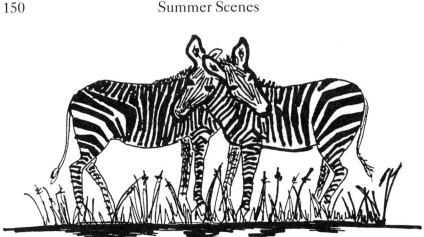

15.2. Zebras resting on African plain, each vigilant and looking in a different direction.

In New Jersey, I have found that piping plovers nest within least tern colonies whenever they are available, and pairs that nest within these colonies hatch and fledge more young than those nesting outside of tern colonies. Partly, the plovers avoid predation when they nest in tern colonies because they are now only one of many potential prey, and their individual chances of falling victim are thereby reduced. This has been termed the "selfish herd" phenomenon, because it was first identified in herds of African ungulates. A zebra is less likely to fall victim to a lion if it is one of a thousand, rather than being a lone zebra walking the African plain.

In late April the plover pairs space themselves out along the shore at Corson's Inlet, and each pair begins to defend its territory. They mark their territory boundaries by giving aggressive displays along an invisible line each recognizes. There is no obvious demarcation to my eye. When a rival approaches, the territory owner rushes to greet it, and the two run in tandem along this imaginary line, hunched down, giving low guttural notes. Usually this is enough, and the birds eventually walk back to the center of their own territory. Sometimes these "boundary walking" rituals erupt into short fights or aerial chases.

With the warming sun of late April and early May, the pair search the upper beach and lower dunes for a suitable nest site. They wander primarily within the least tern colony, looking for a site that will offer them the best view of predators, provide some protection from inclement weather, and be well above any high storm tides. To have a view of predators, the plovers seek a slightly elevated site on the face of a dune that has good visibility in all directions, but I have found that they shun the very tops of the dunes.

To provide protection for their small chicks against heat stress or heavy rains, they search for a site near a large piece of driftwood or vegetation. These objects provide shade and cover for much of the day. To avoid the threat of excessively high tides, the plovers nest well above the wrack line, close to the dunes.

It is not always easy to optimize for all factors, but eventually the pair picks a site just behind a small piece of driftwood, nearly a hundred yards from the water's edge. The nearest seaside goldenrod is only three yards away, not too far for the small chicks to run to when danger is near. The nest is in the center of the tern colony, although the closest tern nest is about fifteen yards away. The nest itself is barely a scrape in the soft sand. The few bits of shell lining the bottom are the only indication that it is a nest. On May 12 the first egg is laid, and one appears every day or two until there are four. This year food must be a bit scarce, because it takes six days for the female to lay the complete clutch.

The eggs are a pale buff, marked with fine speckles of brownish black and purple. They are oval, with a slight point at one end. The female adjusts the eggs so all four point toward the center, making it easier and more efficient to incubate them. The nests of the piping plovers can be distinguished from those of the least terns because the plover eggs are slightly larger, they are more rounded, and the speckling is heavier toward the large end, compared to the eggs of least terns. Besides, least terns usually lay only two eggs, although sometimes they lay three, but never four.

I spend hours sitting on dunes a hundred yards from plover nests, watching the behavior of the adults. I want to determine why the plovers produce so few young each year. Since the birds nest solitarily, there are few pairs on any one beach. I have a number of research assistants working with me, each observing the plovers at a different beach. Debbie Gochfeld observes at Brigantine Beach, Betsy Jones works near Manahawkin, Fred Lesser checks Barnegat Light, and Kevin Staine observes plovers at Corson's Inlet. Still, I must spend many hours watching the plovers' behavior to design the study to assure that observations can be made the same way at each site.

Although the plovers incubate intermittently when they have only one or two eggs, they do not begin full incubation until the complete clutch of four is laid. Both birds take part in incubation, and they shift incubation duties every two to three hours. The relieved bird usually flies to the nearby wrack line or wave edge to feed, always keeping a close eye on its incubating mate.

I watch a dog run into the colony. Immediately the terns swarm overhead, calling loudly and diving toward the dog. In the fracas that follows, the piping plover slips from the nest and runs toward the high dunes. It stands half hidden by the beach grass, watching the dog make its way through the colony. The dog tires eventually of the constant noise and harassment and it leaves, running quickly back to its master jogging along the shore. Of course, bringing dogs to Corson's Inlet is illegal, but there is no one to enforce the law.

Later a young boy ambles through, ignoring the signs that say to keep out of the nesting colony of an endangered species. Least terns are endangered in New Jersey, but it is impossible to guard every colony, every day, all day long. Eventually someone wanders in. Usually the dive-bombing terns are enough to make anyone run screaming from the colony—but this boy continues, no doubt fascinated by the birds swirling overhead. Again the plover slips from the nest and runs toward the high dune.

This time the boy is walking toward the plover nest, and evasive actions are required. The plover runs directly toward the boy, stopping only when the boy has finally noticed the small shorebird running wildly a few yards ahead. The plover leans to one side, droops one wing, spreads its tail, and walks slowly in a zig-zag pattern away from the boy. It looks as if it will topple over at any second. Clearly the bird is injured, and the boy follows, trying to pick up the plover. Each time the boy gets close enough to reach for the bird, it moves just a little farther away, intensifying its broken-wing act.

Little by little the plover leads the boy away from the nest, until the nest is far behind. Only then does the plover lift gracefully in the air and circle out over the beach, back into the safety of the dunes.

I have watched piping plovers perform variations of this distraction display hundreds of times, and I am always amazed that it works so effectively. It works with people, with dogs, with cats, with crows and gulls, and with a variety of other predators. But it does not always work, and sometimes a predator happens upon the nest by chance and eats all of the eggs. Between the crypticity of the nest and eggs, and the effectiveness of the distraction display, however, piping plovers usually hatch their eggs in New Jersey. The cause of low reproductive success does not seem to be a low hatching rate.

The first plover chick in the nest I have been watching hatches after twenty-six days of incubation: a wet, bedraggled, downy mass. Within a few hours it is a dry, adorable, fluffy chick that is brownish black with grayish buffs and browns above, and white below. A black line from the eye to the base of the head serves to break up its outline, and it is difficult to see when it crouches on the sandy beach.

The second and third chicks hatch within a few hours of the first. All three remain in the nest with the pipping fourth egg. Hatching takes nearly twenty-four hours, and the chicks remain in the nest until the fourth chick is also dry, fluffy, and able to walk about. They are all a bit unsteady, but must leave the nest in search of food.

Major problems begin when the chicks hatch, for the parents must keep the brood together, lead them to foraging sites, and protect them from danger. This is not easy with four active chicks all heading in opposite directions. Before people began to use the beaches, the problem was bad enough, because the adults had to find suitable foraging sites and protect them from native predators.

There were few native predators on the salt marshes and barrier beaches of New Jersey before the turn of the century. These included fish crows, mink, and perhaps gray fox. Herring gulls and great black-backed gulls did not breed in New Jersey, peregrine falcons did not breed along the coast, red foxes and raccoons were very rare along barrier islands because they could not get there except by coming across ice in the dead of winter, and rats were not on the barrier islands owing to lack of access and lack of food.

All of this changed when the hordes of people began to build summer cottages along the Jersey shore. Nowadays the plover parents not only have to cope with the increased predator pressure, but they also have to watch for people. Although there are few people on the beaches when the plovers begin to nest in mid- to late May, the number of people increases dramatically just when the chicks hatch in June. School lets out, and families swarm in to occupy homes and summer rentals. Day-trippers come by bus or packed in cars to wander the beaches.

The increased number of people along the beaches in late June and July is a problem for the plovers. Parent plovers must spend time watching for people, defending chicks against intruders, performing more distraction displays to deflect people from their brood, and keeping the brood together. Still, they must continue to forage for themselves.

On a warm July day I watch as plover parents lead their chicks from the safety of beach grass to the water's edge to feed. The chicks stumble along, getting trapped in ruts left by beach buggies, pecking here and there, finding food only occasionally. The parents forage also, turning every few seconds to peer overhead for avian predators, or to scan the beach for people or other mammalian predators. The parents try to keep the brood between them, but the chicks wander about, pecking equally at pieces of driftwood, feathers, and prey items.

When a jogger runs by, the four chicks scatter in all directions, and the adults give distraction displays. First one, and then the other, tilts its body, droops a wing, fans the tail, and scuttles along the ground in a feigned wing injury (Figure 15.3). The jogger is oblivious, and heads on down the beach, splashing through the surf. The parents give up only when the jogger is fifty yards from the chicks. They fly back to where they were feeding and bend low to call the chicks to them. It takes nearly fifteen minutes for both parents to corral the chicks together, and then the family begins to feed.

The parents spend nearly half of their time watching for danger, scanning

15.3. Piping plover giving a distraction display, feigning a broken wing.

the sky, peering over the sand. Then three young children run madly toward the surf where the chicks are foraging. Unaware of the plovers, the children play tag in the tumbling waves. But the chicks have scattered and are now huddled down motionless against the sand. The parents try in vain to distract the children, who remain unaware of the parents' efforts.

Finally the parents fly forty yards up toward the dunes and call frantically. They are too far for the chicks to respond to them. They fly back over the huddled chicks, call softly, and circle back to land on the berm. They succeed at last in drawing three of the chicks to safety. The fourth chick is running toward its waiting family, but a herring gull swoops down and picks up the chick in its bill. Within seconds the chick is swallowed whole, and now there are only three in the brood.

In four hours I watch as the brood dwindles to only one chick, despite the heroic efforts of the parents. The three chicks were lost to gulls, but it was the disturbance caused by people that resulted in the brood being separated. Had the chicks been together, none would have been running frantically and conspicuously across the sand. The frenetic, rapid movement of the young chicks catches the eye of gulls that are not even searching for prey. They cannot resist the lone chick bobbing across the sand.

My studies have shown that the amount of time adult plovers spend foraging decreases as the number of people on the beach increases. On bathing beaches, such as Brigantine or Corson's Inlet, plovers can spend only half as much time foraging as they do on beaches without people, such as Little Beach Island. On some particularly crowded beaches, the plovers are forced to move away, to places where there are few people, but these may not be the best foraging sites.

The problems that people cause are never-ending. Plovers cannot even feed undisturbed at night, because many of our beaches are used extensively at night by fisherman. They drive their vehicles down the beach, just above the surf where the sand is hardest and they will not get stuck. Piping plover chicks are foraging on these same places, and some get caught in the tire tracks or are run over by unwitting drivers.

One mid-July night as I sit on a dune at Corson's Inlet, watching a piping plover family through a night-vision telescope, I cringe when an off-road vehicle drives slowly down the beach. Too late, the parents sense the danger and call the chicks to the safety of higher ground. One plover chick hesitates too long and is crushed beneath the tires.

When another fishing vehicle barrels down the beach, I run for the remaining chicks, leaving my night scope on the dunes. The lights catch me picking up the last chick that had tumbled into the tire track left by another vehicle. I stuff them in my pockets just as the truck comes to an abrupt halt. Three young men rush out, and I suddenly realize I am alone and unprotected. Their large size and alcohol breath convinces me to give them my binoculars when asked. Fortunately, they are not my best binoculars, but still, it is scary being robbed. Realizing my peril, I turn and run for the dunes.

None of them have flashlights, and the sand is too soft for them to drive toward the dunes in their truck. Once safely in the dunes, I huddle down and wait for the sound of the motor to signal their departure. When the motor sounds have been gone for hours, although it was probably only minutes, I slip back down to the water's edge. I remove the chicks from my pocket and squeeze one ever so gently so that it gives a plaintive "contact call." The parents have been listening for the calls and immediately circle back. Placing the chicks on the ground, I watch as they disappear in the black night. I listen carefully to their contact calls, and to the crooning calls of the parents. Within minutes all of the contact calls cease, and I am sure the parents have found all three chicks.

It is such a dark night that I cannot see where I left my night scope. I creep over the dunes, searching in vain, picking up pieces of driftwood and old bottles. I finally edge back toward my car, where I have a stronger flashlight. I stop abruptly when I hear male voices in the parking lot. They may be the three young men I met out on the beach; I certainly do not want to see them again. There is nothing to do but wait in the dunes until morning.

Even in July it is cool at night, and I am ill prepared for the long wait. Suddenly I am starved, and the hours drag by with mosquitoes buzzing around. When daybreak finally comes, I find the night scope only a few feet away, nestled against a goldenrod. I walk back along the beach and find another dead chick. It must have fallen into the tire track of another vehicle. By daybreak it had died, exhausted from trying frantically to climb up the side of the tire impression in the sand. To us, it seems like a small distance, but plover chicks are not strong enough to flap up over the lip, and the top is well above their heads. Along the shore the piping plovers feed with their brood of two chicks.

I return to the car, now standing alone in the parking lot. As I pull out of the lot, heading for home, I watch as a man in a steel blue Mercedes drops a calico cat out of the door and pulls away. People sometimes abandon cats near a bird colony so the "little darlings" will have something to eat. Then the cats breed, and the mother must kill as many as ten to twelve terns or skimmer chicks a night to feed her hungry family. Such feral cats are particularly difficult to eliminate from a nesting colony, because they avoid traps and are born hunters. Around the world, cats are one of the most devastating predators on seabirds nesting on islands, for they are deadly and persistent predators, and they can breed fast enough to populate quickly most small islands.

On a latter visit I note that the pair I have been watching still have one chick. They brood it less now. At nearly three weeks old, it is large enough to avoid the pitfalls of car tracks and to run from approaching predators. In a week or two it will be able to fly, and its chances of survival will be quite high. By this time next year it may have a brood of its own. Its parents are likely to be back here breeding together on the same beach.

Since piping plovers nest solitarily, they are much more difficult to protect than are least terns or black skimmers. It is way too costly to station a warden by each nesting plover, or even to find and locate all plover nests. It is also harder to protect their nesting habitat, because a mile-long stretch of beach can support only about 15 or 20 piping plover pairs, but the same beach could support several hundred pairs of terns or skimmers.

It is critical, then, to protect those remaining beaches where piping plovers still nest. We may have to close part of each beach to the public during the nesting season to reduce human disturbance for foraging adults and young. Part of Holgate, the Barnegat Bay Unit of Forsythe National Wildlife Refuge, has been closed to people and vehicles for a number of years. Reproductive success of the plovers has increased, and there are more pairs breeding than there were before the closures. Such actions have costs in terms of vociferous complaints, even though most of the public is sympathetic to the temporary beach closure. By August first, when the chicks have grown and can fly, the beach can be reopened.

Piping plovers will survive in New Jersey only with the constant vigilance of conservationists, naturalists, managers, and the help of the public. It is not too late to help them, for we have one of the largest, most successful breeding populations along the Atlantic coast. Indeed, with active management and public support, New Jersey's piping plovers have increased from about 100 to 134 breeding pairs in the last ten years. We may have the most densely populated state, but we also have one of the healthiest piping plover populations.

16

Peregrines, Ospreys, and Harriers: Diurnal Predators

The shrill "kek kek kek" calls of least terns mobbing a fish crow flying low over the sandy beach colony at Barnegat Inlet are barely audible above the pounding surf, for a nor'easter has blown in. Whitecaps are building on Barnegat Bay, and the waters of the inlet are too rough even for large boats. The terns circle about the crow, some dive-bomb it, stopping only a few inches above its black body.

As the crow passes the far edge of the nesting colony, the terns disperse and circle back to land at their nests. The nests are not dense this year; the terns have spaced out over the beach, and neighbors are at least ten yards apart. The colony is also smaller—there are fewer birds nesting here this year. All is quiet, as the terns silently incubate. Most birds face into the wind, for the winds are strong enough to seriously ruffle their feathers. Hours pass, and the sky darkens, making it difficult to pick out the incubating terns. Out in the bay the storm rages, but only the fact that all the birds are facing in one direction indicates the severity of the storm. Now and then a mate returns to take over incubation duties, and the relieved tern departs for the foraging grounds. With such strong winds, the terns forage in the back bay, in the lee of salt-marsh islands, where the water is calmer.

The relative tranquillity of the colony is shattered by the sudden stooping of a peregrine. The terns rise in unison and in one tight flock fly out over the bay, in a silent panic. They circle back and begin to mob the peregrine as it rises from the colony. The terns fly in a dense group. At first they stay ten yards away from him, but gradually they come closer, and individual terns begin to dive-bomb him.

The peregrine starts another dive, his rapid movement carrying him directly toward the nesting colony. Then he turns abruptly, and with his talons grabs a least tern from the mobbing flock. One tern came too close for an instant, but that instant cost its life. In only a few seconds the peregrine disappears toward Sedge Island, and the terns settle down to incubate. The terns are not coping well with the frequent visits of the peregrine, and I suspect that the fewer nests and their greater dispersion is due to this new predator. Out on the bay the winds have increased, and the whitecaps are larger, deeper, longer.

Peregrines had never nested along the Jersey shore; they bred instead along the Palisades, selecting rocky ledges for their nest sites. Somehow the image of a peregrine stooping from the high ledges to the Hudson River below evokes feelings of majesty and wilderness—a wilderness that no longer exists along the Palisades.

The peregrine falcon population in the eastern United States was about 350 active pairs in the 1930s and 1940s. They plunged to no active pairs by the mid-1960s, along with declines in other top predatory and fish-eating birds such as pelicans. DDT and other organochlorine pesticides proved to be the culprit. DDT interfered with calcium deposition in eggshells, which became so thin that they broke when the birds incubated. Since raptors and other fish-eating birds are relatively long-lived, and DDT and other toxics can be stored in their fat tissues, the chemicals build up in the body for many years. Such toxics are mobilized from fat, which is used during egg formation, and toxics are deposited in eggs. The pesticides were a two-edged sword, causing adults to lay thin-shelled eggs and exposing embryos to high levels of toxic chemicals. No wonder the population crashed between the late 1940s and the 1960s. There was simply no successful breeding.

Recovery efforts for peregrines began in the early 1970s after DDT was no longer legal for use in the United States. When peregrine populations crashed, Tom Cade began a captive-breeding program at Cornell University, the "Peregrine Fund" with the long-term objective of reintroducing these raptors to the East after the threat of DDT was eliminated. The program continued for many years, as such programs do, entirely contained within the laboratory walls. The time eventually came when DDT levels in the environment had declined and sufficient birds were available for introduction to the wild.

New Jersey was deemed the appropriate place to release captive-bred falcons into the wild, and negotiations began between the Peregrine Fund and the New Jersey Endangered and Nongame Species Program. These were exciting times, as the Program and the Endangered and Nongame Species Council grappled with the hard questions of how and where to introduce the birds. The Palisades were no longer appropriate because of increased populations of great horned owls that interfered with breeding. Great horned owls like cliff sites for nesting, finding it easy to prey on young peregrines from cliff nests. These owls are increasing generally in New Jersey, particularly along the coasts.

Salt marshes along Barnegat Bay were selected for the first introductions, because there were suitable foraging lands for the young peregrines, there were no obvious competitors, and to do so was logistically feasible. To ensure that the birds could adapt to the wild, they were "hacked" from a tower high above the Sedge Island marsh in Barnegat Bay, and fed without being able to see who fed them. During hacking young chicks are placed in an artificial nest and fed natural foods through a one-way door. The young can see the surrounding habitat but are not allowed to see their caretaker. In this way, they imprint to the appropriate habitat and begin to identify appropriate foods. Hacking was exhausting for the caretakers, who had to obtain a constant supply of suitable prey for the birds.

After the successful hacking at Sedge Island, other sites were chosen, and hacking towers were set up. Birds were hacked at six sites from 1975 to 1980. Over the years, fifty-two peregrines were hacked, and fourteen other young were supplemented to successful nests.

The first pair of released peregrines began nesting in 1980. Since then, the nesting population in New Jersey has grown to thirteen pairs. The first pair produced two young, and average production over the years has ranged from one and a half to two and a half birds per pair. Of the fifteen pairs currently in New Jersey, nine nest on salt-marsh towers, one nests on a high-rise building in Atlantic City, and five nest on large bridges. Production is high, and nearly two young are produced in each nest. This is well above the level needed to sustain the population levels in New Jersey.

The peregrine reintroduction program is clearly a success in New Jersey, but it is not without its problems. Introducing any bird into a new habitat creates the potential for competition with native species for nesting space and food, and increases the likelihood of predatory interactions. This happened with the first peregrines that nested at Sedge Island.

I was heartbroken when I learned that a barn owl I had banded as a nestling at Clam Island was forcibly and fatally removed from the peregrine tower on Sedge Island. The owl had hatched in the attic above my Clam Island hunting shack, and I had listened to its parents return with food every night for several weeks. It came home to Barnegat Bay when it was only three years old, found the Clam Island attic boarded up, and set up housekeeping in the peregrine tower weeks before the peregrines needed it. Attempts to dissuade the owl failed miserably, and it had to be removed by force. Although clearly there were more barn owls in New Jersey than peregrines, barn owls are native nesters in salt marshes, and peregrines are not. We chose to put the peregrines there.

Before the peregrine hacking tower was erected on Sedge Island, a large colony of common terns nested on nearby salt-marsh islands. The colony numbered 825 pairs in the late 1970s, but by 1982 had dwindled to almost none. Although hundreds of terns wheeling in the air are a spectacular sight, as they try to avoid a peregrine stooping within their midst, the devastation was swift and final. Day after day the young peregrines harassed the adult terns trying to incubate. Over the course of only two weeks most of the colony abandoned, and only a few terns tried to raise their young. Later the more agile peregrines captured the remaining young terns when they were barely able to fly.

We learned from this reintroduction that the needs of existing wildlife had to be considered, in addition to the needs of the peregrines and the hackers. We learned just how far the peregrines would travel regularly in search of food. Finally we established a five-mile buffer around any hacking tower, and we tried to place peregrine platforms in salt marshes that were more than five miles from any active tern or skimmer colony. It was not a question of preventing the peregrines from eating common terns, but of preventing the devastating effect of a peregrine disrupting a nesting colony on a daily basis.

The five-mile buffer worked, and we reduced the adverse interactions between the peregrines and nesting least terns, common terns, and black skimmers. It did not prevent a peregrine from occasionally entering a nesting colony, but such an event was irregular enough to prevent colony desertion. When a peregrine made a steep dive or swoop at the common terns nesting on Pettit Island, the swarming, swirling terns were forceful enough for the peregrine to sail away. It left only after it captured an adult common tern in mid-air, evidence of the risk birds take when diving too close to a peregrine.

Although the DDT problem is greatly reduced, it has not disappeared. Organochlorines are still important insecticides in tropical countries, and if our birds migrate south they accumulate a toxic burden over the winter. Fortunately, some of the laboratory-reared peregrines are nonmigratory.

The salt marshes and barrier beaches of New Jersey are not without their native predators: Ospreys, harriers, and barn owls prowl by day and night. These species are an integral part of the salt marshes. Few sights are as breath-taking as an osprey plunging from a height of over one hundred feet to grab a large bluefish in its talons. Being top predators, these species also suffered during the DDT era, reproduction decreased, populations declined, and they were in danger of extirpation from the shore. In some places, such as the Delaware Bay shore, the ospreys too must contend with predatory great horned owls (Figure 16.1).

Ospreys were once common in New Jersey, nesting from the salt marshes to inland marshes and lakes, equally at home with trout or saltwater fish for food. In south Jersey, they nested on the flattened crowns of cedars or on large side branches. In Cape May nearly every cedar of any size sprouted an osprey nest, although not all were occupied. The ospreys also nested on old, long-abandoned telephone poles that grace many small barrier is-

16.1. *Great horned owls are predators on tern and skimmer chicks on salt marshes, as well as competing with peregrines and other raptors for nest sites.*

lands. They built large stick nests that grew with each succeeding season. In the early 1930s Brooke Worth regularly followed the fate of a hundred osprey nests in south Cape May alone, and he estimated that up to 500 pairs bred in Cape May County.

In the courtship period, males provide their mates with nearly all of their food. Males that are particularly good providers, bringing back plenty of food, stimulate females to lay earlier than less well fed females. Both take turns incubating, and the haunting whistling call of a male gently soaring in to take his turn inspires awe. The female often leaves before he has touched down. Once the young hatch, the male brings in the fish, delicately passing it to the female, who feeds the young. During the first few days a brood of three wolf down at least six pounds of fish a day, and thereafter their needs increase.

Young ospreys are quite awkward when they first try to fly, and are even more bumbling when they try to catch their first fish. Eventually, they are successful, as they improve their technique day by day. Because autumn waters along the coast are often turbulent, young Ospreys have better luck fishing in the calm waters of inland pools and lakes. Early banders discovered that the juveniles flew directly west until they hit mountains, and only then did they migrate south.

There were still over 500 Osprey nests in New Jersey in the 1950s, but this number fell to only 50 in the 1970s, another sign of DDT. The species was

16.2. Osprey with bluefish.

listed by the Endangered and Nongame Species Program as an endangered species. Listing alone, however, is not enough for a species in such trouble, and an active management program involving restocking was initiated.

Ospreys, harriers, and barn owls are part of the normal food web along the shore, and the birds nesting there have evolved with them. Osprey eat fish from the estuaries, and harriers and owls eat small sparrows or mice from the marshes. Ospreys fish by circling up to one hundred feet above the water, searching for prey. When an osprey spots a fish, it dives at incredible speeds toward the water and snatches the prey in its sharp talons. It never breaks its speed, but continues on to a craggy dead tree or its nest, where it rips its prey apart (Figure 16.2). The osprey is impressive with a wingspan of five to six feet. It is also dramatic, for its upper parts are dark brown, while its underparts and head are pure white. There are black streakings on the head, including a broad eyestrip. With its hooked beak and powerful talons it quickly rips apart the bluefish pulled from the bay.

Ospreys, or fish hawks, have suffered both from environmental contaminants and from decreasing availability of nest sites. When the old hunting shacks, telephone poles, and other buildings on the marshes disappeared, the birds had fewer places to nest. Some resorted to nesting on Coast Guard buoys, but this made them vulnerable to boaters. The Endangered and Nongame Species Program solved the nest-site problem by building them artificial platforms, placed on the tops of telephone poles sunk in the marsh.

The buildup of DDT was a difficult problem, because osprey are long-lived, and once females are highly contaminated, they continue to lay contaminated eggs for many years. Contamination not only causes thin eggshells that break when they are incubated, but the embryos themselves may be inviable. The Endangered and Nongame Species Program, in co-operation with other states, started a restocking plan in which infertile eggs were replaced with fertile, healthy eggs, mainly from Chesapeake Bay.

The nest-site restoration and egg restocking program for ospreys was a huge success, and population increases were sufficient for the Endangered and Nongame Council to remove the bird from the endangered species list. It was an exciting program, and over the years, we all watched with pride and pleasure as the population slowly rebounded; but it was not half as exciting as watching an osprey plummet a hundred feet to the clear bay waters to snatch a fish with its talons.

Along the Atlantic coast of New Jersey, the harrier or marsh hawk populations also have recovered, and their reproduction is normal once again. However, the number of marsh hawks on the Delaware Bay coast has remained low and has not rebounded despite the decreased use of DDT. Eggshells of the marsh hawks nesting on the Delaware Bay shore are precariously thin, and reproduction is still depressed. Their plight indicates the importance of research and vigilance in monitoring our environmental problems. The marsh hawks on Delaware Bay are clearly still exposed to DDT, but the exact source is undetermined.

Marsh hawks once flew low over farmlands, hunting for small rodents, but there are no longer inland populations that breed on farms. They used to build nests on the ground in old, abandoned hay fields, where they foraged. Freshwater habitats are no longer suitable for marsh hawks because safe nesting places are rare.

While the osprey is powerful, the harrier is graceful. Both are an integral part of the salt marshes and bays. Harriers glide effortlessly across a salt marsh in search of small mice or birds. They hold their wings in a V, making them easy to identify at a distance. They dip down to pick up a sparrow in their talons, but often remain on the spot to devour their prey. The osprey nests in prominent places, with good visibility in all directions; the harrier searches for a secluded nesting place among the reeds or low bushes. It builds a nest on the ground, and its small young are vulnerable to ground predators such as rats, cats, or foxes. Both birds build massive nests, but the harrier's nests are protected from high winds by vegetation buffers. Because of their foraging methods and nesting habitats, ospreys and harriers do not compete directly with peregrines. Not so with great horned owls and barn owls. Peregrine hacking towers are perfect places for barn owls to nest, and they arrive back at their breeding sites before the young peregrines are ready for hacking.

Even with the conflicts, however, the sight of a peregrine stooping to pluck a sanderling out of a dense flock flying just above the whitecaps is awesome. The reintroduction of the peregrine into the east coast of North America is one of the successes of conservation and management.

17

Mink, Mussels, and Ghost Crabs

Many creatures spend their whole lives in relative obscurity, invisible to the hordes of people who visit the Jersey shore every year. Most people take the well-traveled roads that lead to the marinas and beaches. They never visit the small salt-marsh islands, or the salt-marsh creeks that meander through vast mainland marshes. They miss the creatures that move at night, travel the tunnels hidden in the salt-marsh grasses, live languidly along the undisturbed salt-marsh channels, or move rapidly over the sand.

Every habitat along the shore has myriad creatures that are less obvious, that catch the eye only in passing. On the outer sandy beach, there is a newcomer to the Jersey shore: the ghost crab. Over the years they have slowly moved north, from one beach to another, until they reached the beaches of Cape May, then Corson's Inlet, and finally along Barnegat Bay. These pale, sand-colored crabs are only an inch or two across. The young, small crabs dig burrows just within the intertidal zone, but older crabs dig them higher on the beach. The burrows go down two to four feet, making it particularly infuriating to try to catch them. Most are active at night, but some scurry about in broad daylight, giving the impression of ghosts that disappear in the sand. They are so quick, and so very pale, that at first they seem like a faint shadow passing over the sand.

Another ghostlike denizen is the mink. I have become interested in the mink that find their way to the salt marshes, because of the devastation these rare predators can cause. Usually there is enough food for mink along the mainland, and they prowl the uplands at night searching for birds or other small prey. Their varied diet includes frogs, turtles, young birds, rabbits, mice, and even muskrat. They have no trouble killing prey much larger than themselves, often several in a night. These small weasels are the most aggressive predators in New Jersey. An average male lives in a territory as large as a square mile, although females have smaller home ranges. Sometimes their territory includes a bit of salt marsh where they come to prey

17.1. Red-winged blackbirds mobbing a mink.

on fish or solitary-nesting species such as sparrows. Once in a while they go
farther out in the marsh.

Mink are nearly impossible to see along the shore, for they slip through
the shallow waters at night, searching for unsuspecting prey. They venture
forth in the early morning and can be located by the blackbirds mobbing
them as they slink through the grass (Figure 17.1).

Creeks pose no obstacle to these strong swimmers, who move easily from
the mainland to the salt marshes and back each night. Their passage is
silent, their stealth cunning, and their aim deadly. I have come upon salt-
marsh islands where they have wrought total devastation in a single night,
destroying all the eggs or chicks of skimmers and terns in nearly seventy
nests. Dead bodies lie piled up on a nest here and there; small puncture
wounds in the neck are the only clues to the predator. No other predator
of the salt marshes kills so many birds wantonly, and leaves the bodies
stockpiled around the marsh.

Foxes, raccoon, and skunks also travel the mainland and barrier beaches
at night, keeping to the vegetation, venturing out on the open beaches or
marshes only to eat eggs or young chicks. For the most part they are dark
shadows moving across the sand, trotting slowly, using their noses to find
food. Raccoons will even go out on the salt marshes at night, searching for
eggs and small birds, or settling for ribbed mussels they can pull from the
peat banks (Figure 17.2).

Two mussels that are widely distributed along the Atlantic Coast are the
blue mussel and the ribbed mussel. Blue mussels, the ones most people eat

17.2. Raccoon eating ribbed mussels along salt-marsh bank.

in restaurants, live in shallow waters exposed at low tide. They grow in dense beds on jetties, rocks, pilings, and channels wherever there is intense wave action. Ribbed mussels, on the contrary, live in the calm waters of marshes, where they are half buried in the mud. They too are exposed only at very low tides.

The larvae of both mussels are planktonic and float in great numbers in the local bays, inlets, and coastal waters during the spawning season. To grow, the larval mussels must find a suitable substrate, to which they attach themselves by means of strong hairlike filaments called byssal threads, secreted by a gland near the foot. The ribbed mussels use their byssal threads to anchor themselves in the creek muds, and the threads act as roots. The threads of blue mussels attach to rocks or jetties, and they must withstand the force of the pounding surf and waves. Those that fail to attach perish, but others hold fast and slowly begin to grow.

Once young mussels attach, they are sedentary and wait for the tidal currents to bring them food and prevent silt from covering them. As the tides recede, the mussels close up tightly so that no air enters their shells. When the waters turn and slowly rise, they open to receive the tides that carry food.

Ribbed mussels grow in dense beds on banks of salt-marsh creeks along the Jersey shore, but the beds are difficult to find. Only at very low tides are the mussels uncovered, and it is no use searching for them at any other time. Even then, only the very tips of the mussels are exposed, and they are often hard to spot against the dark mud of the creek banks.

Ribbed mussels are filter feeders that strain and sort plankton from surrounding waters. They live half buried in the mud, straining the inedible from the edible, binding the inedible with mucous and mud to form pseudofeces. In the calm waters of some creeks, the currents are not strong enough to carry away the piles of pseudofeces, and the mussels must move slowly upward to keep themselves above the piles. The slow movement of the mussels upwards along the creek banks gives them a hummocky appearance, which is a dead giveaway for finding the edible treats.

Ribbed mussels are also interesting because they aid the growth of salt-marsh vegetation. The mussels sometimes attach to the roots of cordgrass with their byssal threads and deposit fecal material on the surrounding sediment. Where mussel density is high, the cordgrass is denser, taller, and flowers more. Mussels seem to stimulate both the roots and the above-ground plants by increasing soil nitrogen, which is responsible for the increased growth of the cordgrass.

I first became interested in mussels as a culinary benefit of working in salt marshes. However, mussels are also studied as bioindicators of environmental pollution. It is clearly impossible to monitor contamination of all organisms in all coastal ecosystems. It would be logistically impossible, and much too costly to consider monitoring most organisms. Instead, it is far wiser to select a few organisms that can be used as indicators of environmental contamination. Then, these chosen indicator species can be monitored regularly.

Mussels are a delightful delicacy, made more so by their dependability and ease of procurement. Ribbed mussels are eaten by crabs, fish, starfish, ducks, snails, herons, egrets, and even crows, if they are desperate. They are ignored by most fisherman and clammers, but I find them a welcome treat when I am camped on salt-marsh islands. They require no refrigeration; can be obtained just before supper; their shells can be returned immediately to the marsh; and they make a tasty addition to spaghetti and tomato sauce.

The blue mussel is the favorite in restaurants and clam bars along the Atlantic coast. It is honored in poems and prose. I think its preeminence is pure snobbery, for the ribbed mussel is just as good eating. Nonetheless, I make no value judgments if you prefer to search for the blue mussels along the Jersey shore. They live in the fast lane, where the tides are splashing against rocks or jetties, where the force of the sea requires them to hold fast. Other than their habitat, their life style resembles that of the ribbed mussel. They filter feed, straining out the edible from the inedible. Their pseudofeces are more easily washed away by the raging surf, and they do not have to migrate up through the soil. Instead they cling precariously throughout their lives to the rocks or concrete.

18

Diamondback Terrapins
at Little Beach

Just off the shallow sandy beach, small dark eyes peer over the water and scan the beach beyond. To the right, another head emerges and then disappears. Not far away, another pops above the water. Looking over the small inlet along the north edge of Little Beach Island, I count twenty-three heads of diamondback terrapins within only three minutes.

It is hard to use binoculars through the mosquito-netting hat that covers my entire head. Mid-June along the Jersey coast means the greenheads have just emerged. Greenheads are just about the worst insect I have ever encountered, and that includes swarms of mosquitoes at Snakebite Trail in the Everglades, no-see-ums in northern Minnesota in the summer, and blackflies in Maine. It is not that they are so abundant, although they are. Nor is it because they sound like miniature helicopters buzzing around your head. It is because they are so persistent and have a sting that continues to hurt for several minutes (Figure 18.1). They can and do bite through thick clothing. It is nearly impossible to sit on the dunes in a short-sleeved shirt or shorts; and I am clothed in a long-sleeved shirt and long pants with thick socks.

Like all insects on the marsh, greenhead females are looking for a blood meal from a vertebrate, but there aren't many here. Swatting them does not help, they just circle around and come in for another landing. Nothing works short of slapping them, which is easy to do because they are remarkably slow on the uptake. The greenheads cannot dissuade me from watching the annual nesting activities of the diamondbacks.

Diamondback terrapins live in estuarine waters from New England to Texas. They are the only turtle specialized for this intermediate habitat between the sea and freshwater ponds and streams. There is a great deal of variation in their appearance, as their shells range from black, to black-and-yellow; from smooth to those whose scales or scutes contain deep concentric growth rings. Adults range in length from four to eight inches. Males, however, never get larger than five inches, whereas females normally attain a length of six inches or more (Figure 18.2).

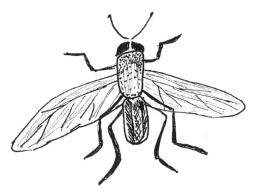

18.1. Greenhead fly, one of the worst insects I have ever encountered.

Diamondback terrapins used to be common along the Atlantic and Gulf coasts. An observer could count over a thousand turtles in a single day. They were so abundant that they were once fed extensively to slaves and other workers, and many states had laws prohibiting plantation owners from serving them more than two or three times a week. The same restrictions applied to lobsters and heath hens, which were equally common in colonial times.

The flavorful diamondbacks became a popular food around the turn of the century. "Bulls" or males sold for $12 a dozen, "half counts" or females between five and six inches sold for $24 a dozen, and "counts" or females over six inches sold for $40 or more a dozen. Terrapins measuring over eight inches brought as much as $125 a dozen in the early 1900s. Retail prices were substantially higher. The fact that they had established prices for females over six inches, and for females that were over eight inches, indicates that these sizes occurred. In the 1970s and 1980s very few females even reached seven inches.

In the late 1800s turtle "farms" sprang up all along the Atlantic coast, and populations quickly declined as they were collected for breeding stock. Only after protective legislation curtailed the species' demise did populations begin to increase. Although there were originally six subspecies along the coast, considerable mixing occurred when they were collected for farms. After protection, restocking practices further mixed up the gene pool, and subspecies were introduced outside their normal range. This contributed to the current mix of color patterns present along the Atlantic.

Now, just when populations have begun to recover, diamondback terrapins face new threats from destruction of salt-marsh creeks used for feeding, loss of sand dunes used for nesting, and death from motor boats, illegal collecting, and inadvertent death in crab traps. Steve Garber, Whit

18.2. Male diamondback terrapins spend most of their time in the salt marshes or in the creeks.

Gibbons, others, and I have documented a decrease in many east coast populations. At present an unsustainable large number of terrapins are drowned in commercial crab traps each year, possibly as many as 1.8 million a year, according to Roger Wood. He has been developing a terrapin excluder that will fit in crab traps, much like the turtle excluders that go into shrimp nets to exclude sea turtles.

"Beware, turtle crossing" signs along major highways fail to slow drivers, who unwittingly crush them when the terrapins try to cross roads to reach nesting grounds. Some roads contain six- to eight-inch high curbs along the edge, just enough to prevent a female from being able to cross the road, and some become trapped on the highway because they are unable to climb over these curbs. The diamondbacks at Little Beach are lucky, for there are no barriers between the inlet waters and the sand dunes they use for nesting.

The female diamondback terrapins are waiting offshore for tidal conditions to be just right for their trek to land to find a nesting place. They wait for high tide and then come ashore to choose a nest site. Waiting for high tide accomplishes a number of things: The females can assure that their nest sites will be above high tide, reducing the risk of tidal inundation; and they reduce the distance they must walk over land before finding a suitable site. Nests that are flooded by seawater for any length of time fail to hatch. In my years of observing diamondback terrapins at Little Beach Island, none ever came ashore during low tide, and most come ashore at peak high tide. Females begin nesting as early as June 9, and egg-laying continues until mid-July, although the peak is in late June.

While on land diamondback terrapins are vulnerable to predators, people, and heat stress. Predators such as fox can catch a terrapin easily and eat their heads or legs. A diamondback terrapin can withdraw its head, legs, and tail within the shell only incompletely, and a determined predator can find something to eat. Those humans also pose a threat who use terrapins in stews or soups; others merely take the animals home for pets.

Heat stress, however, is a greater threat to nesting females than are predators. Once terrapins leave the protection of the estuary they are vulnerable to heat and desiccation. In June the surface sand temperatures can reach over 130 degrees F., and the air above is not much cooler. The turtles must drag their shells across the hot sand, moving higher and higher along the dunes to assure that their nests are not flooded.

The half-mile stretch of sand dunes in the back bay is an excellent place for diamondback terrapins to nest, because it is sheltered from the full force of the surf and ocean waves by taller dunes that fringe the ocean beach. Further, these back-bay dunes are not buffeted by the storm winds that come off the ocean. Winds disturb the fragile dunes, blowing the surface sands and uncovering the eggs.

Here the dunes are stabilized by beach grass and an occasional goldenrod, but for the most part the vegetation cover is sparse. The dunes run for nearly a half mile, fringing the small back-bay lagoon that leads into Great Bay.

Glasswort and a bit of cordgrass separate the advancing tidal waters from the foot of the dunes. The cordgrass is thin and short, and the rising tides soon cover much of the grass, leaving the glasswort still uncovered. The short, stocky stems of the lime-green glasswort are barely a few inches tall. It grows only on the higher elevations of the marsh, where tidal inundation is frequent, but not daily. Patches of it grow interspersed with the *Spartina* beds. Here the glasswort fringes the dunes, providing a clue to tidal conditions, and indicating the upper limit of the tides.

The water seeps into the glasswort, covering the bluish black, rich soil visible through the pale green fingers. When the water has moved halfway through the shallow band, the first diamondback swims slowly in, peering almost continuously toward the shore. As it advances, it swims less and begins to walk, its body more and more exposed until it is completely visible.

The terrapin walks rapidly through the remaining glasswort, into the sandy mud, and swims across the small tidal pool created by a very high spring tide. Having finally reached the foot of the dune, she slows her pace, and moves deliberately upward until she has scaled nearly half of the dune. Turning to her left, she moves steadily along the sand, avoiding the heavily vegetated areas and remaining on the open sand.

Near the crest she stops and bends to sniff the sand before moving on. I remain a discrete distance, walking ever so slowly, stepping gently to avoid any vibrations that might warn her of my approach. Terrapins do not respond to sound, but any unusual movement or vibrations would send her trundling off to sea. To reduce the chances of her seeing me, I huddle down, trying to avoid making any unusual silhouette above the beach vegetation.

Finally she reaches a place where she touches her nose to the ground; she sniffs, raises her head, and lowers her head to sniff again. Turning, she scrapes away one scoopful of sand with her hind leg, then scoops another with her other leg. She turns and sniffs the sand again and abandons that site to continue her methodical search.

For nearly an hour she moves along the dunes, stopping to sniff or to rest, before moving on. She is being particular, for it takes most females from a few minutes to an hour to find a nest site after emerging from the bay. Now her search takes her slightly up, and then slightly down the dune. She sniffs again, but still she has not found the right place. When at last she is satisfied, she begins to dig.

Females do not nest just anywhere on the dunes, but select particular areas. No turtles nest in the high, steep dunes devoid of grass that face the open sea. Instead, females generally choose older, lower, protected dunes covered with sparse beach grass, which ensures the dunes are stable and will not shift for the two or three months necessary for the development of the eggs. More turtles nest in the higher parts of the dune than on the lower, flatter places that could flood out. The turtles avoid the steep slopes, where sand could slide over the nests, burying them too deep for the warm rays of the sun to incubate the eggs, and too deep for the young to emerge successfully. Females also avoid areas with too many roots, for it is difficult to dig there and the roots can grow into the eggs, causing them to die.

Once satisfied with the site, the female digs sporadically for a few minutes with her front feet before shifting forward to continue in earnest. Using her webbed back feet alternately, she scoops out sand rapidly until the four- to six-inch hole is complete, with a round egg chamber at the bottom. Larger females do not necessarily dig larger or deeper holes. She remains propped up by her front legs, her hind end partially in the nest, dropping eggs every few seconds (Figure 18.3). Every now and then a tear drops from her eyes, removing salt from her system. Although most females spend ten to twenty minutes digging the hole, egg-laying takes less than five minutes.

18.3. Female diamondback terrapin laying eggs on the dunes.

Clutches range from eight to seventeen eggs, although most females lay nine or ten white, leathery eggs slightly over an inch long.

Rapid movement starts anew, as the female begins shoveling the sand back into the hole with one hind foot, and then the other. She completely fills the hole, and then camouflages the nest by smoothing over the surface while walking ahead. She scoops sand over the top with one foot, and

18.4. Laughing gull pecking at digging terrapin to make her abandon her nest. The gull will then eat the eggs.

then the other, moving slowly ahead for six or eight feet. Finally she crawls off, directly toward the bay. In only a few hours, gently blowing winds completely cover the nest with a film of sand, and within a day or two the nest is impossible to find.

I walk the dunes daily. Armed with a "search image," I find over 200 nests in a season. I dig up each nest carefully, measure and mark the eggs, and replace them in exactly the same position. Some nests I find by sneaking up on the female, but most I discover by seeing where the sand has been ever so slightly displaced. Some nests I find only after a fox or raccoon has dug them up, but I find far more than they do.

Through the course of the season, I record how many of the nests I located are found by predators, and how many additional nests that I did not find are located by predators.Using this ratio, I determine that there were over 1,500 nests in the half-mile dune area on Little Beach Island.

Any sound, movement, or vibration disturbs digging females, who quickly abandon their hole and move elsewhere. Only when a female has laid more than three eggs will she continue to lay and cover up the hole as quickly as possible. Females that are disturbed when digging the nest, or after laying only an egg or two, move away and eventually dig another nest. If they are further disturbed, they will abandon for the day and return to the bay. Usually I find these females on the dunes a day or two later, again searching for nest sites. When I move slowly and quietly over the dunes, no turtles abandon.

Gulls and crows career above the dunes searching for nesting females. Sometimes they displace a laying female, and then they pull out the eggs to eat, or take them back to their mates or chicks at their nests (Figure 18.4).

The gulls and crows can find a nest only by seeing the female. Even so, they find and destroy nearly 15 percent of the nests during the egg-laying period.

At night foxes and raccoons patrol the dunes, searching for nests. Relying on smell rather than vision, they can find nests days or weeks after egg-laying. Mammalian predators take about 1 percent of the available nests each night during the development period. Since the incubation period is at least 60 days, foxes and raccoons destroyed over 60 percent of the nests.

Fox and raccoon raids are easy to distinguish: Foxes dig out the entire area, destroying the nest while leaving a hole several inches deep, almost a foot wide, and up to two feet long. No eggs or baby turtles survive and only empty eggshells and fox tracks attest to the fate. Raccoons, which are more delicate, make smaller holes as they scoop out the eggs. They are less efficient and often leave an egg or two at the bottom of the nest. Whenever I search the dunes before six a.m., I find nests opened by raccoons with an egg or two remaining. When the nest is near hatching, a hatchling turtle may be emerging, or tiny trails leading from the nest indicate that a turtle or two escaped. When I check later in the morning, the gulls have already found the nests and eaten any remaining eggs or hatchlings.

Terrapins place their eggs four to eight inches below the sand surface, but it is the sun's rays that drive their development. At these depths, temperatures range from 68 to 99 degrees, although sand at the surface often burns at 120 degrees. Prolonged periods of rain depress nest temperatures to their daily low. Deeper nests are cooler than shallow nests, and eggs take longer to develop in them.

Once the egg-laying period is over, I continue to search the dunes every day, checking to see if my marked nests are intact. The beach grass grows taller, the sands blow around a bit, and predators continue to make nightly rounds. The gulls and crows spend less time in the dunes, for no more turtles lay, and they can only search for the scraps left by the raccoons.

Diamondback terrapin eggs should hatch in two to three months, according to the records of the terrapin farmers of the early 1900s. So in late August I delicately scrape away the sand from a nest or two, being careful not to disturb the eggs themselves. Eggs in the first nest begin to hatch at 60 days of age, so I dig up all nests as they reach 60 days of age. I record whether they are hatching, and then cover them back, even if they have started to hatch. Since turtles take 15 to 25 hours to hatch, I can determine the exact hatching time from pipping eggs. The development period for the 200 nests ranges from 60 to 104 days, but most hatch at around 75 days. Within a nest, hatching takes about 4 days, with the bottom eggs that received the least heat from the sun hatching last.

Once I find the hatching date for any nest, I leave it undisturbed, but continue to check it to find out when the hatchlings actually leave the nest. When hatchlings emerge, they leave tiny trails in the sand. By checking every few hours, I can find out exactly when they leave. Turtles from the tops of nests usually hatch first, and emerge first.

Some hatchlings leave the nest immediately upon hatching, but others remain in the nest for up to nine days. They depart from the nest during the day, usually in the early afternoon when it is the warmest. Terrapins hatching during rainy weather remain in the nest the longest, reluctant to face the cold. Terrapins hatching on warm sunny days usually leave immediately, bursting from the nest in a rosette of tiny trails going in all directions.

The warm rays of the sun stimulate the hatchlings to begin swimming movements which eventually bring them close to the sand surface. When they reach the surface, they crawl quickly to the closest vegetation. Hatchlings emerging from nests on level sand spread out in all directions, but those hatching from nests on slopes invariably head down the slope, toward the bay. Once they reach vegetation, they wait for nightfall, and then they move quickly to the bay.

Crows and gulls again begin to patrol the dunes, searching for young terrapins emerging from their nests. Often I find the tiny trail of a hatchling leading toward a bush, only to be interrupted by the tracks of a gull or crow. Raccoons and foxes patrol at night, searching for nests and hatchlings. Once one egg has hatched in a nest, liquid is exposed to the air, and these odors make it easier for mammals to detect the nest.

Last summer Bill Montevecchi and I were able to find only 40 nests; this summer I have developed the "search image" of a predator. I have followed 200 nests on Little Beach, and some eggs hatched in at least 36 percent of the nests, 57 percent were destroyed completely by predators, and the other 7 percent failed to hatch because eggs were infertile, they were drowned by heavy rains, or roots invaded the eggs. Even in nests where some hatchlings emerged, others were eaten by predators, and still others never succeeded in swimming out of the nest. The last hatchling in a nest has difficulty getting out of the nest, particularly if it hatches after all the other hatchlings have emerged. Thus, for all the nests followed, only 16 percent of the eggs resulted in hatchlings that emerged from their nests. Many of these were eaten rather quickly by gulls and crows, some never made it to the bay, and others perished soon after reaching the bay. The path to the bay is patrolled by foxes and raccoons at night, and by gulls and crows during the day. The path is strewn by logs, brush, grass, and other objects that are difficult for a small hatchling to pass.

But some hatchlings make it to the bay and then swim toward the safety of vegetation, where they can again hide in the dark shadows. They will spend the next two to three years in the shallow bays and salt-marsh creeks, eating and growing. In the winter they will hibernate beneath the mud at the bottom of salt-marsh creeks. They will return to Little Beach to breed when they are three or four years old: the males to wait just off shore to court females, and the females to come on land to search for their own nests. Once they make it to breed, they may live to be forty years old, returning each year to breed in the same place. We must ensure that these breeding places still occur along the Jersey shore.

19

Mosquitoes: The New Jersey State Bird

Sunlight reflects from the small pool, all that remains of a large salt-marsh pond. Mostly the sun glistens off the dry, caking mud along the sides, and shorebirds peer into the murky water, looking for insects. Short cordgrass lines the pond, although it is taller near the creeks where there is regular tidal inundation. At the far edge of the pond on the half-baked mud, Forster's terns incubate quietly. Some twenty pairs nest beside the pond, each nest four or five feet from its neighbor. Summer has come to the Tuckerton marshes.

The incubating terns can see approaching predators from most directions, and the short wall of vegetation provides some relief from the noonday sun. In only a few weeks the *Spartina* will provide cover so the young chicks can hide from aerial predators, such as herring gulls and harriers. The ground here is higher than the surrounding marsh, and the Forster's terns will escape flooding unless there are very heavy rains. This shallow pond is not natural, it was made by snow geese who grazed the area so completely that they created this "eat out," a scar on the open marsh that will take years to heal.

Not far away are natural ponds, created when the marsh was formed. These pools are slightly deeper, but they too will dry up if the warm weather continues without any rain. The ponds are isolated from tidal creeks and channels, so their water comes only from heavy rains and spring tides. Without permanent water, they are devoid of fish.

On other marshes in south Jersey, no terns nest along the shores of the ponds, although many more shorebirds feed there. When the warm spring rains come, the pools fill. However, the salt-marsh mosquitoes do not lay their eggs in these ponds. Instead they lay their eggs on the damp mud of small temporary ponds that are not yet full of water. Then the rains or high tides come, flooding the mud and eggs. As long as the muds are salty, the eggs and mosquito larvae can handle freshwater as well as salt water.

With warmth from the sun, the eggs hatch and develop, bringing the ponds alive with thousands of tiny black mosquito larvae writhing at the surface. The larvae wriggle rhythmically through the water, feeding on algae and organic debris lying on the bottom or suspended in the warm pool waters. They molt four times before they form pupae, and the pupal stage lasts for only two or three days. Then the pupal skin splits down the back, and the mosquito emerges, using its shed skin as a raft while it dries its wings. The surface of most pools is black with the larvae, and in only a few days the adults emerge from the surface in black, swarming clouds.

Salt marsh mosquitoes are really quite elegant as mosquitoes go, once one looks beyond the bite. They have an abdomen with a white or yellow stripe down the center, legs that are brightly banded, and wings that have intermixed dark brown and white scales. They have a delightful upturned proboscis, usually up to no good. As with all mosquitoes, only the females bite, for the males are content with sugary plant exudations. Males are distinguishable by their featherlike antennae, while females have rather drab antennae with only a few short hairs.

The mosquitoes spread out over the marsh, the females searching for blood necessary for them to breed. The clouds of mosquitoes are blown by the breezes onto the barrier beaches, or to the mainland. Salt marsh mosquitoes are also strong fliers and can migrate many miles in large numbers, easily reaching mainland communities. Here they swarm around people, seeking a blood meal.

Hordes of mosquitoes coming from the marshes made the barrier beaches unbearable for the Indians, who moved to the uplands far from the coast to avoid their vicious biting. Greenhead flies were an added nuisance when they used their sharp stilettos to bore through thick clothing. The early settlers also avoided the coasts, except when it was necessary to cut salt hay, fish, or shoot waterfowl and shorebirds.

New Jersey is famous for its Jersey mosquito, often referred to jokingly as the "state bird" or "the salt-marsh terror." As long as the mosquitoes ruled the salt marshes, the shore was safe from human development. Once the first batch of mosquitoes emerged, people migrated inland, and the birds that nested on sandy beaches and salt-marsh islands did so in relative peace.

The early salt-hay farmers used the marsh as they found it, but gradually they made small alterations. They discovered that draining the high marsh ensured a good stand of salt hay and made it easier to move about the marsh. Still, few ditches were dug because it was hard work, and the ditches soon filled in. The farmers noticed that there were fewer mosquitoes when they drained parts of the high marsh, which made working the marsh almost bearable.

Many small coastal towns tried to ditch large areas, but it was too time-consuming for farmers, who had to plant their fields, cut salt hay, and attend their livestock. And so the marshes survived for a while. People worked along the shore only when it was necessary, and no one came to the beaches for fun. It was simply too unpleasant.

Between 1912 and 1914, every county along the Jersey shore created a Mosquito Commission to deal with the mosquito problems in their communities. The depression following the first World War brought high unemployment to the land, throwing millions of people out of work and into despair. Work projects were developed as a way to employ great masses of people, and draining the salt marshes was viewed as a perfect project that benefited a huge number of people living along the coast. The workers of the Civilian Conservation Corps (CCC) and the Works Progress Administration (WPA) arrived in the marshes in large gangs, armed with picks and shovels. They dug long straight ditches from the trees at the edge far out into the marshes. No attempt was made to connect mosquito-breeding ponds to the ditches, which were simply dug every hundred feet. All up and down the coast, from Virginia to Maine, one marsh after the other was drained in an endless series of grids.

The task was nearly finished before men found other jobs. Only with the coming of the Second World War did the ditching cease. Although many mosquitoes still emerged from the marshes, their numbers were far fewer than a generation earlier, and people began to come to the shore to swim. They built small summer shacks, crowded next to one another, just behind the dunes. In the middle of the summer, when the mosquitoes were still bad, some folks returned to their towns and cities, but many simply applied repellent, gritted their teeth, and soaked up the rays on New Jersey's fabulous beaches.

During the war years, as people turned to less frivolous pastimes, the shore again was left in relative peace. The massive war effort involved developing effective chemicals for biological warfare and combating the insect pests of the trenches and jungles in far-off lands. Following the war it was a small leap to use these chemicals to control mosquitoes on the salt marshes.

Intense competition developed for mosquito-free beaches: Tourists brought economic prosperity to the shore. Larger, more permanent houses were built, marinas grew bigger, grocery stores moved in, followed by drugstores, ice cream parlors, clothing stores, and finally boutiques.

The State of New Jersey formed a State Mosquito Commission to help the county commissions develop and test new water-control and ditching practices, to test pesticides, and to monitor mosquito problems. Pesticide use was the answer to their prayers. Frequent application of a variety of pesticides followed: The marshes were sprayed on a regular schedule, sometimes regardless of patterns of mosquito breeding, although many commissions targeted their spraying to breeding cycles.

The marshes were sprayed many times throughout the summer. Many shore communities were also sprayed on a regular cycle. Large trucks drove around, fogging the streets. Children rode behind on bicycles, daring one other to get as close as possible to the fog, despite parental admonitions. Pesticides were a panacea, able to control the insects, and reported to be "harmless" to everything else. No one felt the need to warn the public of the human health and ecological effects of fogging. Only a few people who were worried brought their children into the house whenever the trucks passed, and closed all their windows. Entomology departments flourished in universities, and great effort was devoted to systematics, behavior, ecology, and population dynamics of mosquitoes. Mosquitoes come in many different species: There are over three thousand worldwide, and the salt marsh mosquito is only one of a whole host that live in New Jersey. Over sixty different species of mosquitoes have been identified in New Jersey, about a third of the North American list. Nearly half of the Jersey species belong to the genus *Aedes* and the rest belong to *Anopheles*, *Coquillettidia*, *Culex*, *Culiseta*, *Orthopodomyia*, *Wyeomyia*, *Psorophora*, and *Uranotaenia*. The wide diversity even in our mosquitoes implies that we have a special state.

Some mosquitoes are more than annoying; they carry dangerous diseases, and this strengthened the role of the Mosquito Commissions. The salt marsh mosquito is the vector of Eastern Equine Encephalitis (EEE), caused by a mosquito-borne virus that occurs naturally in a variety of wild birds. There have been various outbreaks of EEE over the years, the most recent in 1994, when there were six confirmed nonhuman cases. Horses that are infected always die. No humans died during this outbreak. The highest mortality in horses occurred in 1975 (thirty-eight horse deaths) and 1984 (twenty-six horse deaths).

In the outbreak of EEE in 1959 there were thirty-two human cases. In humans the disease is debilitating and can cause death; it kills 50 percent of the people in cases that show overt symptoms. Since 1959, EEE has been transmitted to humans in six different years. It is particularly problematic along the shore because of the high human density and the prevalence of mosquitoes.

Wild birds act as the primary hosts for EEE, and small songbirds often have high levels of antibodies, indicating that they have been exposed to the virus. Songbirds, or passerines, are the primary amplifying host. But passerines are not prominent in avifauna of coastal ecosystems, which prompted Wayne Crans and Don Caccamise of Rutgers University, and others to search for an avian host in the larger species that nest in colonies.

19.1. Glossy ibis serve as reservoirs for EEE.

Snowy egrets, among the most common birds in the salt marshes, have relatively low antibody levels for the virus. However, they found that glossy ibis have high levels of infection, and they may serve as the reservoir for both the equine and the human forms of EEE (Figure 19.1).

Mosquitoes also spread malaria, although it is the *Anopheles* mosquitoes that are implicated, rather than the salt marsh mosquito. Malaria in New Jersey was never really a coastal phenomenon, and controlling mosquitoes in the salt marsh will have no effect. Nonetheless, malaria was no doubt a serious problem for the early settlers in New Jersey, but by the late 1870s the average number of malaria deaths was only about 330 per year, dropping to an average of 120 cases a year during the 1890s, and remaining at about 10 to 15 cases a year from the 1900s to the 1930s. Today there are very few cases of malaria, usually the result of imported transmission, since there is no documented, indigenous transmission. There were two confirmed cases of locally acquired malaria in 1991, however. The early mosquito control that occurred along the coast helped to eliminate the carriers.

In the early 1960s when Rachel Carson published *Silent Spring*, the world woke up and recognized the widespread harm caused by pesticides to birds, bees, and even to ourselves. She cautioned that unless we changed our ways, no butterflies would grace our gardens, no birds would sing each spring, and few fish would migrate into our estuaries. Through the 1960s, case after case came to light of wildlife injured or killed by pesticides.

Gradually the realization dawned that controlling larval mosquitoes was easier than spraying for adults, because once mosquitoes dispersed to the barrier beaches and mainland it was impossible to control them. People were getting worried about large-scale spraying around their homes, and the days of communitywide fogging ceased, although aerial spraying continued in many communities.

Although they are always annoying to people, salt marsh mosquitoes actually take their blood meal more often from other animals. Most blood
meals of mosquitoes come from deer, and another 8 to 13 percent come
from small mammals such as rodents and rabbits. Only about 1.4 percent
of the blood meals can be linked to birds, mostly herons and egrets in the
salt marshes.

Mosquitoes often hide in the thick vegetation during the day, but will bite
anyone invading their haunts, even in full sunlight. Only by obtaining
blood can females return to the marsh to lay their eggs. They search for
just the right salt-marsh pools, with wet mud. There the eggs lie until the
warm rains cover the mud.

Sometimes the pools dry up before the eggs can hatch or the larvae can
emerge. Nearly always a pool or two is suitable for mosquito breeding.
Amazingly, not all the eggs hatch with the first flooding of the mud. Many
remain as eggs through the flooded state and through another drying period; some of these hatch with the second flooding. Nitrogen deprivation
seems to stimulate hatching. And so it goes, with eggs hatching throughout the summer from the very first egg-laying period. With each new dry-
down, other females lay, and the cycle continues. Although we have learned
much about mosquito control through opening up mosquito-breeding
areas to predatory fish, new pools develop, and the process of mosquito control will continue. Future mosquito control will surely involve less destructive measures and lower application of pesticides. Our salt marshes are too
important to destroy or alter, for they serve as nurseries for our coastal and
oceanic waters.

Fall Changes

20

The Shorebirds Return

In late July, it is mid-summer along the shore, the young terns and skimmers are still at their nesting colonies, and the piping plover young are barely able to fly. Crowds of people are heading for the beaches, and the Garden State Parkway is jammed with cars most of the day. Many roads on the barrier islands are like parking lots, with cars moving imperceptibly. The beaches ring with the sounds of happy children, boom boxes, and teenagers congregating in an age-old ritual of playing volleyball, hanging out, learning the rules, and finding special friends. The beaches may be crowded, but everyone can find a space.

A few hundred yards away from the nearest parking lot, the beaches are empty. Along the surf sanderlings run in and out with the waves, frenetically picking up invertebrates gleaned from the sand. A lone sunbather lies quietly, reading the latest real-life court drama. Shorebirds adapt readily to people who lie quietly in one place. Not far away a flock of laughing gulls sleep with their bills tucked in their back feathers. There are no young gulls with the flock, for it is early July, and the chicks have not fledged yet.

Farther down the beach a flock of nearly seventy semipalmated sandpipers feed at the edge of the waves. It has been several weeks since these small peeps graced the Jersey shore—they were off breeding in the tundra of northern Canada. Most of the shorebirds seen in New Jersey in the late spring are migrants, bound for the far north. Only willets, oystercatchers, spotted sandpipers, piping plovers, and killdeer breed in New Jersey. Although killdeer nest in a variety of habitats throughout the state, the others breed only along the shore on the barrier beaches and marshes.

Many shorebirds that breed in the Arctic nest near pools, ponds, or streams that cut across the tundra, and they forage near their nests. Some shorebirds, such as yellowlegs and solitary sandpipers, nest in lone stunted trees, where they can survey the tundra, watching for jaegers and other predators.

When shorebirds arrive in northern Canada in the spring the ground is still frozen, and ice and snow linger in low spots. Insects are few, so shore-birds rely on fat stores laid down thousands of miles to the south in Delaware Bay or other stopover areas to sustain them, and to produce eggs. Birds that arrive in early June have little time to breed, for by late July the food supply is already dwindling, and they leave for the south once again.

Almost immediately the new arrivals must decide whether to breed or not. When food is scarce on the tundra, the shorebirds fly about, search-ing for a better place. If the snow cover persists too long, many birds forgo breeding that year. In 1986, for example, when I spent two weeks in the High Arctic near the northern tip of Baffin Island, many birds were not breeding, owing to the late snow and ice cover. Others may make a valiant attempt, and fail. Even in a good food year some shorebirds lose their eggs or chicks to predators, or their chicks die from starvation or disease. By late June, some shorebirds are already leaving the tundra to start their south-ward migration to the tip of South America.

By early July the first southbound migrant shorebirds are hitting the Jer-sey shore. Unlike spring, the summer offers no superabundant food sup-ply like the horseshoe crab eggs, and the birds are not funneled through one or two stopover places. Instead, the shorebirds spread out along the shore and linger wherever there is food and little human disturbance.

As July turns to August, large concentrations of shorebirds build up wherever there are extensive mud flats, and the birds can feed at low tide. Shorebirds in the tens of thousands concentrate at Jamaica Bay, Brigantine National Wildlife Refuge, and along the beaches of Raritan and Delaware Bays. At high tide they fly to high marshes, where they can rest or continue feeding. The pressure to feed all day long is low, for in the fall they are not so time-pressed. They do not have to make a long journey in only a few days, and they do not have to arrive on southern wintering grounds with large fat reserves. They only have to leave northern regions before cold weather eliminates their food supply.

During July, August, and September of one fall Julia Chase, Caldwell Hahn, Marshall Howe, and I decide to find out just how the fall shorebirds use the intertidal habitats at Little Beach Island, near Brigantine. Vast ex-panses of mudflat are exposed each day as the tides recede, while at high tide no foraging space is left uncovered. Then birds are forced to feed on the outer beach along the surf, or they move onto the high marsh to feed in the tidal pools.

Each day at high tide we anchor our boat over the same part of the mud-flat, now hidden below nearly a foot of water. We wait for the tidal waters lapping against the *Spartina* to recede. The sun is high overhead, and we have no protection from its penetrating rays. Slight breezes prevent the

20.1. Black-bellied plovers feeding on beds of algae on tidal flats.

mosquitoes and greenheads from being impossible, but still they are annoying.

At first the tidal waters ebb gradually from the creeks, exposing only a narrow rim of mudflat near the grass. Then the outward tidal flow gains force, and the mudflat uncovers rapidly. Some shorebirds appear when a bit of the mud is exposed, and gradually the numbers build up as flocks career in. Oystercatchers come first, followed by black-bellied plovers, dowitchers, semipalmated sandpipers, and finally by Red Knots and semipalmated plovers (Figure 20.1). Most species seem to prefer the rapidly falling, or rapidly rising tides, and numbers of feeding birds drop off around dead low tide. Only semipalmated sandpipers continue to build up in numbers through the low tide, reaching a peak an hour after the tide turns.

Although the mudflat looks homogeneous, the conditions vary subtly. In some places the mud is covered with a lush, ragged film of the algae sea lettuce; in others the algae is scattered and sparse. The wet mud is lumpy with thousands of tiny snails called periwinkles; in other places periwinkles are few and the soil is sandier. The periwinkles are marine and have a horny operculum they draw into the opening of their shells to keep themselves from drying out at low tide. They seem almost dead, lying on top of the wet mud, motionless. When the tide rises and they are safe below the water, they open and slowly move about the mudflat, feeding on microscopic algae.

With our boat high and dry now, we are marooned far from any water. The birds have grown used to our boat and feed all around us. As water drains from the mud, the periwinkles sink ever deeper, burrowing to keep moist. They look like tiny raisins pressed into freshly baked bread.

Many of the shorebirds have particular feeding preferences. Dowitchers and oystercatchers feed where the algae is thick, and they pick their way through the algae, turning it over, pecking at the moist mud. The oystercatchers walk about by themselves, ignoring the other shorebirds, while the dowitchers feed in tight flocks, nearly "waist" deep in water. When one

20.2. Semipalmated plovers feeding along the surf.

dowitcher moves, they all move. As the tidal waters recede the birds follow the leading edge and probe with rapid up-and-down motions.

Black-bellied plovers, semipalmated plovers, and semipalmated sandpipers feed on the wet film of water that covers the periwinkles. Two large brown shorebirds stand out, much larger than any other individuals. These marbled godwits are looking for large marine worms called *Nereis*. The larger species of shorebirds stay in the wetter places, often walking out into the tidal waters. Only a few Yellowlegs are present, and they are in the shallow water. The smaller species feed where the mud is exposed, often remaining on the drier places. There is enough space for everyone on the vast expanse of exposed mud, and there is little fighting because they are spread out.

After three and a half hours, the tide begins to creep back in, and the pattern is reversed as one by one the shorebirds leave the mudflat. It is not always clear what prompts the birds to quit feeding or leave. One moment they are probing away, the next they look up, a few stretch their wings upward, and they all take off, wheeling over the mud and out of sight over the marsh. Semipalmated plovers often remain the longest, feeding on the bits of exposed mudflat up near the *Spartina*. For nearly six hours the shorebirds used the mudflat, but now they must find foraging sites elsewhere.

Our boat is floating once again, and we make our way to the ocean side of the bay, where most of the shorebirds have flown. Many fly directly to the outer beach, where they feed along the surf line (Figure 20.2). Not as many species feed on the ocean front compared to the mudflats, for some are in the high marshes feeding in the pools. Some rest in dense flocks, their bills tucked in their feathers. Many others walk along the edges of the pools, probing in the mud. Some snap at emerging insects, but most seek invertebrates buried below the surface. Some even forage in the marsh in the wetter places in the sparse grass. Where clouds of beach fleas hover over wet vegetation, several species of shorebirds dash in and feed frenetically for many minutes.

On the outer beach, feeding habitat is much less diverse. Sanderlings and turnstones feed at the tide line, while other sandpipers run along the windrow probing at the seaweed debris washed up by the last high tide. Minor skirmishes sometimes break out, as the birds battle for space in the waves. The larger species engage in little aggression, for the smaller species give them a wide berth. The intermediate-sized and small species fight often, however, for the outcome is less clear. They are fighting over foraging space, for the food is not limiting. It is just difficult to push their way into the dense flock feeding at the edge.

As high tide approaches, many shorebirds fly to the bay side of the barrier beach and feed on the protected shores where there is little wave action. They wait, many of them asleep, watching the mudflats across the water. Hours later, as soon as even a small bit of mud is exposed they begin to fly over, standing at the edge of the cordgrass, waiting. Anxious to begin feeding again, the large oystercatchers and black-bellied plovers wade out in the shallow water. Long-legged godwits and willets are the first species to feed on the flats, even before the mud is exposed.

Along many Atlantic coast beaches migrant shorebirds reach a peak population in August, although the flocks are never as large or as dense as the spring flocks feeding on horseshoe crab eggs, and the migration period is prolonged. By late September, numbers have already decreased. The southward migration of shorebirds is leisurely, and some species will linger in New Jersey well into the fall. Several species remain in fair numbers into November, decreasing precipitously in early December.

A few shorebirds, such as dunlins, sanderlings, and turnstones may remain until nearly Christmas, or even later if it is a particularly mild winter. They need to time their final departure so that they will have enough food without depleting fat reserves necessary for their southward migration. One species, the purple sandpiper is unique. It does not even arrive until November, and it passes the winter probing wave-washed seaweeds on rocky jetties in northern Jersey such as Caven Point, Manasquan, and Barneget Light.

Though it is still summer along the Jersey shore, the first migrant shorebirds suggest that fall is not far away. The vast numbers of people playing on the beaches do not read the signs of impending fall, for the days are still long, the sun still bright, and the waters invitingly warm.

21

Migrating Monarchs at Cape May

In the late summer the nights are often chilly, but the sun is still warm, the clouds fluffy, and the sky a delicate blue. The cool breezes blowing from the ocean suggest that fall is nearly here. A soft fluttering motion draws our attention to a tree festooned with hundreds of bright orange-and-black monarch butterflies, each seeking just the right place to spend the night. Other nearby trees are similarly dressed with so many it is difficult to identify the tree. Now and then a monarch moves from one tree to the other, but for the most part they flit only from branch to branch. Monarchs do not fly at night, and when the sun begins to sink and the temperature drops, each seeks a place to roost for the night. Guy Tudor, Michelle LeMarchant, Mike, and I have come to observe the monarch migration, just as hundreds come to view the spectacle of the fall bird migration. Cape May is a wonderful place for butterflies; Pat and Clay Sutton and Jim Dowdell have recorded nearly as many butterflies in Cape May as are found in the rest of New Jersey.

Every year the same trees are visited by the monarchs. Some scientists have suggested that migrants leave an odor on the tree that attracts migrants the following year. When a traditional roosting tree is cut down, however, butterflies simply transfer to another nearby tree the following year. It is more likely that they are attracted visually to a particular group of trees, and choose a given tree because it has large clusters of leaves. Most monarchs roost on the leeward side, away from the strong winds and driving rains. There is some indication that they are attracted to one another, but whether pheromones or visual cues are the attractant is unknown.

Each monarch flutters around a potential roosting tree, circling many times, seeking space on the sheltered side of the tree. The first monarchs to land drop their bodies, close their wings, and finally hang nearly upside down, their wings folded. The butterflies pile in, until their folded wings nearly touch one other. They do not land on each other, for if one approaches too closely, the resident opens its wings in a startling signal. The tree pulsates with orange-and-black wings fluttering gently. Small clusters of up to fifty butterflies may form on a single branch. Here and there a tree has only ten or fifteen clusters, but most have three hundred or four hundred. Some have many hundreds.

A steady stream of butterflies wafts along the shore, their undulating flight catching the sun as they flutter into the roost. Each seeks a resting place before they begin the long journey across Delaware Bay and beyond. Hundreds of thousands of monarchs move through south Jersey on their migration to wintering grounds in the highlands of Mexico. When they reach Texas they slow down and feed voraciously, swelling until their bodies are nearly 50 percent fat. This will enable them to be relatively inactive through the cool winter on their Mexican roost.

Though less well-known than the shorebirds that migrate through Delaware Bay in the spring, or the hawks and songbirds that congregate in south Cape May each fall, the monarchs are as predictable and as spectacular. They are certainly more incredible, for despite their small size and fragility, they migrate as far as many of the birds. The journey is surely more perilous, for their wings are fragile, and they can be blown off course by even the slightest breezes. Unlike avian migrants, they cannot control their own body temperatures, and are at the whim of the weather.

The migration of monarchs through Cape May occurs in the early fall. A few arrive in mid- to late August, but the massive clusters form in the trees in mid- to late September. Although hard to discern at first, there are waves of migrating monarchs, just as there are waves of migrant hawks and songbirds. Their movements are influenced by the weather. The number of migrants piling into the trees in Cape May increases dramatically with each passing cold front. The butterflies apparently move in the warm air masses ahead of the front. Eventually the cold air overtakes them, and as their bodies slow, they seek roosting trees to wait out the cold. They wait for the cold air mass to pass before beginning to migrate anew; in the meantime they flit around Cape May, nectaring on whatever flowers remain.

The monarchs have come from their northern breeding grounds in southern Canada and New England to migrate through New Jersey, following the coastline. They fly across meadows, through forests, and over busy highways, where hundreds are smashed by passing cars. They brave heavy winds and violent rains. Tropical storms cast migrants against trees, grasses, bushes, and buildings. Many damage their wings, others drown in the ocean. Many of the millions of migrating monarchs that pass through Cape May will reach their destination in Mexico, but most will perish along the way. Yet, tens of millions of monarchs congregate at the Mexican overwintering sites from the United States and Canada.

Even in Cape May dead monarchs or parts of their wings lie scattered beneath the roosting trees, along highways, and over the meadows. Many are victims of bird predators, though most have been injured by migration. Even so, the trees are still filled with thousands upon thousands of Monarchs, ready to fly again with the new dawn.

In the first rays of sunlight, the roosting migrants spread their wings to absorb the warmth. They remain in the sun for an hour or so until their bodies warm, and then they take off, their undulating flight carrying them toward Delaware Bay. They must cross the bay in one flight, for there is no place to land, and their wings become waterlogged if they land on the water. With a wingspread of only about four inches, they accomplish quite a feat. From Delaware Bay they head southwest, eventually reaching the Gulf of Mexico, another formidable water barrier. Millions more will die crossing the gulf, but some will make it.

They are on their way to the Neovolcanic Plateau or the Cross Mountain Range that extends across Mexico from the Gulf of Mexico to the Pacific Ocean. The monarchs overwinter in several locations in the mountains at elevations that range from 8,000 feet to 15,000 feet. Here they will roost in the millions on trees, bushes, and even on the ground. They form curtains on the trees and carpets on the ground, in a dense vibrating mass of orange and black.

Monarchs from other parts of North America also migrate. They leave the Great Lakes region and head southwest along river valleys to Mexico, bypassing the treacherous Gulf of Mexico. Others from the western regions migrate to California, where many thousands of monarchs overwinter on traditional trees in coastal sites such as Pacific Grove. They overwinter from Muir Beach to Ventura, but the numbers at each site vary. Indeed, these wintering sites were known before the Mexican roosts were found. In California they gather on pine and eucalyptus trees, where they hang upside down, making it almost impossible to see the branches. Their warning colors and scents reinforce one another, although their bright orange is muted when they hang with their wings folded together. The light pale orange between black veins suggests stained glass. A rim of white spots on black serves to break up their pattern, though these large aggregations are clearly visible.

The monarchs leave the Northeast in the fall partly because the milkweeds that are so integral to their life cycle are dying even before the temperatures have dropped. Those that did not migrate would die, leaving no nonmigratory genes in the next generation.

The life cycle of milkweeds affects monarchs in many ways, for the monarch is closely tied to milkweeds from the time the egg is deposited on the plants' leaves until the monarch reaches the pupa stage. This plant influences the distribution and density of monarchs all along the Jersey shore.

Milkweeds come in many shapes and sizes, and their flowers range in color from white and pink to a hot orange. Milkweed flowers are so close together that they form dense terminal or lateral clusters, creating lovely visual and aromatic flower heads. As the seeds within develop, the plants begin to form artistic, oblong pods, thin and slightly curved at the end. As the pods split open in the fall, they reveal an intricate pattern of overlapping seeds attached to the pod by a white thread. Within hours, the threads dry and feather out into a fluffy plume. At the first wind, the seeds are borne away and float on a fluffy floss familiar even to the early American settlers, who collected them to stuff pillows. The colonists also used the strong stems as a fiber instead of flax or hemp. The common milkweed ranges throughout North America, providing food for millions of monarch larvae. They usually occur in little colonies or dense clusters of plants, as most of the seeds fall to the ground at their parents' feet, while the wind-blown seeds establish new colonies at a distance.

The milkweed flowers have a rich perfume, which draws many species of nectar-feeding insects, including a variety of butterflies. Several monarchs may feed at a single flower head, and dozens of monarchs may grace a large clump of plants.

A female monarch about to lay eggs seeks the young tender leaves of the milkweed, rather than the old leathery ones. Grasping the upper surface of a leaf, she curves her abdomen so it touches the undersurface. She then deposits one tiny, yellow, conical egg on the undersurface of the leaf, where it is less visible and not directly exposed to the sun. Through a microscope the egg appears gemlike, with tiny longitudinal ridges with dots that reflect light. Smaller ridges cut across them, forming tiny cells.

Over three to five days, depending upon the temperature, the tiny egg changes to dark gray. Just before hatching, called "eclosion," the tiny black head of the larva moves slightly within the egg, chewing its way out. This hatching process, from the first tiny slit to the larva's emergence, may take two to three hours. The small larva consumes its eggshell, and then begins to eat the small hairs on the underside of the milkweed leaf. It wanders awkwardly about the leaf for a while, but then returns to gnaw through the leaf, producing the minute holes characteristic of young larvae.

Slowly the larva grows, shedding one skin to reveal a translucent one underneath. A clear molting fluid is produced, which dissolves the old skin. The transition period is called an "instar." The larva grows larger and larger, through five instars. The monarch larva, or caterpillar, has striking bands of white, black, and yellow around its body. When disturbed, it rolls into a tight ball and falls to the ground, where it blends with grasses and weeds.

Monarch caterpillars feed exclusively on milkweeds, in the family *Asclepiadaceae*, which contain varying amounts of heart poisons similar to digitalis.

Birds that eat these caterpillars gag, choke, and vomit, and will not eat any more monarchs. Since the larvae are so boldly colored, birds do not have trouble learning not to eat them. This is called warning coloration.

The noxious taste of the monarchs depends upon which of the milk-weeds they eat, since the milkweeds vary in their toxicity. Some milkweeds are innocuous, and so are the monarchs that feed on them. In some places, only a quarter of the monarchs are distasteful, and the rest are innocuous. But they all are protected, since birds who eat a noxious caterpillar first will learn to avoid the species as a whole. This allows the whole population of monarchs to feed on both toxic and nontoxic milkweeds, yet still retain the advantages of warning coloration.

The larva grows and feeds until it reaches the final growth period, the fifth instar. It has been nearly two weeks since the tiny egg hatched, and now it must enter one of its most dramatic stages, the pupa or chrysalis. It will undergo an incredible transition from a wormlike creature to a beautiful butterfly with colorful wings. It is this single miraculous process that has made many of us naturalists forever.

The caterpillar leaves the milkweed only after eating an enormous final meal, and looks for a safe place to pupate. It falls or climbs to the ground, and may crawl up to sixty or seventy yards away from its milkweed to find a suitable site on the undersurface of herbaceous plants, logs, trees, fences, or even windowsills (Figure 21.1). It needs a safe place away from direct sun and heavy rains.

The larva hangs upside down and tests the suitability of the site by swinging gently back and forth, testing for objects that might interfere with its movements. Then it lays down a layer of silk on the supporting surface, called a silk mat. Satisfied, the larva lays down more and more silk on the mat, forming a "button" that it can grasp tightly with its anal prolegs. Hanging thus in a J position, the larva goes through a series of changes in its larval skin. The body elongates as the thorax straightens out, and it changes color from bright yellow to a bluish green. The fully formed pupa now must shed its larval skin. A split appears and, with a series of peristaltic waves, the skin is moved back toward the button. The pupa then engages in such active wriggling that I fear it will lose its hold on the button. Gradually the skin of the pupa becomes firmer, and changes within have resulted in the formation of legs, wings, and antennae. Finally the smooth, waxy, mature pupa is formed, with ornate gold spots that may relate to the final pigmentation of the scales on the head and abdomen of the adult butterfly. It remains a pupa for about ten days (Figure 21.2).

Toward the end of the pupal stage, a hint of the orange-and-black butterfly is visible through the pale green, transparent shell. A small crack appears in the pupal shell, enough for the legs to emerge and grasp the shell

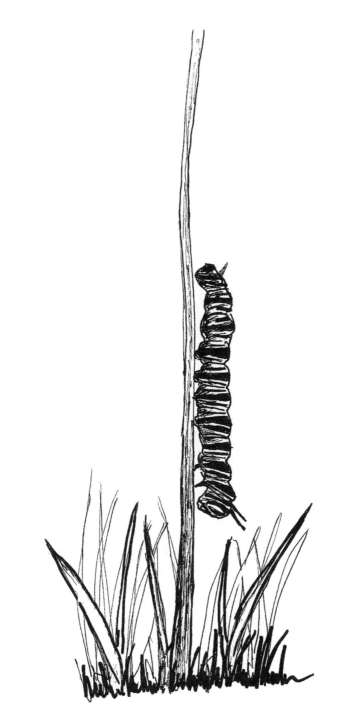

21.1. *Monarch caterpillar crawling to the ground to find a good site to pupate.*

21.2. Chrysalis of monarch hanging on a windowsill next to a swamp milkweed.

21.3. Recently hatched monarch, just drying out and expanding its wings.

firmly. The shell continues to fracture, and the small butterfly emerges. The small, oval-shaped wings are swollen. Slowly, body fluids are pumped into the spaces between the upper and lower membranes of the wings, and the wings begin to expand (Figure 21.3). It takes at least an hour for the wings to expand and dry, during which the butterfly is vulnerable. If the day is damp and rainy, however, the butterfly may not even fly the first day. When the warm sunrays hit it the next morning, the monarch takes its first flight.

I remember watching a monarch pupa attach itself to a bench in my parents' greenhouse in Niskayuna, New York. I anxiously guarded it for days, until the butterfly emerged. Last summer, nearly fifty years later, I watched with my nieces and nephews as another monarch in the same greenhouse emerged, dried, and fluttered away for its first flight. Their pleasure brought back my own delight of that first wonderful marvel.

Finally the butterfly is dry and ready to face the world. The transformation is complete, and one of the loveliest creatures in the world takes wing. It flits over the fields, searching for nectar in a variety of flowers such as goldenrod, knapweed, milkweed, and butterfly bush. It may avoid avian predators because it tastes bad, but not all have a bitter taste, for it depends upon the toxicity of the milkweed it fed on as a caterpillar.

Viceroy butterflies mimic the color pattern of monarchs, thereby making use of the warning coloration of the foul-tasting monarchs. This is called Batesian mimicry. Since some monarchs are innocuous, they also mimic the distasteful monarchs, and this is called automimicry, because they are mimicking their own species.

That monarchs are taken by birds is obvious on the wintering roosts in California and Mexico, where thousands upon thousands of partially eaten butterflies and broken wings lie strewn beneath the roosting trees. Birds eat several hundred thousand monarchs on the wintering grounds in Mexico. On their wintering grounds, the monarchs are less emetic than elsewhere, allowing increased bird predation. Remarkably, the birds capture the butterflies randomly, but eat only the ones that are less emetic.

Bird predation is one possible reason why the monarchs cluster in such large overwintering concentrations. It is another example of the "selfish herd" concept: any given butterfly is less likely to be eaten if it is in a extremely large group compared to a smaller group. Studies on partially eaten butterflies on the forest floor indicate that predation rates are lowest in large monarch groups compared to smaller groups.

The butterflies are inactive during the winter, but as February approaches and the days become warmer in the mountains of Mexico, the migrants become more agitated. Many leave the trees to find beds of flowers, pairs begin courting, and some even mate. By late February a frenzy fills the roosts, and activity crescendos.

The butterflies fly northeast, stopping to breed along the way. Many if not most of the overwintering females return to their northern breeding grounds in spring and early summer, according to Fred Urquhart, who has studied and tagged them for many years. They may stop in Georgia or South Carolina to mate and lay eggs, but they continue. They are followed north in June and July by their offspring hatched along the migration route. Thus in July there is a mixture of very old, worn migrant females, mixed with the brightly colored, untattered first and second generations produced along the migration routes. If this is so, then females from the Jersey shore have migrated to Mexico, and returned to New Jersey to breed and nectar in the flowers in our gardens or along the shore. They will not survive much longer, but they use their last strength to flutter from milkweed to milkweed, laying a few more eggs before death concludes their long journey.

Migrating monarchs pose several conservation problems that are similar to those faced by migrant birds: loss of habitat both en route and in Mexico, human disturbance, and direct mortality by cars and other vehicles. They face additional problems. Virtually none of their roosting trees on migration routes are protected from the ax. The trees are indistinguishable for most of the year, making it difficult to protect them under the best of circumstances. In other cases, trees are deliberately cut down, as happened recently when seven of the forty-seven known overwintering sites in California were destroyed deliberately by developers. About 10 million monarchs used these seven sites.

In many states migrating monarchs are not protected, and the masses of butterflies roosting in trees are collected for hobby or the biological trade. Thousands can be collected in a single night, and the butterflies are absolutely defenseless. This practice has been halted in New Jersey by action of the Endangered and Nongame Species Program, but it still continues in other states along their migratory route.

The masses of migrating monarchs wafting over the dunes, through the trees, and above the meadows in southern Cape May is a truly remarkable sight. Although they migrate along the shore throughout New Jersey, nowhere else are the concentrations as great. Not only is the color spectacular, but the sight of many thousands of butterflies hanging from a few trees is breathtaking.

22

Hawks in Cape May

An orange red shaft of light glances over the smooth water, only a ripple or two reflecting the rays. Within minutes the sun rises, changing the red to a warm golden yellow. The dark silhouette of a gannet moves along the horizon, diving occasionally from a height of thirty or forty feet.

In the near waves a flock of Bonaparte's gulls wheels and turns, hovering low over the water to pick up small fish schooling at the surface. Their frenzied activity indicates that predatory fish must be nearby, forcing the baitfish close inshore to the wave edge. The much larger-bodied predatory fish cannot pursue them in such shallow water. It seems as if the gulls will crash into the sand when they dive, for the water must be only inches deep there. Yet they are barely dipping their bills into the surf. The early morning light glances from the white leading edge of their wings. Nearly every dive results in a fish, attesting to the efficacy of feeding with predatory fish.

The frenzied activity soon ceases, as the predatory fish turn and head for deeper water. Without the predators, the small baitfish scatter, darting back into the ocean, swimming deeper, out of reach of the gulls hovering above.

Cape May Point is deserted now, only an occasional jogger moves along the water's edge, scattering a flock of sanderlings in her path. It is easy for the sanderlings to adapt to the jogger, for otherwise the entire stretch of beach is deserted, and the shorebirds can spend most of their time foraging. On a crowded summer day, joggers can disrupt foraging for hours, because the birds have a difficult time finding another stretch of beach not occupied with sunbathers, swimmers, or children building sand castles.

The sanderlings circle behind her, and land only a few feet away, feeding in a tight flock along the water's edge. Following the waves, they run in and out, in and out, stopping to peck at tiny invertebrates that are exposed at the leading edge of the wave. They are refueling for their southward journey to wintering grounds in Florida and South America.

The foraging flock of sanderlings is one reminder that summer has passed, and winter is close behind. The full flush of fall is here, the leaves

22.1. Common snipe feeding at Cape May before migrating south.

are reds and yellows. Away from the small woods it may not be obvious to the infrequent visitor, but I have learned to take pleasure in the subtle seasonal changes of color of even the smallest beach plants.

The once-green beach grass has turned amber. Many of the leaves are broken, battered by the early fall winds. It is an exciting time, for each fall hundreds of thousands of raptors, songbirds, snipe, and woodcock funnel through Cape May peninsula (Figure 22.1). The seasonal raptor count, sometimes over 80,000 individuals, is the highest and most diverse in the entire United States. Over 200 species of songbirds migrate through Cape May, including sparrows and warblers. They rely on the fruiting shrubs, grass and weed seeds, and a supply of late fall insects. Since many of these migrants are neotropical migrants that have suffered severe losses in recent years, Cape May Point is critical to their continued survival. There are also other important migratory corridors in New Jersey, including the Kittatinny Ridge, Central Highlands, and the Atlantic Coast corridor that includes Island Beach State Park.

On a good fall morning following a brisk northwest wind, the passerines tumble from the sky, some exhausted from a long flight, others anxious to find food. The trees drip with them, and the potential for a new, exciting, rare bird is everywhere. There are birds on the ground, low in the bushes, and at the tops of the trees. They have dropped in on lawns and on the streets. Even the countless multitudes of common migrants such as catbirds, yellow warblers, black and white warblers, and red-eyed vireos are overwhelming. We count over 20 different species of warblers in a small row of trees. Deep within the woodland trails the numbers drop, it is difficult to find as many, but the sounds of peeps, cheeps, tzits, and other calls and moving birds are lively.

As September gives way to October the species change slightly, as wave after wave of neotropical migrants move through the Cape. Now yellow-rumped warblers, white-throated sparrows, and flickers predominate, and the diversity of species drops somewhat. On a good day when the cold breezes have dropped and a front has passed, the numbers are still high.

Sharp-shinned hawks zip through the trees, targeting the weak, finding it easy to catch their prey among the bedraggled and exhausted warblers. On a branch over our heads a sharpie tears at a warbler, feathers flying in every direction. Sometimes it seems hard for the hawks to select prey, there are so many birds flying in every direction. The exhausted yellow warbler sitting on the ground is easy prey, however, and soon provides energy for the continued southward migration of a Cooper's hawk that swooped down.

A marsh hawk courses low over the nearby fields, searching for small mice, while a stately red-tailed hawk sits disdainfully in the trees, resting and watching. At the very top of an old dead snag, an osprey holds a large fish in its talons, bending to rip the flesh bit by bit. Several kestrels are perched lower on the branches, watching for passersby. Everywhere there are hawks, some moving, some resting, some hunting. The winds are calm, and most will rest and feed here for the day. The few that will cross the bay are up and about early in the day, circling ever higher in the air to catch the winds.

Many species of raptors move through Cape May each fall, including, in order of abundance, sharp-shinned hawk, American kestrel, red-tailed hawk, broad-winged hawk, and marsh hawk. Others that pass through in lower numbers include turkey vulture, Cooper's hawk, osprey, merlin, peregrine falcon, goshawk, red-shouldered hawk, and eagle.

As we stand on the platform at Cape May Point, most of the hawks over our heads are young birds, and this is true of many songbirds as well. Young birds find it easier to follow the coastline, and to forage and hunt in the calm of the bays and coastal forests. High on the ridges the winds are strong, and it may be difficult for hawks to hunt and capture prey.

The raptor migration at Cape May is one of the largest and most diverse in the country. Hawks from the Northeast and Canada move south in the fall, pushed by the dominant northwest winds. The winds, and the inexperience of young raptors, push them toward the Atlantic Coast. Rather than go out to sea, they follow the coast that shunts them to Cape May Point.

Cape May is a long narrow extension of the New Jersey Coastal Plain. To the east is the Atlantic Ocean, and to the west is Delaware Bay. Many birds are reluctant to fly over broad expanses of water, and so they are funneled down the point. At the tip of the point they encounter Cape May. Some fly directly across the bay, a distance of eleven miles. Others pause for the right winds, while many fly back north along Delaware Bay shore, following the coastline around until the bay is so narrow they can cross easily and head south again over land. A major factor concentrating the birds at the Point is the influence of adverse weather conditions that delay birds from crossing the bay.

During the day the hawks hunt and rest in the forests and edge areas of the Dennis Creek Wildlife Management Area, Belleplaine State Forest, Heislerville, and Egg Island, and other forest patches before finally crossing Delaware Bay. They will continue to their destinations in the southeastern United States, Central America, and South America.

Because the hawks and songbirds pause at Cape May, these lands are a critical stopover habitat, providing safe resting, roosting, and feeding places. The large fallouts of small birds provide an ample food supply for several species of migrant hawks, which pause to replenish energy reserves as well as to wait for better winds.

The Cape May Bird Observatory has been counting the hawks that pass through each year since 1976, and Pete Dunne and others have followed the same procedures each year. This is critical, for trends in bird populations are difficult to ascertain unless methods are comparable from year to year. These censuses have proven invaluable in determining long-term population trends of hawks. In some years nearly 90,000 raptors have passed the counting tower at Cape May Point, and nearly half are Sharp-shinned hawks.

Since 1976, several species have been increasing, including Cooper's hawk, bald eagle, harrier, osprey, peregrine falcon, and merlin. Peregrine falcons have increased over five-fold, partly owing to reintroductions. Population levels of these species had been severely depressed by DDT and other chemicals. Numbers of red-tailed hawks and turkey vultures have remained relatively stable since 1976. Other raptors, however, have continued to decline since 1976, including sharp-shinned hawk, red-shouldered hawk, American kestrel, and golden eagle (Figure 22.2). It is remarkable that kestrels have declined, given that the other falcons have increased. Even so, as many as 22,000 Kestrels can pass one spot at Cape May Point between the first of September and the end of November.

The migration of hawks and passerines at Cape May draws myriads of birders each fall, some seeking rare birds, others coming for the spectacle. Birding is big business in Cape May, for birders spend over six million dollars there each year. Nowhere else in New Jersey is the incentive so strong to allow birders and birds to coexist in harmony.

Tourism is the state's second largest industry, and much of this tourism involves coastal areas. Natural phenomena such as the mating horseshoe crabs and migrating shorebirds in the spring at Delaware Bay, wintering birds at Port Liberte and Sandy Hook, and the fall migration at Cape May

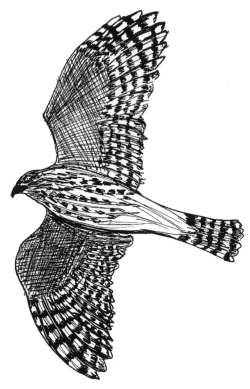

22.2. Sharp-shinned hawk hunting for small passerines during migratory stopover.

attract vast numbers of tourists. They come for the day, or they come for the week. But come they do. If we are to protect birds adequately, we must learn how people affect them, while still allowing people to enjoy them.

Two problems migrants face are habitat loss and human disturbance. With development, there are fewer and smaller patches of forest available for passerines and hawks. Larry Niles, Mandy Dey, and I have embarked on a study of landscape resources so that the state may best manage and pre-serve these migrants. Both passerines and hawks need large, undisturbed tracts of forest for nesting and foraging. Charlie Leck at Rutgers was one of the first scientists to recognize that birds need large contiguous forest patches rather than small isolated ones.

Higbee Beach, near Cape May Point, provides an ideal place to exam-ine the effect of people on birds, for nowhere else in the state is the con-centration of both so great as it is during fall migration. For several years Larry Niles, Kathy Clark, and I have examined the effect of people on birds at Cape May and along the Delaware Bay shore. At Higbee, we compared the presence of hawks in fields with and without people. Our objective was to determine how best to manage access to Higbee Beach to maximize both raptor and passerine migration while allowing the best viewing possibilities for birders and other naturalists.

Some hawks used the protected fields more often than those open to the public. Sharp-shinned hawk, Cooper's hawk, and merlin that prey on small birds found it easier to hunt where their songbird prey were not disturbed or warned by the presence of people. Kestrels and red-tailed hawks, species that often live near human developments, did not differ in their use of the fields. At Higbee the best approach is to restrict human use of some fields to allow undisturbed hunting places for some hawks, while allowing complete access to other fields. In this manner both the birds and birders can coexist comfortably.

One of the major problems for migrants is loss of habitat, making these accommodations far more difficult. Between 1973 and 1986 over 30 percent of the wild habitats on the Cape May peninsula were lost to developers. This rate of loss has continued, increasing the value of Higbee Beach and other public lands for the migrants. It also increases the importance of thoughtful management. Birds and birders can coexist amicably, but only when careful consideration is given to controlling the duration and closeness of human encounters.

As more and more habitat disappears around Cape May, the songbirds and hawks rely more completely on Higbee. The winds still bring thousands of migrants that are funneled down the narrow strip of land between the bay and the ocean. There they must choose between waiting or crossing. Many have no choice, for they are exhausted and their fat reserves are expended. The magic of the Cape will continue, the trees will fill with myriads of warblers each fall, and they will be pursued by sharp-shinned hawks as always.

Winter Solitude

23

Nocturnal Wanderings at Higbee Beach

The sun seems unusually large as it disappears over the Bay at Higbee Beach. Shafts of light dance on the water of the bay, glancing off small white-caps fueled by winter breezes. It is cold and damp, and with the disappearance of the last sunrays, all hope of warmth disappears.

Sanderlings and a lone red knot feed along the surf. Sanderlings are primarily visual foragers, looking for prey before they probe in the sand. They glance ahead, to the left and right, then dash a few steps forward to pull a small worm from the damp, surf-splashed sand. Sanderlings can also forage by pecking staccato-like for the small invertebrates that live just below the wet film of sand. This time of year there is far less daylight, and the birds are pressed to find enough food during the day.

The beach is deserted, the sand swept smooth by erratic winds. Small drifts of snow nestle against the shallow dunes. A bit of ice clings to the driftwood in the wrack line. In the lee a solitary sanderling stands on one leg, still sleeping, preparing for the night.

Not far away the vibrant yellow of the seaside goldenrod has turned to a dull brown (Figure 23.1). Gone are the shades of greens, yellows, and delicate tans of summer. The leaves are broken, most bend haphazardly to the sand. Even the goldenrod flowerheads have been blown over or broken by storm winds. Distracted by a plant I don't recognize, I pick a long stem to take back to Rutgers for David Fairbrothers to identify.

A cool breeze blows in off the bay, across the open sand, toward the gentle dunes. The beach grass sways ever so gently. The grass is bent, away from the ocean. Tiny circles are brushed in the sand around each clump of grass, a result of the constant movement of the black tips. By early November even the most hardy grass has turned a delicate shade of tan or yellow.

Along the leading edge of the dune the grass is sparse, each clump standing alone, guarding the dunes that rise behind. Beyond, the grass grows thicker, the edges of one blending in with the next. The dunes form nearly a complete band along the beach, broken only by a path here and there,

23.1. Dried goldenrod flower head.

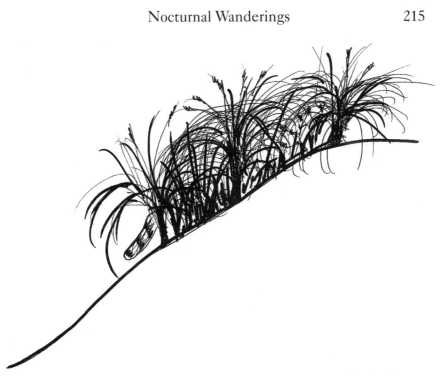

23.2. Bushy tail of an animal disappearing around a dune at Higbee Beach.

a reminder that in summer this beach is packed with swimmers, sunbathers, and solitary joggers. The path is clear now, a well-worn trail that winds through the uplands and dunes. In a few months the path will be less clear, obliterated by sand swept across the beach by winter winds.

A dark shape disappearing around the dunes catches my eye, and I follow slowly, hoping to identify the creature caught in the last light of evening. Ahead, a bushy, partially stripped tail dissolves behind the beach grass, suggesting perhaps a skunk or raccoon (Figure 23.2). The tail seems a bit thin. The sand is so soft that the tracks are fuzzy and indistinct, merely depressions.

The tracks lead between the dunes and loop up toward the crest. The golden yellow clumps of beach grass are picking up the last rays of light, and swirling grass gently describes circles in the sand. A Savannah sparrow bursts from the dunes, flies low over the grass, and disappears—frightened by my quarry, no doubt. Using its initial location as a clue, I change directions, heading away from the shore.

The beach grass here is invaded by goldenrod, beard grass, asters, Queen Anne's lace and other species, now mostly dried and brown (Figure 23.3). The once vibrant yellow flowerheads of the goldenrod are now a rich

23.3. *Dried Queen Anne's lace, cockle burr, and aster on dune.*

chocolate brown, the stems a drab tan and gray. The seed heads are shriveled, turned inward against the winds and rains.

The goldenrods ahead shake violently, suggesting the animal is moving through them. Two hundred herring gulls take wing and circle in a dense flock, calling loudly. The swirl of gulls drifts ahead, tracking the slow movements of the predator, for they would not long pursue anything that was not a direct threat. Occasionally a gull swoops toward the ground, but for the most part they remain ten to twenty feet above the moving animal.

Still following, I come across a small freshwater pool, the remnants of a recent storm. Freshwater obviously gathers here often, for the sloping shores are lined with *Phragmites* that are over six feet tall. They too are brown, but the delicate, lacy flower heads that have gone to seed are a pale tan and mauve. The animal has moved into the *Phragmites*, for the gulls rise above them. The circle gradually widens, and the gulls career back and alight next to the water. Still nervous from their interruption, they preen perfunctorily, their movements quick and jarring. Some hold their wings slightly out from their bodies, signaling that they are ready to fly at any moment.

The *Phragmites* ahead of me are still, and not wanting to disturb the gulls, I circle around the edge, keeping well within the vegetation so they cannot see me. I stop to listen for any rustling that might indicate where the animal has gone. The gulls are quiet, and the stiff, still reeds give no clue to the animal's whereabouts.

The sun has moved well below the horizon, the last rays shimmering off the dunes. The air is filled with an early evening chill. With less light, the bouquet of browns, tans, mauves, rust, beige, chestnut, rufous, umber, and burnt sienna has turned to dark browns and blacks. The sky beyond is a pale blue, laced with pinks, reds, and oranges that reflect from the billowy clouds.

Beyond the thin band of reeds is a fringe of bayberry. A few dark brown leathery leaves cling to the craggy branches. The bushes are short and stocky, their thin limbs intertwined. Tiny, whitish gray berries form small clusters along the edges of most branches. When pinched they give a faint, bayberry smell reminiscent of old-fashioned candles. Not all the bushes have berries; only the female bushes are festooned with them. There are only a few male bushes in this group. They stand apart, but actually many are interconnected underground by an elaborate root system, all one plant.

As I brush against the bushes in pursuit of my quarry, I release the sweet bayberry smell, and a few berries fall to the sand. I am no longer sure I am moving in the same direction as the animal, for the stiff bayberry bushes do not yield to such a small animal. The sharp, brown spurs of sand burr touch my leg, and the prickers still hurt (Figure 23.4).

A flock of horned larks bursts from the bayberry a hundred yards ahead, indicating that I may still be on the trail. They fly swiftly in a tight flock over

23.4. Dried sand burrs rise menacingly from the dunes.

the dunes to land on the high tide berm. They disappear amid the old *Spartina* and reed stems, driftwood, whelk egg cases, and shells, fading into the long shadows and dark recesses.

I move carefully to the edge of the bayberry, where the larks last burst from the shallow dune devoid of most vegetation. Only sea rocket and pearly everlasting grow here. The sea rocket is dead, hardened by the fall winds, and looks like miniature sagebrush. Along the edge of the bayberry are a number of sea rocket clumps, blown here by the wind. The pearly everlasting that creeps along the ground still retains a bit of its silvery green, the tiny white hairs along the leaves giving it a fuzzy feel. Although it will die back even more as winter progresses, in the spring new life will emerge from the strong, underground root system.

I come upon a mangled horned lark, blood spilling from its severed neck. It lies on its back, its wings outstretched. It dies within seconds—attesting to the predatory habits of the animal I am following. What could be fast enough to sneak up on a flock of larks? I lament its passing, and regret that the predator did not even finish its meal. Perhaps it will return after dark, when I have gone. It may be waiting nearby, waiting for me to leave.

The trail of tracks in the sand continues, and I move on to another area of *Phragmites*. With so little light it is easy to follow the trail, for each track is a dark shadow in the light sand. I pick my way slowly and quietly through the tall grass so as not to spook the animal, or I will never be able to identify it. Still the tracks are not clear enough to identify.

Suddenly the air is pierced by a loud scream and plaintive cries. Not far behind, I move quickly under cover of the chilling sounds. When the sounds cease, I stop and wait. The reeds are now merely silhouettes against a dark sky. The gulls drifting overhead are black shapes that cry softly in the night. In the silence, the pounding of the waves rises above the wind and the sound of my heartbeat.

There is a softer cry, and then silence. I have meandered through the reeds to the edge of the dune, expecting to find two animals in deadly combat. There are two animals, but instead they are locked in combat of another kind, and the creation of yet more cats. For nearly two hours I have been following a black-and-white pussycat—albeit a wild cat accustomed to fending for itself along the barrier beach. But still a cat.

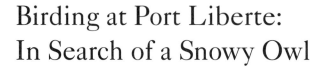

24

Birding at Port Liberte:
In Search of a Snowy Owl

A cold wind sweeps in along the shore, driving the snow against our faces, reminding us that winter can come in early December in the New York Harbor. Visibility is low, and the World Trade Center is barely visible across the bay. The skyline of New York City is but a pale gray outline against a swirling white sky. It is almost impossible to find the Empire State Building. The Port Liberte Science Center is but an outline behind me. Much closer, the Statue of Liberty stands proudly, her torch pointed skyward, catching the slight shafts of sunlight that filter through the wind-driven snowflakes.

Port Liberte is one of the best places in New Jersey to look for rare gulls in the winter, and the occasional snowy owl. Even though it is so close to New York City, and surrounded by urban sprawl, the shoreline itself is fairly deserted. The New Jersey Turnpike cuts off this part of the harbor from everyone but those who know that a bit of nature still survives, that a protected shoreline shelters flocks of migrant shorebirds in the spring and fall, breeding killdeer in the summer, and foraging gulls in the winter.

For years the area was a fenced military base, off-limits to most people. Old abandoned vehicles and buildings still linger amid the fields and grassy meadows. Cottonwoods, which have grown up around the old remains of military activity, sway gently in the wind and snow. Fences still prevent access to much of the area, but the roadways are now free and the gates stand open.

Snow-covered paths lead through the fringe of *Phragmites*, toward the open beach. A small *Spartina* marsh is nestled at the leading edge of the land, a reminder that with care and reduced pollution a flourishing salt marsh can gradually build up. A creek meanders through the *Phragmites*, into the *Spartina*, and out onto a narrow mudflat. It is almost high tide, and the usually wide mudflat is nearly covered. A few ring-billed gulls, herring gulls, and Bonaparte's gulls linger, pecking at the mud in search of food. A lone great black-backed gull picks at the remains of a large fish washed ashore by last night's high tide.

We follow the path toward the tip of the peninsula, through the higher ground, where old goldenrod heads are covered with snow, and only the stiffest stems protrude through the drifts. The tall flower stalks of sea rocket also poke through the snow, each dead flower like a small cup (Figure 24.1). The path is easy to follow, for countless other birders have made this same trek in search of the same rare gulls and snowy owl. Even through the snow it is possible to see that nice upland vegetation covered the area during the summer, providing places for small mammals, raccoons, and other urban wildlife.

The snow beneath our feet covers the soil deposited here years ago by Maxus and by Allied Chemical involved in the chromate industry. This fill containing chromium waste was dumped in various places in Hudson County from the early 1900s to as late as the 1960s. Chromium is a widespread problem in the entire area, because it was used for fill in many places that now support warehouses, schoolyards, and homes. One of the waste sites was Port Liberte.

The health problem that chromium posed to humans and other animals was only beginning to be appreciated in the late 1940s. In the early 1950s the mayor of Jersey City praised this fill because rats could not live on it, and the city did not have to worry about annoying rats running wild at night. This should have been a clear sign of danger. Surely, if the rats cannot live there we all need to worry, but it was years before the chromium issue became a real public concern.

We now know that chromium is a lung carcinogen, an intestinal-tract carcinogen, a skin sensitizer, and it damages the nasal mucosa of humans. It causes similar problems for other vertebrate animals.

Chromium pollution is clearly not as severe along the Port Liberte shore as in some parts of Jersey City and other surrounding areas, for there is a good small mammal population here. Chromium apparently has not prevented vegetation from growing on the Port Liberte spit, but it has no doubt influenced the kinds of plants that live here.

A wide expanse of mudflat is still exposed at the tip, and a large, dense flock of gulls stands huddled against the driving snow. They all face into the wind, so their feathers are not ruffled, and they lose less heat. Most stand on one foot, another adaptation to the cold. A bird can reduce heat loss by nearly 20 percent just by standing on only one leg and keeping the other neatly tucked into its belly plumage. By tucking its bill in the feathers of its back it can prevent another 30 percent of heat loss. Although they sleep with their bills tucked into their back feathers, these gulls have their eyes open, and are watching for predators. In extreme cold, birds will sit on their bellies, with both feet tucked within their feathers, allowing them to conserve still more heat.

24.1. Sea rocket dried flower head.

The flock of gulls is mostly herring, ring-billed, and Bonaparte's gulls. They face into the wind, making it difficult to look over every gull to find a rare one. Besides, most have their heads tucked in, making it even more challenging. Using a telescope, we carefully look at each gull in turn, checking the head and wing patterns. We are looking for black-headed gulls.

It would be nice if a hawk would fly by and get them all up, allowing us to see their patterns in flight. Of course, there are no hawks in sight. Anyway, with the swirling snow it would be difficult to see them clearly.

As the tide edges in, a few of the gulls lift up their heads and amble up the beach. This disturbs their neighbors, and suddenly the whole flock is edgy, moving up toward the shore. Toward us. Rapidly we scan the flock for any bird that looks different. Quieting again, one by one they tuck their bills in their backs, still warily watching us.

It is quiet and peaceful here, with New York City sleeping across the Hudson River, and the Statue of Liberty guarding the harbor. We are low enough along the shore so that the *Phragmites* and poplar trees shield us from Jersey City and the rest of the urban sprawl. The dense flock of gulls huddled together seems surreal against the backdrop of snow and the outline of New York City. Mike and I shiver in the cold winds.

This flock, however, contains no rare gulls. No snowy owl sits silently on the ice. Discouraged, we begin to trudge back through the drifts, toward the large, broken pier at Caven Cove that juts out into the harbor. A light dusting of snow covers the few pilings in the open water, the worn tires and abandoned car to our right, and even the *Spartina* flattened by recent high tides.

The rickety pier before us is covered by ice and snow, obliterating the broken boards and the holes used for fishing last summer. The pier is clearly dangerous, even when it is free of ice and snow. It should have been torn down years ago. The planks are old, broken, and worn away. Here and there are gaping cavities, big enough to fall through. Small holes can easily catch an ankle, or cause us to fall over the edge.

A large chain-link fence bars the entrance to the pier. Long ago fisherman or birders cut an opening in the fence, and by ducking only slightly, we can climb through. The pier, such as it is, extends as far as we can see. Slowly and carefully we pick our way along the pier, stopping every few feet to search through our binoculars for a snowy owl.

Halfway out the going gets far worse, for the storm waters have swept the pier, and every board is covered with ice. By staying in the middle of the pier we can avoid slipping and falling off the edge. We inch along, checking our footing with each step, making sure the drifting snow covers wood, and not just treacherous ice or a small hole.

We finally reach an impasse where half the pier has broken into the

24.2. Female snowy owl.

harbor, leaving only a narrow passageway to the next section. Through the swirling snow we can make out neither the end of the pier nor the beginning. We could almost be in a frozen arctic tundra, for we are surrounded by water, ice, and snow. Only the barest outline of the World Trade Center reminds us that we are close to one of the largest urban centers in the world.

Minutes go by as we peer into the snow ahead, looking for the owl. It was here yesterday, at least according to the New Jersey Birders Hotline. As the last snowflakes drift down, the sun begins to filter through the clouds. The end of the pier gradually materializes, and we begin to look over each lump of snow. One lump seems larger than the rest, but we are still too far to make the shape into our quarry.

Unable to contain ourselves, we inch across the narrow path on all fours, clinging to the slippery boards with our hands. The icy waters below are dark and menacing. Finally we reach the other side, and the pier widens. Free again, we walk slowly toward the end, stopping every few feet to stare at the large blob through our binoculars.

Then the blob turns its head, and two grand, soulful yellow eyes watch us. It is a large, magnificent, female snowy owl (Figure 24.2). Female owls are larger than males, perhaps so they may adequately protect their offspring from the male during the breeding season. Since the males do all the hunting, they could be tempted to kill their own young. A female snowy owl is less white than the male and has more distinct black-and-white markings. Still, she blends in almost perfectly in the snow and ice.

Snowy owls breed in the northern Arctic and usually remain there throughout the year. They nest on windswept hummocks and boulders in the open tundra. It is only when food is particularly scarce that they fly south in search of small rodents and other prey. In the cold Arctic winters, snowy owls normally survive on lemmings, rabbits, and other small mammals. In a good lemming year, one snowy owl may eat over 1,600. The population levels of snowy owls, and their nomadic wanderings in the nonbreeding season, depend on the population levels of the small mammals. They differ from all other owls in being diurnal, and their low, undulating flight over the tundra is awe-inspiring.

During the breeding season, snowy owls adjust their clutch size according to the prey base. When there are few lemmings or other small mammals, the owls abstain from breeding or lay only a very few eggs. In a good lemming year, they may lay up to twelve or fourteen pure white eggs. The total clutch weight can be equivalent to 25 to 43 percent of the female's body weight, quite unusual for a large owl. If the food supply remains abundant they can raise a dozen young. Otherwise, some will starve if the rodent population dips before the young are fledged. It is usually the smallest and youngest that starve, for by the time they hatch they are unable to compete with their larger and stronger siblings for food.

When winter comes, the owls wander about the Arctic in search of a good food supply, but if there is none, they travel south. Their irruptions are cyclic, seeming to mimic the cycles of the lemmings. The food supply in the tundra is patchy, and local differences influence the movements of the owls. Since the lemming cycles are not synchronous all across Canada, the irruptive pattern of snowy owls is unpredictable in any region. Snowy owls usually move to southern Canada once every four years or so. Their movement into the Northeast is even less predictable, but it may relate to snowfall and temperature conditions, as well as lemming availability.

It is hard to pull ourselves away from the majesty of the lone snowy owl, silently watching us. We are anxious to cross the icy narrow strip to the safety of the land. Besides, there may be a rare gull waiting. The walk back is tedious and slow, but not so discouraging as it would have been if we had missed the snowy owl.

Once on land we make our way through the snow and tangles of dead raspberry bushes. The prickers on the dead stems seem to find our hands and shoulders even easier than when they were lush and green. We walk slowly so we will not disturb the gulls that may be resting on the sand spit at the edge of the water. However, there is only one great black-backed gull amid a small flock of ring-billed gulls.

Without the blinding snow, it is easier to look out over the old pilings and broken pier abandoned in the small inlet. The pier that remains is no longer attached to land, and a long stretch just stands in the water, coming from nowhere and going nowhere. It provides a nice resting place for gulls throughout the cold winter, and nearly every available space is occupied. Great black-backed Gulls and herring gulls have the solitary pilings to themselves, and the smaller ring-billed gulls are standing on the large, open part of the pier. A dense flock of nearly 200 Bonaparte's gulls sits along a thin strip of dilapidated pier that is precariously leaning toward the water. Next to the larger gulls, they seem delicate, shorebird-like, and very elegant.

Out comes the telescope, and we deliberately look over each member of the flock. Sometimes there may be a lesser black-backed gull or a black-headed gull, species of the Old World, which occur in very small numbers in North America. Looking over gulls is fun and challenging, because there are so many possibilities. The color pattern differences among species during the nonbreeding season are often subtle and difficult to spot.

By now the sun is bright, the sky is a pale blue, and the storm has moved east, out to sea. The wind having died down, the weather is positively balmy. It is much easier to concentrate on looking over each group of gulls. Slowly and painstakingly we study every large gull, looking for a glaucous or an Iceland gull.

One large herring-like gull takes off, flying toward us and a flock of about twenty gulls that stand on the ice at the edge of the land. They face in every direction, because there is no prevailing wind. A few preen quietly, rearranging the feathers displaced by the high winds that raged only minutes ago. Suddenly they all raise their heads and look toward the stiff, brown-topped *Phragmites*, a few stretching their wings in anticipation.

A golden tan collie runs along the edge of the grass, stops to glance at the gulls, and moves on, followed by a young boy. The boy is watching the ground, picking up pieces of driftwood, and then discarding them. He is unaware of the commotion his dog is causing among the gulls, for the gulls react to the dog as if it were a fox. They can clearly outfly either, but they must take off well before the potential predator approaches.

Suddenly the collie veers and dashes straight for the gulls, scattering them. Their vigilance was well justified, their intention movements for flight gave them the edge. Lazily they swirl in the air around the dog and return to land on the pier, protected by an expanse of open water.

Our scrutiny of the gulls continues. Despite the sun, it is still cold, and the light breeze burns our face. It is a birdwatcher's ritual, this looking over the gulls for an unusual one. A long line of gulls floats on the waves behind the broken pier. Most are ring-billed gulls, but there are several Bona-

24.3. Small flock of Bonaparte's gulls at Port Liberte.

parte's gulls, small dovelike birds with rounded white heads (Figure 24.3). Each has a dark spot behind the eye, the remnant of the black hood which they wear in the breeding season. Each winter they remain in Caven Cove until it ices over, moving south just ahead of the freezeup.

With a loud hoarse cry a dark juvenile herring gull plunges into the midst of the resting gulls, apparently attempting to seize prey. In unison the Bonaparte's gulls take to the air, and among them we see one with blackish underwings, a black-headed gull. Very similar to Bonaparte's gull, the black-headed gull is a European species that has only recently invaded North America. Small numbers breed in the Canadian Maritime Provinces and around the Great Lakes, and our bird may well be one of these, rather than a transatlantic vagrant. When it settles again on the water, it looks very much like a "Boney," with the same dark spot behind the eye. We notice that it is slightly larger and it has a dull red bill, but it did not stand out the first time we scanned the resting flock. In summer, the black-headed gulls also develop black on the head, but it forms a mask, reaching only to the top of the head. They nest across Europe and Asia, often building floating nests in marshy lakes.

Among the Ring-bills remaining in a tight flock on the water, a ghostly pale Iceland gull captures our attention. It is slightly longer than the others, with faint gray marks on the wingtips. Like the young ring-bills, it has a pinkish bill with a dark tip. Iceland and glaucous gulls are two Arctic species that appear regularly each winter, but in very small numbers. It is always a treat to spot one among the thousands of gulls along beaches or at garbage dumps. They nest from eastern Canada to Greenland, but the dark marks on the wingtips identify our bird as a Canadian visitor.

We have lingered longer than we intended, and the sun has slipped lower in the sky. The temperature has dropped precipitously. The slight wind is colder now, and even the gulls seem to huddle in the lee of the broken pier. The bushes behind us take on the odd yellow tinge that signals the sun is sinking behind the tall buildings of nearby Jersey City. Within minutes only the tops of the bushes are tinged with light, and the reeds are dark and dreary. Cold, but content, we take our leave. Behind us, a lone female cardinal drifts into the dense shrubbery, and disappears for the night.

25

Snow Geese and Brant at Brigantine and Barnegat Bay

On a cold wintry day, patches of ice and snow linger in the protected spots beside the dike at Brigantine. Light whitecaps dance on the bay beyond and snow blows in off the nearby shore. Snow geese rest in long strings in the impoundment, huddled against the light winds. As the day warms, the geese spread out, and a gentle cackling or barking drifts across the marsh. Suddenly the flocks of snow geese take wing, ducks rise from the marsh, and the roosting gulls circle out over the bay. Our eyes search the sky.

A young bald eagle soars high overhead and swoops down toward the marsh. Bald eagles have suffered serious declines over much of their range. Prior to 1960 there were at least twenty-two pairs nesting in New Jersey, but by 1970 the population dwindled to one pair. The accumulation of chlorinated hydrocarbons, particularly DDT, was the major cause of the decline. These chemicals caused thin eggshells that broke when parents incubated them. High levels killed the embryos and disrupted normal parental behavior. Most raptors and fish-eating birds were affected by DDT.

Working with only one nest, Larry Niles and Kathy Clark of the New Jersey Endangered and Nongame Species Program have slowly introduced several captive-bred chicks into it. Most of these have fledged, and they now soar over south Jersey. The team also launched a "hacking" program, much like the Peregrine Fund project, and have hacked over sixty eaglets into southern New Jersey. The number of pairs with nests has gradually risen to five. It is a long and painstaking process, but the majesty of seeing a bald eagle capturing a duck is well worth the effort. Unsuccessful, it soars up to a dead snag, where it waits. The snow geese resettle, and the marsh is again calm.

As the tides change, flocks of snow geese fly out to distant marshes, looking for stands of grass peeking through the snow. The higher places on the marsh are mostly bare, where the winds blow continuously. The geese land in a tight flock, but slowly expand out over the marsh, digging out fresh roots, exposing others. Snow geese are migrants that usually frequent New

25.1. Brant feeding on eelgrass in Barnegat Bay.

Jersey beginning in November, moving south only if the bays freeze completely. Otherwise they remain in New Jersey, leaving in April for their Canadian tundra breeding grounds.

It has been an unusually cold winter and the bay is largely frozen, wisps of snow blow across the bay. Gusts drive the snow sheets higher, and just as quickly they collapse. Here and there flocks of brant drift in small open-water leads, facing into the wind. Some dip under the water, searching for eelgrass or sea lettuce (Figure 25.1). A bit still remains in the bay, and they eagerly plunge in. Brant are unusual in that they are terrestrial grazers on the Canadian tundra during the breeding season, but they switch to feeding on submerged aquatic plants in the winter. They are surprising loud, and their incessant cackling calls build to a crescendo just before the raft takes off for other foraging beds.

Brant prefer to remain in the tidal bays, whereas Canada geese and snow geese return to freshwater and brackish-water impoundments with high tides. In open water the brant sit in large rafts between foraging bouts, moving to good foraging beds of eelgrass as the tides fall. In late fall the brant feed on the edge of the marsh where the sea lettuce forms a dense carpet. Whereas other geese and ducks often feed high on the marsh in the shallow ponds and pools, brant prefer the open water or marsh edge. In some pools in the salt marshes a thick carpet of algae and widgeon grass abounds, but these are the first to freeze over (Figure 25.2).

When the bay begins to freeze, the brant are forced to search for grass

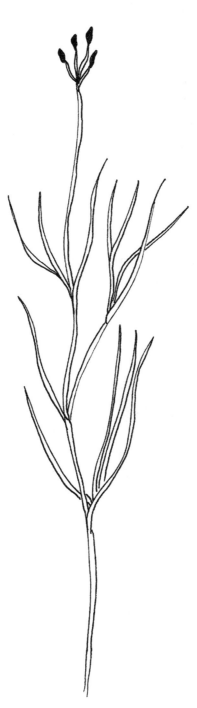

25.2. Widgeon grass.

beds in the open waters of the bay. They congregate in strings of hundreds to feed in the open leads in the ice. Over the years the eelgrass beds have varied in size, and when the beds are small, the brant concentrate in dense foraging groups. In the 1930s a blight hit the eelgrass beds, almost wiping it from the bay. It has been recovering slowly since then, and beds are strewn around the bay, where there is a sandy bottom. In the 1930s the brant learned to feed on sea lettuce; it was that or starve. Now they actively look for the rich, deep green beds of algae blown up on the edge of the marsh.

Almost no eelgrass grows in the northern part of Barnegat Bay, and brant rarely venture to the north. Nice beds of eelgrass start a mile or two north of Barnegat Inlet, continuing to the south end of the bay. In mid-winter, flocks of 10,000 to 15,000 brant drift just inside of Barnegat Inlet, moving from place to place to find new beds of eelgrass. They are usually quite noisy, and their barks and calls create a continuous chorus that wafts across the ice and open water.

If the bay freezes over, most brant will migrate further south. However, in some years they get caught by surprise, and the bay freezes before they have a chance to leave. The shallow-water areas with dense eelgrass are the first to freeze, forcing the brant to deeper water. The three or four large flocks of 10,000 each may be concentrated in the few open-water areas. Brant cope with the frozen bay by looking for beds of sea lettuce on the edge of the marsh or even higher on the marsh, and some have adapted to grazing on lawns. When the ground is covered with snow and the bay freezes, the brant are food stressed, and many die. Severe winter conditions of 1963, 1976, and 1984 resulted in starving flocks of brant in Barnegat Bay.

On the nearby ice edge, a tranquil flock of brant huddle against the cold. Most birds stand on one leg to prevent additional heat loss, but some sit on the ice. The ice is comparatively warm, for it is only 32 degrees, while the air is far colder. A few edge birds are alert, periodically looking over-head for aerial predators. They are too large for most avian predators, and are relatively safe from ground predators because they are so far from land. Gusts of wind blow across the ice, picking up snow, sending sheets shim-mering everywhere.

Under cover of blowing snow, a red fox prowls across the ice, bearing down on the geese. The snow settles, and in an instant the flock takes wing, drifting majestically over the bay toward distant marshes. The brant fly low to avoid the winds. The fox detours and heads out toward Hither Island. He skirts the open water, staying far from the thin ice along the edge.

His vibrant red coat gleams against the ice and snow. Red foxes have adapted to people and are not as shy as the gray fox. They also are faster and stronger than the gray fox, and a bit bolder. This red fox has lived for many months on the nearby barrier island, and has moved under cover of darkness among the homes, marinas, and other buildings. Gray fox cannot compete with a species so well adapted to the presence of humans, and has declined in many places in New Jersey. This fox prefers swampy areas and dense forests, where the species is holding its own.

The red fox disappears in the reeds, and minutes later reappears high on the island, walking slowly across the spoil, picking his way between the cockle burr (Figure 25.3). Most foxes eventually go back to the mainland, for there is little food here on such a small island. Yet, small mice and rats can sustain a fox through the winter, so he could remain. When spring comes, this fox will pose a serious problem for the ibis and herons that nest here, as many nest on the ground. A fox on one of these islands could eat many eggs and young chicks, causing total disruption to the colony.

Many years ago, when the bay froze over, a fox made it to this same island. Within a few days he dug a small burrow in an old knoll on the island. Here the sand was mixed with decaying vegetation, and marsh elder roots stabilized the sand enough to sustain the small lair. He took up hunting in the warmth of the day, and at night he rested in the burrow. Stiff winter winds blew sand in his burrow, which required constant repair. He stayed for the winter, and was marooned on the island when the ice broke up in the early spring.

When great black-backed gulls and herring gulls arrived in late February they settled in clubs on the edge of the marsh elders. Under the cover of darkness the fox stalked and captured a herring gull, which gave up only after shrieking alarm calls and wails. In the dim moonlight, some of the other gulls mobbed the fox, floating far enough above his head to prevent their own capture. Although the fox was annoyed, the swirling gulls did not deter further hunting. The gull was the biggest meal he had in weeks. The next night he again patrolled the bushes, sneaking up on another unwary gull. Within three or four days the gulls abandoned the island and shifted to a nearby island with fewer bushes.

The fox was still there when the herons and egrets returned in early March. As the sun settled for the night, the fox stalked a snowy egret sitting low in the bushes, and he lunged upward. Sensing the fox just in time, the egret burst from the bushes with loud squawks and croaks. Nearby egrets saw the fox trot across the island, and they climbed higher in the bushes. For a few days they sat around the heronry, remaining in the tops of the shrubs and reeds. Great egrets stood on their old stick nests near the crowns of the highest bushes, but snowy egrets never shifted to the lower nests near the ground. They never quite settled down, and no waders moved from the tops of the gently swaying reeds. As days passed, the herons grew more agitated. They never saw the fox again, but they knew he was there. One by one they left the island. Within a week the heronry

24.3. Cockle burr.

was deserted. A late-arriving cattle egret stood about on the reeds for only an hour, and then left to search for its colony-mates.

The fox remained during the spring, feeding on insects, toads, and small mice running through their grass passageways. Sometimes it followed the tunnels, but usually it waited, peering intently, for a mouse to scamper into view. Now and again it caught a clapper rail or a small sparrow, but the pickings were thin. The fox was swimming toward Holgate last time I saw it, but I am not sure it could make it that far. Lack of food and a mate no doubt drove it toward the distant barrier island.

The following February the herring gulls came to Hither Island and again took up residence. They were wary and remained far out in the cordgrass, where they could see approaching danger. When several days passed without mishap, they edged closer to the bushes, finally slipping under them and giving plaintive long-calls to solicit mates.

It was three years before the herons and egrets moved back to Hither Island, even though it was one of the best colony sites in the bay. For several years the herons and egrets squeezed all their nests in the tops of the vegetation, and the colony covered all of the available space. Eventually the colony consolidated, and the lower branches of the bushes were used for nest sites once again.

I hope this fox will assess the food supply quickly and leave before the ice breaks up. It is remarkably difficult for foxes to find enough food in the winter, so they rely heavily on berries as well as small rodents. There may be as many small rodents out on Hither Island as there are on the barrier island. In the dead of winter, Hither may seem as hospitable as anywhere else.

Brant still stand in dense flocks on the edge of the ice, not far from open water. The loud roar of cackling has decreased to a soft clucking and cooing that drifts across the water. They are calming down as dusk falls, and will spend the night here on the ice far from any land. It is time for me to head up the Parkway toward home.

Tomorrow we must check the Brant at the Shrewsbury River and farther north—part of a census to determine how they are doing in New Jersey. The weather forecasters were wrong, although they did change their minds late last night. It does not seem like a good day.

No one in her right mind would venture out on a day like today. The weather forecasters said "Maybe six inches in the highlands and in North Jersey, less along the shore." Remembering the heavy snows of 1978 and 1993, people stopped on their way home for bread, milk, and videos. Others brought out the snow shovels, stocked up on salt, and opened up the bird seed. Some even bought snow blowers at the last moment. Everyone prepared in his own way, sure the weather forecasters were exaggerating, but not willing to count on it.

Just after midnight the snow began in Somerset; although it was light at first, gradually the flakes grew bigger and wetter, and the snowfall heavier. It was pretty, with the large snowflakes drifting down in sheets, blown by light winds. Every rock and imperfection on the lawn made a slight lump in the otherwise smooth blanket. The branches began to bow gently with the weight of the snow. Somehow snow at night, when the house is quiet and everyone is safe and snug, always fills me with a primitive sense of humanity against the elements. The hustle, stress, and excitement of the university world might not actually exist, and I am safe in my own little lair, like a fox, wrapped in a warm blanket of snow and darkness.

In the morning, the snow is still falling in heavy sheets. Nearly a foot covers the ground, and the branches of the shrubs are bent low. The green boughs of the yew bushes are barely visible below the mounds of white snow forming dollops and drifts within the branches. It is silent, for even the birds are hiding.

Gradually, through the morning, the snow peters out, the flakes grow smaller, and I can see the trees a hundred yards away. When it finally ceases, there is nearly fourteen inches on the ground. The branches of the black locusts are laden with wedges of snow, the shrubs are bent nearly to the ground with their burden, and the rocks around our pond look like miniature woodchucks startled from sleep.

Trudging out, we shovel trails to the bird feeders and clear a wide place on the ground for bird food of all kinds. Light breezes riffle the branches, and globs of snow fall to the ground. The lightened branches sweep upward, dislodging still more snow. Within an hour the trees are alive with blue jays, juncos, cardinals, flickers, crows, starlings, and house finches. They pick up food voraciously, for the sky is still dark gray, and more snow is imminent.

As the air temperature increases, the snow settles into a wet blanket, still clinging to the branches. The cedar boughs, curving downward with the weight of the wet snow, are nearly breaking. They are bent so far that the snow will soon cascade to the ground. Within minutes of my putting out birdfood, the flocks of starlings arrive, blanketing the ground. Even with their frantic foraging they pause now and then to watch for a sharp-shinned hawk or other predators that could be lurking in the snow-laden yews.

Despite the snow, the beach beckons, for winter storms often bring in unusual gulls, snow buntings, and snowy owls. The radio still warns "Don't go out unless you have to, some roads are not plowed, others are impassable, others are blocked by five-car pile-ups." Yet the call of the Jersey shore is still strong and overpowering.

Succumbing, we shovel for two hours to clear a path to the road, and drive cautiously toward Sandy Hook. Few cars are on the road, and everyone is driving slowly, keeping a buffer around themselves. Our car skids to a stop before every light, reminding us that the wet snow can be like glass. We pass the odd car in the ditch, up against a telephone pole, or coupled with another car or two. We forge our way to the Garden State Parkway, where only one lane is plowed. Few cars have ventured out, and we are nearly alone.

Remarkably, a path is plowed across the Highlands bridge, leading out to the Hook. Great mounds drift across the road, but giant plows cut a narrow swath through. Snow blows across the tops of the drifts, high above the roof of the car, over to the bay beyond. We are heading for the very tip of the Hook.

The drifts are too deep to walk very far. Heavy winds off the ocean have blown mounds of snow in all the valleys, and only the tops of the dunes are clear. A flock of snow buntings, feeding in the partially bare land blown clear of snow, search for seeds among the few weeds that peak through the snow patches. They blend with the snow, and only their movement gives them away.

From the Hook we head to the Shrewsbury River to look for the brant and any unusual ducks. There is supposed to be a tufted duck—very rare for New Jersey. The Shrewsbury is wide, with several tear-drop islands in the middle. Some are quite old, for dense trees that are nearly twenty feet tall grow in the center, surrounded by small clumps of sumac. Reeds grow on the leading edge, where gulls sit in a dense flock, sheltered from the wind.

Thousands of brant are rafted up near the other side, where the water is still open. Mostly they are feeding, dipping to get the eelgrass, widgeon grass, and sea lettuce lurking in the bottom. The swiftly flowing river is still open here where the brant have congregated. Their loud barks, cluckings, and cooings drift across the bay, growing louder and then softer as they respond to a red-tailed hawk flying overhead.

In the mouth of the river, nestled in the lee of the island, is the pair of tufted ducks. They are like our scaup, except they have an all-black back and elongated crest feathers. Although these ducks turn up throughout North America now and then, they do not breed in North America. They breed in the Old World. It is always nice to add a new bird to our New Jersey list. But for me, the thousands of brant are more exciting, and I never tire of their jostling and loud cackling calls that waft across the water.

Signs of Spring

26

A Killdeer's Plaintive
Call on the Rutgers
Campus

Snow blankets most of the Rutgers campus, but here and there a bit of mud shows through. It is late February, and the weeks of cold and snow are wearing. The wind may blow strongly now and again, but spring cannot be far away. A wide swath of green grass shows above an underground heating pipe, where the last lingering snow buntings and horned larks search for seeds. The air is balmy, warmed by the sun moving higher and higher in the sky each day.

For some, the first white snowdrops that peek above the snow indicate that spring is not far away; for others it is the awakening of buds on trees, buds that are just a little swollen, buds that are waiting for the first real warmth of spring. Then one day I hear my own signal of spring, the plaintive cry of a killdeer flying over the snow, searching for any little seeds that will have to do because no worms or insects are available. I hear it from my window while I am teaching Behavioral Biology to a class of one hundred, and I long to see its solitary flight, to follow its path as it makes its way across Livingston campus. It searches now for food, but in only a few weeks it will be courting a mate and looking for a nest site in a warm place, exposed to the full sun, one that will not be trampled by the thousands of students who walk across campus each day. Truly it must avoid the beaten path. How often I have marveled at the hundreds of students who never see the incubating killdeer only inches from their path, or the students who glance curiously at the killdeer with a broken wing, unaware that it is feigning injury to draw them away from its nest (Figure 26.1).

Unlike many shorebirds, killdeer have adapted to the presence of people. As long as they can find a safe nesting place where they can see approaching predators, and can find enough food, they will nest. Although it will be many weeks before the killdeer actually nest, I can feel spring in their plaintive calls. They herald the crocuses, daffodils, and tulips. They stand quietly on the patches of grass amid early March snowfalls, waiting

26.1. Displaying killdeer on Rutgers campus, feigning broken wing.

for spring, certain it will come. They stand in the lee of college buildings during the high winds of mid-March, emerging to court when the warm sun drenches the campus.

Killdeer have arrived in a variety of habitats, from farmlands in Niskayuna, where I first saw them on my parents' farm, to grainfields in northern Minnesota, to beaches and sand dunes along the Jersey shore. Killdeer hold a very special place in my heart, for when I was a young child my father showed me a killdeer nest in a tomato patch, and I eagerly kept vigil until the eggs hatched. When the chicks arrived, I put different colored paint on each one and followed their movements around the farm.

Unlike many other shorebirds, killdeer have adapted to the ever-increasing hordes of people with their farms, towns, and suburbanization. The birds cannot cope with urban centers and dense industrial complexes of concrete and stone, but they nest happily in expansive industrial parks or corporate headquarters with rolling lawns and spacious gardens.

Killdeer always nested along the Jersey shore, staying in the upland areas, rather than breeding on the sand beaches directly exposed to the sea. The changes brought by agriculture probably increased the number of killdeer in New Jersey, for killdeer can nest in open places on the bare soil and can find insects amid the grasses and weeds. When farmers cleared the land, they provided ideal nesting habitats for killdeer. All the killdeer had to do was find places to nest that would be undisturbed for the month required to lay and incubate eggs. Then they could lead their chicks to safety.

Along the shore, however, encroaching human development no doubt decreased the nesting habitat for killdeer by placing buildings on upland

26.2. Killdeer with clutch of eggs.

areas that were their prime nesting sites. Being fairly flexible, though, the birds adapted to nesting close to human habitations. The problem became one of predators, especially cats, which are annoying to killdeer because the adults are also vulnerable. Fortunately, cats are not interested in eggs, and if killdeers sit very quietly they often go undetected.

In early May, the killdeer pair who court outside my office window make a scrape in the ground, not too far from a student pathway between Nelson Biology and the Chemistry buildings. Over the course of five days, four speckled eggs appear in the nest (Figure 26.2). The eggs are slightly pointed at one end and fit tightly together in the nest. The eggs are quite large with respect to the female, as is the case with most shorebirds, for the young are developed fully at hatching and are able to move about almost immediately.

The adults take turns incubating the eggs for the twenty-four to twenty-six days it takes to hatch. Each parent incubates for two to three hours, and then the parents exchange. The off-duty parent wanders about not far from the nest, picking up insects from the ground. Should a student walk too close to the nest, the incubating parent often sits tightly, while its mate performs an elaborate distraction display, feigning a broken wing, a broken leg, or a badly injured body. Invariably the student moves toward the injured bird, anxious to pick it up, perhaps to bring it to my office for help.

As the student bends to catch the injured killdeer, the bird bursts up gracefully in an arc and disappears behind the Biology Building. The student, usually observant in the laboratory, stands puzzled, wondering how such an injured bird could fly, totally unaware that only ten yards away its mate is quietly incubating, huddled in the grass.

This scene is replayed hundreds of times during the three weeks of incubation, and every time a student is skillfully led away from the nest. No cats roam the Rutgers campus, and the efficacy of the distraction display is not tested against a skillful predator.

By the end of May, the first egg hatches, and a wet chick pecks its way out of the shell. In three hours it is dry, just when another chick begins to hatch. The first gangly chick stands on long legs, barely able to walk. It is cute and fluffy, and within two hours is able to walk quite strongly. Since the parents are busy incubating the remaining eggs and guarding the wet chicks, the older chick sits in the nest or crouches nearby. Over the next twenty-four hours, when all four chicks hatch, the parents lead them away in search of food. They will no longer use the nest, although they may remain in the same general area.

Killdeer chicks are precocious, meaning that they are able to walk and forage almost immediately. Although the parents provide protection and guidance, they do not feed their young, nor do they teach them what foods to eat. Instead, the parents keep the brood together and protect them from predators.

Killdeers were my first research subjects when I was in Van Antwerp Junior High School. My father showed me my first nest, hidden alongside a tomato plant, and I watched each day when I was picking tomatoes. When the chicks hatched, I marked them with colored markers and followed their movements. I drew maps of the farm, recorded where they were each day, and noted how far the parents were from the chicks. I learned how to find the chicks by carefully watching the behavior of the parents. Years later, when I was a freshman at Albany State, I again studied their behavior, and this became my first publication in the *Kingbird*.

Killdeer parents give an alarm call to signal when a predator is near, causing the chicks to crouch and freeze in place. Since they are grayish and white, the birds are cryptic and blend with their background. When they are absolutely still, they are nearly impossible to spot. Only when they move can they be detected, particularly because their gait is halting and unsteady.

While the chicks freeze, the parents engage in elaborate distraction displays to draw the predator from their chicks. These displays are very interactive, and the parents watch the predator to decide how best to lead them away. They allow a predator nearly to capture them before moving only inches away. When one type of distraction display fails, they try another, or move in another direction.

Gradually the chicks improve their ability to find and catch insect prey, learn to distinguish food from nonfoods, and begin to follow their parents closely. They are more steady on their feet, because their body size has caught up with the length of their legs. Their fluffy body becomes less soft as down is slowly replaced by body feathers, and then by wing and tail feathers. Within a month they are fully feathered and as large as their parents. Still the youngsters remain with them, wandering across campus in search of insects such as beetles, grasshoppers, ants, and flies. The brood remains together for most of the summer, moving around the campus, avoiding the busy student paths. They will remain together for most of the fall, but eventually they head south beyond the snow.

27

Herring Gulls: Newcomers to the Jersey Shore

A herring gull pecks furiously at a large dead bluefish washed up by the tides. Down the beach a small group of gulls is preening, resting, or sleeping. To many people, the large gray-backed, white-headed gulls along the wind-swept beach are the essence of the shore. For many years herring gulls have careered noisily over New Jersey sand dunes, dropped clams on stone jetties and parking lots, followed fishing boats, and stood serenely on rain-beaten pilings. These birds, however, were only transients, sporadic visitors to our shores. Before the 1960s, only one or two pairs nested in New Jersey.

Herring gulls used to nest only in Canada and Maine in North America. For centuries they nested in the frozen north and migrated to warmer climes in the winter. Even in Maine their numbers were kept low first by the eggers, and then by the market gunners and millinery trade. Their white feathers looked particularly fetching on ladies' hats, and they were easy to shoot in breeding colonies. Eventually the destruction to our herons and egrets led to protective laws and treaties that included all migratory birds, and herring gull populations began to recover.

Since the turn of the century, herring gulls have increased by a factor of 15 to 20. Inevitably they spread into Massachusetts, and then into New York, where they nested on sandy and rocky islands. Soon they began nesting in the median strips between highway lanes, and finally in grassy areas of public beaches and parks.

I have watched a herring gull incubate casually beside a green picnic bench on Long Island while noisy kids munched hot dogs on the table above, their feet dangling only inches away. Time passes, the picnickers change, but the herring gull relinquishes its nest only to its mate—the same mate who then steals French fries from an unsuspecting grandmother reading a mystery on a nearby bench.

Eventually herring gulls moved to New Jersey, where rocky or sandy islands were unavailable for colonization. The large, determined gulls responded by invading a new habitat—salt marshes. The soft, short salt hay looks a bit like a clipped lawn, and they readily adapted to the salt hay meadows. The bothersome high tides required construction of larger, more substantial nests, which the gulls easily built. They found other species nesting on the salt meadows: laughing gulls, common terns, black skimmers, and clapper rails. The more northern-adapted herring gulls arrived at colony sites weeks and months before the other species, when they had the marshes all to themselves.

The southward expansion of herring gulls has continued into Delaware, Maryland, and North Carolina. Once they adapted to nesting in salt marshes, they made use of the ribbon of green that extends all along the Atlantic coast. Not limited to North America, they also expanded in Europe, and their numbers increased. Herring gulls have expanded southward nearly throughout their breeding range, which is circumpolar. My father-in-law, Alex Gochfeld, has translated Russian articles that chronicle their increase in Eurasia.

They increased when many other species, such as least terns, piping plovers, and black skimmers, were declining. Birds can invade a new area only when they have enough food for themselves and adequate space to rest and roost. They increase, however, only when they have sufficient food for their young and safe places to nest. We have provided the food in the form of garbage dumps in a series of gull fast-food joints located all along the shore. It is not so much that the adult gulls require the dumps, although they are happy to forage there, but that many young gulls use them, young that would otherwise starve when they must learn to forage on their own. Dumps provide a dependable food supply when fish, clams, and other foods are hard to find. The average gull can find enough food for the day in only fifteen or twenty minutes on a good dump. In the past five years, however, herring gulls have actually started to decline on nearby Long Island, probably owing to the closing of many of the landfills.

When the first killdeer calls on the Rutgers campus, that is my call to the Jersey shore. I am unable to resist the warm sunshine and clear skies, and I am drawn to Clam Island as surely as if I were possessed by some primeval need to return home. I will spend the next three summers living on the island, studying competition between herring gulls and laughing gulls, and examining the relationship between territory size, aggression, and reproductive success in herring gulls. The conventional wisdom is that the most aggressive pairs with the largest territories should be the most successful—but I think pairs with intermediate-sized territory may fare better. Such pairs can devote more time to caring for their chicks than very aggressive pairs. This study will take hours and hours of painstaking observations over several years to sort out.

Only the rhythmic sound of Barnegat Light's foghorn indicates the short distance from Clam Island to the deserted beaches, empty houses, and the comforting, always open Coast Guard station there. This time of year Long Beach Island is nearly deserted, and many stores and restaurants are still closed. It is amazing how often it is bright and sunny on the mainland, but foggy out on the bay.

My small rowboat drifts quietly over the water, heading for the island hidden in the fog. A herring gull long-call slicing through the fog indicates I am near. In early March the marsh is a sullen brown, and the grass is bent by the weight of winter tides that rolled over the island. No leaves grace the bushes. A few herring gulls stand about in the salt hay, one or two giving long-calls to prospective mates. I hurry to the cabin to secure my boat, stow my food, settle my belongings, and sort my field gear. The old hunting shack, weathered and gray, has withstood many years of winter storms. Winds whistle through the cracks, and the dampness of the marsh has settled permanently in the bunks. It is home, and I feel safe surrounded by the vigilant gulls.

Within a few days, more gulls arrive, and the courting club on the salt-hay meadow commences with earnest long-calls, chases, and mew-calls. Females solicit courtship feeding by pecking gently at the bill or neck feathers of their mates. The birds' numbers build to nearly a thousand. In early April a few mated pairs walk tentatively to nearby marsh elders, staking out territories, standing guard silently near their chosen plots. The elders grow only on the high spots, the last to be flooded, and then only by exceptionally high tides.

Another gull comes too close; in the ensuing fight the gulls call, wing-flap, chase, peck at one another, and finally pull at the grass in exasperation. The fight goes on for a few minutes, when abruptly the intruder walks a few yards away. He is then ignored by the original territory owner, who almost always wins these fights, and the intruder must move away or fly to another part of the colony. Throughout the marsh, the pattern is repeated: Gulls stake claims to a territory near the marsh elders, they defend it, and they court their mates. With these interactions the gulls firm up their territory boundaries, and aggression slowly decreases throughout the colony. Aggression rates are highest during this territory-acquisition stage, and they decrease thereafter, although they will increase again at hatching when their young chicks are vulnerable to merciless, and sometimes fatal, attacks by other adults.

I erect a canvas blind among the marsh elders to watch the skirmishes across the marsh. No longer are gulls standing about in the middle of the salt hay; they have all moved to the bushes on the high marsh to escape tidal flooding. For most of each day the pairs stand about on their territories, courting, resting, or defending their space. Although the birds all seem

27.1. Female herring gull begging from male for courtship-feeding.

the same size at first, when pairs stand together, one bird is always larger, with a longer, thicker bill and a thicker neck. The larger bird is the male, who engages in more defense than the female. Only when the male is absent or when a neighboring pair initiates a fight does the female join in. She usually attacks the other female, while the males battle it out together.

In early April the pairs begin a joint venture to select their nest site. One gull moves to a place next to a dense elder, bends down, and rattles its body furiously as if it were choking to death. This immediately attracts its mate, who stares fixedly at the spot, but then moves to another and begins the same "choking" display. This pattern goes on all day, in pair after pair, as first one, then the other, indicates its chosen spot for the nest. Eventually both members of the pair choke in the same place, side by side, and the nest site is chosen. Slowly, and then in earnest, each bird walks around the territory pulling up bunches of grass, placing them on the well-trodden ground. The female then sits in the mass, swishes her body to and fro, and begins to place bits of material around the rim. Within days a nice firm nest is constructed. Selection of a nest site is critical, for the nest must be above flood tides, defendable from neighbors, easy to escape from if a predator approaches, and protected from predators and the sun. Further, there must be enough space around the nest so that one day the chicks can wander about, free from the attacks of neighbors.

As egg-laying approaches, the female begs for food from the male by pecking at his bill or neck (Figure 27.1). He slowly regurgitates food that she will use to produce her clutch. Male gulls provide a significant proportion of the food that females use for egg production.

27.2. Herring gull at nest with two eggs.

Egg-laying begins in mid-April. Three to eight days elapse between the laying of the first egg and the third. The olive-brown eggs are heavily speckled with browns and blacks, and they would be camouflaged if the nests were not so conspicuous. The color and pattern reflects the not-so-distant past when herring gulls nested on rocky shores, as so many in New England still do. After the first egg is laid, they stand about the territory, ready to defend the nest, but unwilling to incubate. Incubation only begins with the laying of the second or third egg (Figure 27.2).

By early May nearly everyone is incubating quietly, there are almost no fights between neighbors. The grass has started to grow, and a green shadow covers the brown blanket of grass as the new shoots peer through. The bushes are beginning to leaf out. Both parents incubate, taking turns of a few minutes to several hours while mates are off feeding along the bay or on tidal flats.

As I walk back to my shack at dusk, I stop along the mudbank to see if the tide is low enough to expose the ribbed mussels buried in the mud. The mussel beds grow only just above the low tide line, and on many low tides they are not exposed. The bed by the edge of the island has only a few mussels, which are too small to bother with. Closer to my shack is a bed with clusters of large blue-black shells. Their threads penetrate deep in the mud, holding them fast. I lie on the salt grass and reach over the bank to pull the ribbed mussels from the soil; ten ought to do it. The mussels nestled in the bank must last me all summer, for there is no refrigeration in my shack, and this is my only source of protein. I restrict my take to twenty a week, except on the rare and very special occasions when Mike Gochfeld, Bert and Patti Murray, or others visit for the day.

For most of May the colony is quiet, each pair incubates serenely, waiting. An infrequent visit by a marsh hawk creates a panic as the gulls all rise from the marsh to surround the intruder, escorting it quickly to the edge of the colony. Only a few follow the hawk, dive-bombing it, harassing it until it disappears beyond Barnegat Lighthouse. At night the lull of the colony is interrupted by the silent soaring of a barn owl in search of food for its six young nestled in the attic of my hunting shack. I can hear the patter of tiny feet as the young owls scramble to take the food from the female, who has landed softly on the window ledge.

In late May the first herring gull egg hatches, and the wet, bedraggled chick lies awkwardly in the nest, still brooded by its parents. Eggs usually hatch in twenty-five to twenty-nine days. Hatching takes more than a day, as the chick saws its way out with the tiny white egg tooth on the tip of its bill. It is a long, exhausting process, and a few chicks die trying to break free. The parents remove the shell, for the white inner surface of the egg is like a flag to aerial predators. In three to four hours the chick dries, the down fluffs out, and it begins to call to its parents.

Just as the herring gull eggs are beginning to hatch, large flocks of laughing gulls arrive on Clam Island. At first they land near the herring gulls, but they are chased unmercifully. Although they return to the same spot, they are chased again, and again. Finally, one by one, the laughing gulls move farther from the bushes, until they are no longer chased by the larger gulls. The laughing gulls have been forced to the edge of the herring gull colony. A few still stand about on the salt hay, but only far from nesting herring gulls. Most have moved out into the lower regions with cordgrass.

Within a few days the overt interactions between laughing gulls and herring gulls cease. There is an intermediate zone where salt hay and cordgrass mix, and here the two species of gulls overlap. Even within this zone the laughing gulls are in the lower parts and the herring gulls are at nests on the higher elevations. The herring gulls were here first, and claimed all the best spots. Only a few years ago this island was entirely occupied by laughing gulls, and some even nested on the higher places near the marsh elders. The smaller laughing gulls are being forced to abandon the safer, higher nesting areas, and are nesting in the lower places that are more vulnerable to tidal flooding.

The laughing gulls stand about in the cordgrass, moving from place to place as the high tides lap at their feet, indicating that nests built there would surely flood out. They shift territory boundaries with each high tide, as pairs try to find a place that appears to be above the daily high tides. They

27.3. Young herring gull chick begging from parent for food.

will wait for nearly an entire lunar cycle before building nests, for it is critical to find just the right spot.

On marshes all along the Jersey shore laughing gulls are coping with the invading herring gulls. The competition is unbalanced because herring gulls are three times heavier. Herring gulls arrive on the breeding colonies three months before the laughing gulls, whose eggs and chicks they prey upon, while laughing gulls are not generally predators. Their only chance is to nest on islands shunned by the herring gulls.

By the end of May, most herring gull eggs on Clam Island have hatched, and the colony resounds with low, moaning mew-calls and soft long-calls given to tiny chicks that are barely able to stand. The day after hatching most chicks are up and about, walking unsteadily around their nests. In most nests the first two chicks hatch within an hour or two of each other, but the third chick hatches a day or two later. This chick has a hard time. Since the third egg is usually smaller than the other two, the chick is smaller than its siblings as well, and it competes less well for food. The first few days are critical, for parents must bring them enough food that is small enough for them to eat, and must guard them from the cold, from predators, or from just getting lost. Fighting increases, as nervous parents chase neighbors they have ignored for weeks.

Parents brood the chicks for the first few days and remain with them constantly until they are about three weeks old. The chicks are not only vulnerable to hawks and owls, but to other cannibalistic herring gulls that course above the colony searching for food to feed their own chicks. When a parent returns with food, chicks initiate feeding by pecking at the red spot on their parent's bill, which triggers the regurgitation of fish, clams, insects, or other food (Figure 27.3). At Clam Island the parents feed their chicks almost entirely on natural foods, although there are garbage dumps nearby. Parents seldom feed their chicks junk food, preferring to give them food from the bay.

At first the parents must nudge their chicks, pushing food at them, but by the time they are five or six days old the chicks actively assault their parents for food, and by twenty days, the parents stagger backward under their combined attack. When an approaching parent calls, the chicks all run madly to their usual feeding station, jumping frantically up and down. The parents regurgitate larger pieces and they drop them on the nest, where the chicks greedily grab them.

An alarm call from any adult sends each chick dashing for cover, and they soon find favorite hiding places. The same chicks can be found day after day under the same clumps of grass. I know they are the same chicks because I have banded them with numbered, metal leg bands (Figure 27.4). For more than three weeks they hide in the same place, until their bodies are so large they no longer fit these spots. As they grow, they are less vulnerable to predators, and there is less worry from other gulls.

When neighboring gulls lose their eggs or chicks to predators, cannibals, or starvation, pairs expand their own territories, giving their chicks more room to wander about. For the most part, chicks remain relatively near home, standing about their nests for most of the day. In the heat of high noon they stand in the shade of the marsh elders, but otherwise they prefer to stand on their nests.

As the chicks approach fledging at about six weeks of age, they begin to exercise their muscles by flapping vigorously up and down for hours on end. They jump higher and higher, crashing down on their siblings now and again. In late June they make their first flights. Aerodynamically inept, they crash into bushes, grass, and each other. They land in neighboring territories and scramble frantically back to their nests on foot.

By early July the fledging chicks congregate in pools and ponds amid the salt hay and in shallow channels that meander through Clam Island. When parents call, the chicks break up into family groups, clamoring noisily to be fed at the nest. The marsh seems empty, and the chicks are scattered about away from the colony. By early August the marsh is nearly silent. Only the scattered, bedraggled nest scrapes attest to the eight hundred pairs of herring gulls that have nested here. A nagging image of a solitary herring gull standing on the marsh, calling its chick in early August suggests that I must look at this post-fledging period more closely. Even as I pack my things and look at the Clam Island shack for a fleeting moment, I know I must return to find out how the young really become independent.

The winter passes quickly, with teaching classes, analyzing data, writing papers, and attending endless committee meetings. Soon enough the killdeer

27.4. Young herring gull chick with metal, numbered, U.S. Fish and Wildlife Service leg band.

return to the campus, and the call of Clam Island overpowers me. Having packed my car with food, sleeping bag, and field gear, I head back to the Jersey shore. This year I travel in style. Fred Lesser and I cram all the things into the helicopter and whirl over to Clam Island. I am being partially funded by the New Jersey State Mosquito Commission to find out if their new practices of connecting the few mosquito breeding ponds with the creeks affect the nesting gulls. They have taken extra care to broadcast the dirt from the ditches over the marsh, so no spoil piles are left for bushes to invade.

The herring gulls have already arrived and are established on territories, most likely the same ones they occupied last year. I have two tasks for this and the following years: to determine the relationship between territory size, aggression, and reproductive success, and to examine the post-fledging period.

I spend my days in the blind, from before dawn to well past dusk, following the behavior of over twenty pairs of gulls. I suspend little cups filled with red dye above the nests, and attach the bottom of the cup to a string leading to my blind (Figure 27.5). When the gull is incubating quietly, I

27.5. Herring gull with paint suspended above its head. When I pulled the string from the blind, the paint spilled on its head and back, making it individually identifiable.

pull the string, tipping the dye cup, which splashes dye in irregular and unique patterns all over the gull. Each gull in twenty nests is thus marked with a different pattern. With a carefully drawn map I can now plot the location of each territorial clash, noting the winner and the loser. By connecting the points of these fights, I can draw the exact territory boundaries at different times in the reproductive cycle.

The gulls proceed through the breeding season, from incubation to hatching, from baby chicks to fledglings. Territory boundaries are not static, but change with their activities. Territories are larger during the territory-acquisition stage, when pairs have nothing to do but fight over space. The areas shrink slightly during the incubation stage, when the birds must only protect their eggs, and their most important task is to preserve the eggs from predators. It is not effective to chase intruders from the far reaches of the territory, exposing the eggs to heat stress or marauding gulls.

When the chicks hatch, the parents again become more defensive, chasing any neighbor that comes close. They shift their emphasis to protecting not only the chicks, but also defending enough space for the chicks to wander about unharmed by neighbors. Territories gradually enlarge, and parents take over any unoccupied space not defended vigorously by neighbors. In some sense, territories are like elastic disks that shrink or expand depending upon the needs of the parents, eggs, and chicks.

Surprisingly, the most aggressive pairs, those that engaged in the most fights throughout the breeding cycle, did not raise the most young. These pairs often continued defending territory boundaries when they should have been protecting their eggs or chicks. The pairs that had intermediate aggression levels fledged the most young. These pairs were aggressive enough to protect their eggs and chicks, but were not so intent on defense that they forgot to protect and feed their chicks. The least aggressive pairs raised few or no chicks because they did not adequately defend their eggs or young chicks from cannibalistic gulls, and they did not provide enough space their chicks to live in once they began to move about.

It is now near the end of the breeding season, and many chicks are practicing flight. Some pairs have already lost their chicks to predators or the cold rains of spring. The remaining pairs have usurped some of the territorial space of these neighbors. The chicks spend their time practicing short flights, and at first they career carelessly around the colony, blown hither and yon each time they are airborne. Gradually their aim improves, and they learn to circle purposefully and return to their territory. Finally the day comes when the young can make long powerful flights over the marsh, into the surrounding bay. The colony quiets down, but here and there a few chicks remain, and I am determined to see this through to the bitter end, even after spending fifteen weeks here.

Virtually all studies of seabirds cease at this point, when most of the young have fledged, with good reason. Much as I love the marsh, it becomes less attractive on hot, still midsummer days when there is little to watch or record. Fortunately, my blind keeps the greenheads out, because they seek the sun. Hours of tedium set in.

I have come prepared with plastic bags of multicolored yarn. I will spend my days crocheting shawls for my mother and sisters while I wait and watch the marsh from the tiny windows of my blind. The summer sun is very hot overhead, but the canvas provides some protection from the glare. It is dark in the hide. Hour after hour I wait, anxious to make sure that the marsh is indeed empty, that the gulls have finally fledged.

Here and there a parent returns to the nest, with its chicks careering close behind. The parent opens its bill and regurgitates mass after mass of partly digested fish, crabs, and clams. Sometimes the birds bring back whole blue crabs or clams (Figure 27.6). Within seconds, the fledgling chicks gobble up the food and fly from the nest. The parent leaves also, and the nest site

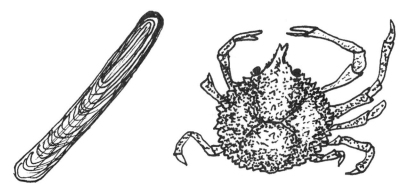

27.6. *Razor clam and spider crab are food for fledgling herring gull chicks.*

is quiet for the rest of the day. Later in the day, the pattern is repeated at another nest, and then at another.

Within only a few days it is clear that although the marsh seems deserted, for there are few gulls standing about, they are still using their territories. They are returning to the nest as a place to meet and feed their chicks. Sometimes a parent returns without the chicks, and then it leaves, circling around the island calling loudly. Eventually it finds its chicks, and then the whole family returns to the nest, where a brief feeding frenzy ensues.

Day after day, week after week, in nest after nest, the parents and their chicks return to the nest site two or three times a day to engage in these feedings. The parents are working exceedingly hard to maintain contact with their chicks, ensuring that they have enough food. I am glad I dyed the adults, for I can discern that both parents come back every day to feed their chicks. Mid-August comes, and still they are returning to their nests for their daily feeding. Other parents who lost their chicks early on come back to stand at their nest site for a while, defending it now and again against a neighbor.

For most of the day the colony is deserted because each feeding bout takes only a few minutes. It is easy to see how this extended period of post-fledging care has been missed. When the last chicks make their first flights from the colony in July, it seems empty. When I walked across the colony then, few birds were around, and those that remained flew easily from the colony to the nearby beach. It looked deserted. Only by spending long hours in the lonely blind could I see that the colony is still acting as an important meeting place for the families. Even my patience is taxed by the few events I observe each day.

Between feedings the chicks fly about the bay, learning to find food on their own. They peck at both edible and inedible objects, and try in vain to open clam shells. Once or twice each day the parents return, to look for the chicks, to ensure that the chicks have enough food to survive this difficult transition period.

Until nearly the end of August I sit in the blind; still the families return to their nests, still the chicks are fed. Although the timing of the feedings is sporadic, the chicks are all fed each day. For up to six weeks following their awkward first flights, the chicks continue to be fed at their nest sites. I wonder vaguely if I have to sit here all fall, enduring the cold fall winds. Having already crocheted six shawls, I have nearly run out of yarn, not to mention sisters and sisters-in-law. I guess I will make an extra one or two, so Mom, Tina, and Barb can have a choice of colors.

The rate of feeding is relatively constant until the chicks are seventy days old. Gradually with approaching fall, fewer families return to their nests. Finally the parents come no more, and I spend four consecutive days in the marsh without a single gull family visiting. The marsh falls silent in early September. Surely I can pack up for the season.

These observations on extended parental care beyond the time when chicks can fly is controversial because Trivers and others have proposed that there is conflict between parents and young over parental care; scientists proposed the theory that parents should invest as little as possible, so that they will survive to reproduce in another year, while chicks should demand as much care as possible to ensure their own survival. My data contradict their theory, because the parents are working very hard to prolong the parental care. But to me, it makes more sense that parents would give the chicks as much care as possible to ensure their survival; trying to give as little care as possible may result in never fledging any young. This extended parental care is ensuring that even more herring gulls will return to breed in our salt marshes.

Herring gulls now nest in the three largest laughing gull colonies in New Jersey: Stone Harbor, Clam Island, and Brigantine (now called Forsythe National Wildlife Refuge). Indeed, the herring gulls have already won at Clam island, for at this writing no laughing gulls nest there. They have been forced to nest on the lower reaches of nearby High Bar and Vol Sedges. In some years all of the laughing gull nests in these low cordgrass marshes are flooded out, and no young fledge. The situation is even more severe, for high tides in recent years have forced the gulls from Clam Island and High Bar.

The effect of herring gulls on common tern and black skimmer colonies is even more disastrous. If laughing gulls cannot defend their nesting sites against herring gulls, the smaller species have even less of a chance. When Fred, Mike, and I survey the salt-marsh islands in Barnegat Bay we find that predation on common tern eggs on islands with nesting herring gulls ranges from 10 percent to over 80 percent, whereas on islands without gulls the rates are lower than 10 percent. In Barnegat Bay, herring gulls now nest on nineteen of the thirty-five islands that have harbored nesting common terns since 1976. The terns have already deserted nine or ten of these completely, and they too are being forced more and more to nest on lower salt marsh islands, where they search for wracks that might be safe from storm tides. At last, the rapid increase in herring gull numbers has stopped, and herring gull populations are increasing only slightly in New Jersey. The closing of landfills has helped, for fewer young survive the winter without this dependable food source when snows cover the shore and fewer fish lie exposed. But the herring gulls are here to stay, they have adapted to the salt marshes. If the other native marsh-nesting species are to survive and prosper, they must learn to coexist with the highly successful herring gulls.

28

Herons and Egrets at Barnegat Bay and along the Kills

A great egret stands near the shore, its neck craned forward, peering into the clear water. It darts its head slightly to the right and left, gauging its aim, and then plunges its strong yellow beak into the water, pulling out a large, plump killifish. In one swallow the fish is gone, and the egret returns to its statuesque stance. It waits in silence for another fish to pass close by.

A flock of twenty herring gulls preen on the wide mudflat that slopes gently up to the salt marshes. One gull pecks at a dead fish stranded on the mud. Soon the flock is joined by another dozen gulls, and they call and jostle until everyone is satisfied with their position. Most tuck their bills in the feathers of their backs, close their eyes, and sleep. One or two remain vigilant, alert for passing danger.

Mudflats are exposed on both sides of the river, for it is low tide. The tiny salt-marsh creeks that bisect the marsh are nearly dry, but the tide will turn soon. Beyond the mudflats a wide expanse of salt marsh waits for spring. Winter browns, buffs, and beiges have not yet turned to green. It is late March, and the warm sun belies the season.

A male marsh hawk, strikingly gray and white, sails low over the marsh, peering intently toward the ground. The gull that is acting as sentinel gives an alarm call, and the other gulls wake up, stretch their wings, and watch the hawk's progress across the marsh. The hawk dips, tilts left and right, sails on without landing, and then dips again. This time he lands, picks up an unwary vole that was scurrying through the dried grass, and begins to tear it apart. This hawk poses no threat to birds the size of herring gulls.

From a small boat in the middle of the river, the mudflats and salt marshes loom large, nearly obscuring the piers, buildings, and oil-tank farms beyond the marshes. They are there, however, for the Arthur Kill is bounded by some of the most heavily industrialized areas in all of New Jersey. Although this part of the Kill is wild, just beyond are the densely populated cities of Elizabeth on one side, and Staten Island on the other. To

28.1. Male red-winged blackbird displaying.

the north over the Kill we can see the New York City skyline, a grim reminder that the marsh sits in one of the most urbanized parts of the world.

Ahead lies Prall's Island. The seventy-acre island located in the middle of the Arthur Kill is made of "spoil" dredged from the Kill. It is just north of the Rahway River, and just below the Goethals Bridge, which connects Bayonne and Staten Island. Once nothing but barren mud and sand, the teardrop island is protected by rocks and concrete rubble. Salt hay, panic grass, reeds and miscellaneous grasses, wild roses, goldenrod, and a variety of upland plants grow along the shore. A male red-winged blackbird displays on the edge of the reeds, his brilliant red shoulder patch glistening in the sun (Figure 28.1). In the middle of the island there are gray Birch, black cherry, sumac, poison ivy, and many smaller shrubs.

In the center of the small stand I lose touch with the urban world beyond. Gone are the sounds of cars, horns, boats, and industry. The gentle
sound of the wind rustling through the trees masks the soft croaks of courting night herons. In the crotches of most of the taller trees there are stick
nests. Some are large and bulky affairs nestled against the trunks, while
other small, flimsy nests are placed far out in the tangles of branches. Most
are still empty, but here and there a black-crowned night heron incubates
quietly. They are usually the first to return to these heronries in mid-March
when there is still snow on the ground. Within a few days they claim their
old nests, using them for resting platforms. A yellow-crowned night heron,
a species that is endangered or threatened in both New York and New Jersey, sits on a bulky nest low in a birch tree.

The trees on the edge of the stand buffer the inner trees from the wind,
and hide the nests from the scrutiny of boats passing close by the island.
The nests here are high and well protected from mammalian predators and
high winds. Once the leaves burst open, the nests will be shielded from
avian predators as well. The stand is more extensive than it appears from
the outside, and hundreds of nests are hidden within.

Herons, egrets, and ibis, collectively known as waders, have not always
nested in the Kills. As their populations rebounded following the plume-
hunting days of the late 1800s, herons and egrets searched for suitable
colony sites. Water quality in the 1950s and 1960s was so poor, and dissolved
oxygen was so low, that many native estuarine organisms did not survive in
the Kill. From the 1960s on, improved environmental regulations required
industries and municipalities to reduce the effluent that contaminated this
and many other rivers. Slowly water quality improved, invertebrates moved
back into the kill, followed by killifish and a number of other small estuarine fishes.

In 1974 a small colony of herons nested on Shooters Island located in
nearby Kill van Kull, a few miles to the north. Gradually the number increased, and birds spread to Prall's Island and Isle of Meadows. The three
heronries in the Kills grew to 800 pairs of herons, egrets, and ibis by the
mid 1980s, and increased to 1,300 pairs by the 1990s. These heronries are
significant, for nearly 30 percent of the total wader population of New York,
and 20 to 30 percent of New Jersey's coastal waders breed here. They are
well worth protecting, not only for their numbers and diversity, but because
yellow-crowned night herons breed here.

In only a few weeks the heronry will be bustling with the breeding activities of great egrets, little blue herons, tricolored herons, snowy egrets, and
glossy ibis, but for now, only the night herons are incubating. The nests are
high and difficult to see. Reluctantly, I turn from the inner quiet of the birch

stand, leave Prall's Island to Kathy Parsons, who has worked here for many years, and head the fifty miles south to Barnegat Bay, where the herons and egrets are easier to watch.

The wide salt marshes of Barnegat Bay extend for miles to the mainland beyond. We are a bit farther south, and the small green cordgrass shoots peering up through last year's growth indicate spring is here already. Hundreds of salt-marsh islands dot the Jersey shore, nestled in bays and estuaries. Most are unsuitable for heron colonies, because they require nest sites that are well above the high tides. Dense reeds, small shrubs, or taller trees will do nicely, but most of the islands are too low to support them.

Hither Island looks deserted as we approach. Short cordgrass fringes the island, and salt hay grows in the higher places. The middle of the island, where spoil was carelessly dumped years ago, is now covered with a dense stand of reeds, marsh elders, and poison ivy. Summer tides almost never reach these bushes; only the very high storm tides of winter wash over the island, killing rats and other small predators.

As we approach, the elegant white shapes of a dozen snowy egrets appear at the tops of the reeds, along with the larger great egrets. The herons here are circumspect, and one by one they abandon their reed nests as we approach, circling the area once or twice. They land in the marsh behind us, objecting with only a soft croak or two. They silently await our departure, their heads raised to watch our progress. We tarry only long enough to note that they have not laid eggs yet.

We run on up the bay to Lavalette Island, where the silhouettes of herring gulls form a menacing cloud above the island. Although the island is mostly cordgrass and salt hay, there is a sandy knoll in the center covered by dense reeds. In the highest places poison ivy bushes grow, along with a few twisted marsh elder. Our approach through the reeds is greeted with the loud crashes of black-crowned night herons scrambling from their nests. Mostly they tumble onto the ground, but some fly awkwardly from the reeds and disappear, along with masses of snowy egrets and great egrets.

We quickly bring in the blind and other supplies to set up shop, and away Mike goes, leaving me alone in the heronry. After I hear the motor moving across the bay in the distance, all is quiet. The rays of the setting sun form halos around last year's majestic reed heads. With the island to myself, I am safe and snug in a canvas blind just big enough to sleep in. Within minutes the birds slowly begin to return, first the night herons, then the snowy egrets and glossy ibis, and lastly the great egrets. They cling precariously to the tops of the branches and reeds, or stand awkwardly on the sandy knoll. After peering at the blind from all directions, they suspiciously settle down, one by one. The black-crowns return to their nests to incubate, but the egrets and ibis return to land on the vegetation. Most of the herons and egrets here do not have nests, and I am interested in how they interact with one another to choose territories and nest sites.

There are fewer black-crowned night herons nesting here than there were ten years ago, a cause for concern because this has happened all over the bay. Heronries that once contained many night heron nests now have only a dozen or so. Black-crowned night heron populations have declined drastically throughout New Jersey. There were 1,470 pairs counted in 1978, 359 pairs in 1985, and only about 200 in 1989 and 1995. Although aerial surveys miss a proportion of the night herons, some fail to leave colonies when the plane flies overhead; there is no reason to assume this bias differs among years. If this decrease continues, the species should be listed as threatened, as the yellow-crowned night heron is.

Heronries are fascinating places because it is unusual for so many species to nest together in mixed species groups. Although many seabirds nest together on islands, they usually do so in discrete subcolonies of only one species. Even on cliff ledges where many species of alcids and gulls breed, they often nest on distinct places, on different-sized ledges. In many heronries the habitat is homogeneous and the vegetation is uniform. I have spent many years examining habitat partitioning in heronries in the United States, Mexico, South Africa, Kenya, and Argentina.

Generally the nesting pattern depends upon whether there are differences in vegetation structure, plant species, or general aspect. When there are differences in vegetation patterns, the herons use these to partition the space. Different herons and egrets prefer different species of vegetation, and their weight influences where they can nest. Heavier herons or egrets must build nests where the branches are strong so that the nests will not collapse, while lighter species can build flimsier nests further out on branches or on the ground (Figure 28.2).

In homogeneous vegetation, however, the herons and egrets must divide the space differently, for there are no variations in vegetation structure or strength. In these heronries they sort themselves out with the largest species on top, and the smallest species farther down in the vegetation. From dense cattails in Minnesota to thick tules in Argentina, the largest species always occupies the top positions.

I am now interested in watching how the different species determine the nesting pattern. Patiently I record, day after day, the aggressive interactions between the species: who initiates a fight, who wins, and what happens to the winners and the losers. Lavalette Island is a good place to watch this behavior, for several species nest here, and there are different types of vegetation. In some places the reeds are uniform, in others there is a mixture of reeds and shrubs of different heights. I have already spent some time

28.2. *Great egret nesting high in the vegetation, with glossy ibis nesting on the ground.*

examining heron aggression on Islajo Island near Atlantic City, but I want to confirm the patterns here.

It is difficult to keep track of the fights here because they can occur on many different planes. Herons can fight with neighbors who are above or below them, or to the right or left. I settle on recording both the horizontal distance and the vertical distance of each interaction.

A pattern emerges: Larger species gravitate toward the top, forcing the smaller species lower in the vegetation, and each species defends a space around themselves that relates to their body size. Large birds, such as great egrets, defend a larger space around their nest than do snowy egrets or glossy ibis. A great egret will walk or fly farther from its nest to chase any intruder than will a snowy egret. It also matters who the intruders are. Each species will go farther to chase a large intruder than they will go to chase a small intruder (Figure 28.3).

With each day there are fewer and fewer aggressive interactions, as most birds have secured a nest site. The highest spots in the reeds and bushes are held by great egrets, who have bent over lots of reeds to form a dense platform that will bear their weight. Below them are tricolored herons, and below these are snowy egrets. Each pair has carefully constructed nests of reeds that are suspended above the ground. Glossy ibis, the smallest of the species, are all nesting on the ground, or only a few inches above the ground. In nearby reeds, the heavy bodied black-crowned night herons are also on the ground, but this is by choice. They were already on nests when the other species arrived.

The pattern in the bushes is similar. The great egrets have secured most of the bushes at the edge of sandy knoll, and they have built their nests as high as they could, given the strength of the branches (Figure 28.3). On some of the lower crotches there are a few black-crowned night herons, and still lower are snowy egrets. Here and there a pair of snowy egrets nests on the ground, far below the great egrets.

With each passing day there are more completed clutches of pale blue eggs, and the parents take up incubation duties with a vengeance. They take turns incubating the eggs, the off-duty parent going to forage along the edge of the island or on the nearby mudflats.

When Mike comes I show him the nesting pattern, easily identifying the nests by the size, color, and shade of the eggs. Great egret eggs are easy to identify: They are large and a beautiful robin's-egg blue. Snowy egret eggs are similarly colored, but they are much smaller. They are the same size as the glossy ibis eggs, but the ibis eggs are greener. Tricolored heron eggs are a darker blue and a bit larger than the snowy egret eggs. The black-crowned night heron eggs are not as light blue as the others, and they are rounder, with less of a pointed end. The differences are subtle, but with

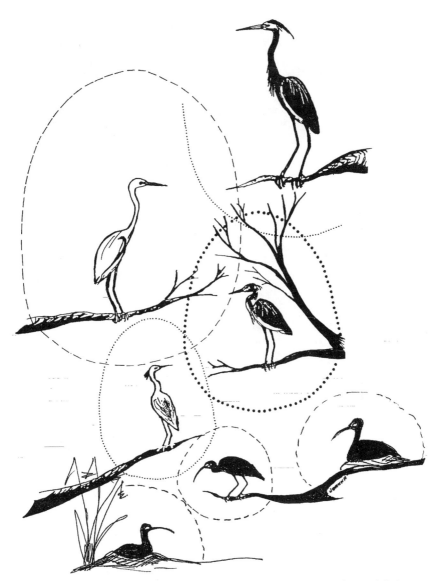

28.3. Spacing patterns in herons, egrets, and ibis as a function of size of their body. Smallest species nest the lowest.

28.4. Glossy ibis pair nesting on the ground.

practice the identity of each heron or egret egg is as clear as if its name were signed on the edge of the nest.

Waders keep their eggs covered continuously, not only to keep them at the appropriate temperature, but also to prevent marauding gulls and crows from stealing them. Since there is an active, thriving herring gull colony on the island, the herons must be particularly vigilant. Fish crows also visit the colony periodically to eat eggs.

There are no rats on the island to eat the eggs of the ground-nesting ibis, night herons, and snowy egrets (Figure 28.4). These birds are also safe from another threat—high winds. I watch in horror as a nor'easter wallops the island for three days. The herons and egrets cling to their nests, while sticks and grasses fly in every direction. Now and then an egg topples to the ground. When pairs awkwardly exchange incubation duties, the winds blow them about the minute they open their wings, and pieces of the nests tumble to the ground, carrying eggs with them. In one such nor'easter, nearly a quarter of the nests lose at least one egg, and some blow down completely. The eggs still remain on the ground, unbroken, half-developed, and dead. I cannot rescue these eggs, for my movements would scare the birds off their nests at a time when their best strategy is to sit tight, hunkered down against the wind and rain. In the dead of night the heronry is lighted up by bolts of lightning. I count the seconds between the light and thunder to assure myself that the bolts are still a mile away. The reeds sway menacingly and some bushes crack in the violent winds. No one will come to rescue me, for the bay is impassable. I can only imagine the deep waves and angry whitecaps that cover it.

When the sun breaks through the clouds and the storm has passed, the herons stand upright for the first time in days. They shake their wings and begin to preen their bedraggled feathers. Mates hurry off to fish, which they have been unable to do for three days. They do not tarry in the marsh creeks, but return almost at once to allow their waiting mates to go in search of fish. Fortunately only the night herons have small chicks, for the other young would have surely starved. Night herons can always find a few fiddler crabs in protected salt-marsh creeks, but the rough waters make fishing difficult for most herons and egrets.

In the sunlight I notice that the new green reeds have grown taller than the old brown flags from last year. The vegetation is dense and lush, the heron nests are almost hidden from view. I can risk a few minutes outside of the blind to check nest contents, to remove a few leaves for better visibility, and to collect a few of the fallen eggs for heavy metal analysis. It is bad enough that the eggs have died, but there is no sense in not getting some information from them.

Only one small black-crowned night heron chick lays dead outside the nest, a victim of the cold and rain. Otherwise the young night herons survived, attesting to the effectiveness of their parents' brooding. Their raucous cries are music to my ears. I do not appreciate their vile regurgitations of well-digested, slimy remains of fish and rodents, but at least it indicates that they are being fed regularly.

The eggs in many of the great egret nests are pipping, and in one nest a tiny, wet, bedraggled chick glares back at me. The storm was indeed well-timed, for the adults now can forage in the relatively calm bay. It is a critical time for the birds, and I hurry back to my blind to let the parents resettle. Within a few hours, the soft coos and croaks of concerned parents indicate that more and more eggs have hatched. With dispatch, the parents flick the empty eggshells from the nest, scattering them about the ground.

As increasing numbers of eggs hatch, the parents hustle about the heronry, bringing back food in their crops to regurgitate to their waiting chicks. Since the parents started incubating with the first egg, the chicks in each brood hatch over a few days, and the chicks in every nest range in size from tiny to quite large. The older chicks can climb higher to grab the food from their returning parent, and the smaller chicks are forced to wait until the largest chick or two is satiated. Exhausted, the large chicks wander to the sides of their nests and fall asleep, their bare greenish bellies distended. Only then can the smaller chicks compete for food.

The food supply seems to be stable, and few chicks starve. In bad food years, or when storms prevent foraging, the smaller two or three chicks in every nest starve, and only the largest fledge. The intense competition between brood mates, coupled with their age and size differences, ensure that at least some chicks in every brood fledge. By this brood reduction method, the smallest and youngest chicks starve. Although it seems wasteful to produce the last two or three eggs, in some years they all survive. This is one of those years, and many great egrets, black-crowned night herons, and snowy egrets are feeding broods of four and five healthy chicks.

When most chicks are two weeks old I go out to band them, for they are old enough to find their nest sites if they run a bit. It is easy to identify a true heron lovers, for only they understand the subtle pleasures of a great egret chick vomiting and defecating on them at the same time. The chicks' near-perfect aim attests to their obvious intent. Both are the most odoriferous fluids I know. I have taken to wearing sun glasses in the dim light of the reeds because at least none goes in my eyes.

Diligently, however, I collect the vomit, also called regurgitations, which will allow examination of their last meal. Several such specimens give a good indication of their diet. It is a smelly business, however, and my sample of several plastic bags is stored inside a larger, air-tight container. Mummichogs seem to make up a high proportion of the excreta in most of the young herons.

The next stint in the blind passes rapidly, as the hours fill with watching healthy chicks growing stronger and larger each day. No more bad storms blow through, and after five weeks, the egrets and herons take their first flights in relative calm. They are awkward at first, but gradually they learn to fly from one branch to another or to the ground without tumbling down head first. The parents, who are seldom at the nest now, must spend all their time flying to and fro with food. It is never enough, and a great commotion breaks out whenever any parent returns with food. From every direction chicks climb up or down bushes or reeds, or fly in to fight for every morsel. It has been a good year; almost every nest that weathered the storm raised two or three chicks, and many raised four.

Comparing notes with Kathy Parsons, we find that the young did well at the heronries in the Arthur Kill also. It has been five years since the Exxon oil spill in the Kill coated the mudflats and Cord Grass with oil, and things are almost back to normal. The snowy egrets and glossy ibis that suffered the most following the oil spill, because of their dependence on fiddler crabs, have achieved reproductive success rates equivalent to pre-spill levels. Young snowy egrets clamber through the trees as they did before the spill, seeking cover, hiding from predators, and crashing down to parents waiting to feed them.

In the days to follow, the marshes of the Arthur Kill and Barnegat Bay will be packed with young herons and egrets, standing silently along the creeks, learning to fish. They wait for the plump killifish to move past their sight, and plunge their bills in awkwardly. They will try their luck at the edges of the salt-marsh creeks on slightly larger and faster moving fish. For more than a month they will wander the shore aimlessly, learning to fish, practicing their skills. In time they will turn purposefully to the south and leave the Jersey shore for the warmer climes of south Florida.

Although it is early fall, I am already waiting for next spring. Each spring brings the possibility of finding birds that I have banded along the Jersey shore. Over the years I have watched as young cattle egrets and snowy egrets returned to their parents' heronries to breed, followed their breeding activities, banded their young, and located these same young on other heronries in the following years. I have captured common terns at Cedar Beach, Long Island, that I banded as young in Barnegat Bay, and I have followed skimmers as they moved from island to island in Barnegat Bay. Each year brings new changes to the birds along the Jersey shore, and with it come new research challenges. Over the years my interest in natural history and social behavior has only intensified as I have realized the importance of figuring out how wildlife can survive and flourish along the coast that is equally vital to the survival of man. Their survival and ours are intimately linked; when they suffer, so ultimately do we.

Appendix A: Scientific Names Mentioned in the Book

Plants

Asters, *Aster* spp.
Baobab tree, *Adansonia digitata*
Bayberry, *Myrica pensylvanica*
Beach grass, *Ammophila breviligulata*
Beach plum, *Prunus maritima*
Beard grass, *Andropogon* spp.
Black cherry, *Prunus serotina*
Black grass, *Juncus gerardi*
Black locust, *Robinia pseudoacacia*
Butterfly bush, *Buddleia* spp.
Cattail, *Typha* spp.
Cedar, *Chamaecyparis thyoides*
Coastal sand burr, *Cenchrus incertus*
Cockle burr, *Xanthium strumarium*
Common milkweed, *Asclepias syriaca*
Cordgrass, *Spartina alterniflora*
Eelgrass, *Zostera marina*
Glasswort, *Salicornia* spp.
Goldenrod, *Solidago* spp.
Gray birch, *Betula populifolia*
Holly, *Ilex americana*
Hydrangea, *Hydrangea paniculata*
Knapweed, *Centaurea nigra*
Marsh elder, *Iva frutescens*
Marsh mallow, *Althaea officinalis*
Panic grass, *Panilcum virgatum*
Pearly everlasting, *Anaphalis margaritacea*
Pinks, marsh pink, *Sabatia stellaris*
Poison Ivy, *Rhus toxicodendron*
Poplar, or cottonwood, *Populus deltoides*
Queen Anne's lace, *Dauca carota*

Raspberry, *Rubus* spp.
Reeds, *Phragmites australis*
Salt hay, *Spartina patens*
Sea lettuce, *Ulva lactuca*
Sea myrtle, *Baccharis halmifolia*
Sea rocket, *Cakile edentula*
Snowdrop, *Galanthus nivalis*
Spike grass, *Distichlis spicata*
Sumac, *Rhus* spp.
Swamp rose mallow, *Hibiscus palustris*
Switch grass, *Panicum virgatum*
Widgeon grass, *Ruppia maritima*
Wild rose, *Rosa multiflora*

Invertebrates

Barnacles, *Balanus* spp.
Black flies, *Simulium damnosum*
Blue crabs, *Callinectes sapidus*
Blue mussel, *Mytilus edulis*
Brackish-water fiddler crab, *Uca minax*
Bryzoans (phylum = Bryozoa), several species
Buckeye butterfly, *Junonia oenia*
Channeled whelk, *Busycon canaliculatum*
Fiddler crab, *Uca* spp.
Flatworm (phylum = Platyhelminthes)
Ghost crab, *Ocypode quadrata*
Grass shrimp, *Palaemonetes vulgaris*
Greenhead flies, *Tabanus americanus*
Horseshoe crabs, *Limulus polyphemus*
Lobster, *Homarus americanus*
Monarch butterfly, *Danaus plexippus*

Mud fiddler, *Uca pugnax*
Mussel (see blue mussel, ribbed
  mussel)
No-see-ums (sand flies, diptera),
  Culicoides spp.
Periwinkle, *Littorina littorina*
Ribbed mussel, *Modiolus demissus*
Salt marsh mosquito, *Aedes sollicitans*
Sand fiddler, *Uca pugilator*
Slipper shells, *Crepidula fornicata*
Sponges (phylum = Porifera), many
  species
Viceroy butterfly, *Limenitis archippus*
Whelk (channeled whelk), *Busycon
  canaliculatum*

Fish

Atlantic silversides, *Menidia menidia*
Atlantic sturgeon, *Acipenser oxyrhynchus*
Bay anchovy, *Anchoa mitchilli*
Black drum, *Pogonias cromis*
Bluefish, *Pomatomus salatrix*
Cod, *Gadus morrhua*
Eel, *Anguilla rostrata*
Herrings, *Clupea* spp.
Killifish (mummichog), *Fundulus* spp.
Mummichog, *Fundulus heteroclitus*
Sheepshead minnow, *Cyprinodon
  variegatus*
Sticklebacks, *Apeltes quandracus*
Striped bass (striper), *Morone saxatilis*
Summer flounder (fluke), *Paralichthys
  dentatus*
Tautog (also known as blackfish),
  Tautoga onitis
Weakfish (sea trout), *Cynoscion regalis*
White perch, *Morone americana*
Winter flounder, *Pseudopleuronectes
  americanus*

Herptiles

American toad, *Bufo americana*
Diamondback terrapin, *Malaclemys
  terrapin*
Fowler's toad, *Bufo fowleri*
Garter snake, *Thamnophis sirtalis*
Snapping turtle, *Chelydra serpentina*

Birds

American kestrel, *Falco sparverius*
Bald eagle, *Haliaeetus leucocephalus*
Barn owl, *Tyto alba*
Black duck, *Anas rubripes*
Black skimmer, *Rynchops niger*
Black-bellied plover, *Pluvialis squatarola*
Black-crowned night heron, *Nycticorax
  nycticorax*
Black-headed gull, *Larus ridibundus*
Blue jay, *Cyanocitta cristata*
Boat-tailed grackle, *Cassidix major*
Bonaparte's gull, *Larus philadelphia*
Brant, *Branta bernicla*
Broad-winged hawk, *Buteo platypterus*
Brown pelican, *Pelecanus occidentalis*
Canada goose, *Branta canadensis*
Cardinal, *Cardinalis cardinalis*
Cattle egret, *Bubulcus ibis*
Clapper rail, *Rallus longirostris*
Common snipe, *Capella gallinago*
Common tern, *Sterna hirundo*
Cooper's hawk, *Accipiter cooperii*
Dowitcher, *Limnodromus* spp.
Dunlin, *Calidris alpina*
Fish crow, *Corvus ossifragus*
Flicker, *Colaptes auratus*
Forster's tern, *Sterna forsteri*
Gadwall, *Anas strepera*
Gannet, *Sula bassana*
Glaucous gull, *Larus hyperboreus*
Glossy ibis, *Plegadis falcinellus*
Golden eagle, *Aquila chrysaetos*
Goshawk, *Accipiter gentilis*
Great black-backed gull, *Larus marinus*
Great blue heron, *Ardea herodias*
Great egret, *Egretta alba*
Great horned owl, *Bubo virginianus*
Herring gull, *Larus argentatus*
Horned lark, *Eremophila alpestris*
House finch, *Carpodacus mexicanus*
Iceland gull, *Larus glaucoides*
Jaeger, *Stercorarius* spp.
Killdeer, *Charadrius vociferus*
Kingfisher, *Ceryle alcyon*
Laughing gull, *Larus atricilla*
Least tern, *Sterna antillarum*

Lesser black-backed gull, *Larus fuscus*
Little blue heron, *Egretta caerula*
Mallard, *Anas platyrhynchos*
Marbled godwit, *Limosa fedoa*
Marsh hawk, *Circus cyaneus*
Merlin, *Falco columbarius*
Osprey, *Pandion haliaetus*
Oystercatcher, *Hematopus palliatus*
Passenger pigeon, *Ectopistes migratorius*
Peregrine falcon, *Falco peregrinus*
Piping plover, *Charadrius melodus*
Purple sandpiper, *Calidris maritima*
Red-shouldered hawk, *Buteo lineatus*
Red-tailed hawk, *Buteo jamaicensis*
Red-winged blackbird, *Ageliaus phoeniceus*
Red knot, *Calidris canutus*
Ring-billed gull, *Larus delawarensis*
Ruddy turnstone, *Arenaria interpres*
Sanderling, *Calidris alba*
Scaup, *Aythya* spp.
Seaside sparrow, *Ammospiza maritima*
Semipalmated plover, *Charadrius semipalmatus*
Semipalmated sandpiper, *Calidris pusilla*
Sharp-shinned hawk, *Accipiter striatus*
Sharp-tailed sparrow, *Ammospiza caudacuta*
Snow bunting, *Plectrophenax nivalis*
Snow geese, *Anser caerulescens*
Snowy egret, *Egretta thula*
Snowy owl, *Nyctea scandiaca*
Solitary sandpiper, *Tringa solitaria*

Spotted sandpiper, *Actitus macularia*
Starling, *Sturnus vulgaris*
Tricolored heron, *Egretta tricolor*
Tufted duck, *Aythya fuligula*
Turkey vulture, *Cathartes aura*
White ibis, *Eudocimus albus*
Willet, *Catoptrophorus semipalmatus*
Woodcock, *Scolopax minor*
Yellow-crowned night heron, *Nycticorax violaceus*
Yellowlegs, *Tringa* spp.

Mammals

African buffalo, *Syncerus caffer*
Deer, *Odocoileus virginianus*
Elephant, *Loxodonta africana*
Gray fox, *Urocyon cinereoargentatus*
Jumping mouse, *Zapus hudsonius*
Lion, *Panthera leo*
Masked shrew, *Sorex cinereus*
Meadow mouse, *Microtus pennsylvanicus*
Mink, *Mustela vison*
Muskrat, *Ondatra zibethica*
Norway rat, *Rattus norvegicus*
Rabbit, *Sylvilagus floridanus*
Raccoon, *Procyon lotor*
Red fox, *Vulpes fulva*
Skunk, *Mephitis mephitis*
Weasel, *Mustela* spp.
White-footed mouse, *Peromyscus leucopus*
Wildebeest, *Connochaetes taurinus*
Wolf, *Canis lupus*
Zebra, *Equus burchelli*

Suggested Readings

General References

Burger, J., ed. 1994. Before and After an Oil Spill: The Arthur Kill. New Brunswick: Rutgers University Press.

Carlson, C., and J. Fowler. 1980. The Salt Marsh of Southern New Jersey. Pomona, N.J.: Stockton Center for Environmental Studies.

Duncan, W. H., and M. B. Duncan. 1987. Seaside Plants of the Gulf and Atlantic Coasts. Washington, D.C.: Smithsonian Institution Press.

Dunne, P. J., ed. 1989. New Jersey at the Crossroads of Migration. Franklin Lakes: New Jersey Audubon Society.

Garber, S. D. 1987. The Urban Naturalist. New York: Wiley & Sons, Inc.

Gosner, K. L. 1979. A Field Guide to the Atlantic Seashore. Boston: Houghton Mifflin Company.

Kaufman, W., and O. H. Pilkey, Jr. 1983. The Beaches are Moving: The Drowning of America's Shoreline. Durham: Duke University Press.

Kennish, M. J., and R. A. Lutz, eds. 1984. Ecology of Barnegat Bay. New York: Springer-Verlag.

Moonsammy, R. Z., D. S. Cohen, and L. E. Williams, eds. 1987. Pinelands Folklife. New Brunswick: Rutgers University Press.

Nordstrom, K. F., P. A. Gares, N. B. Psuty, O. H. Pilkey, Jr., W. J. Neal, and O. Pilkey, Sr. 1986. Living with the New Jersey Shore. Durham: Duke University Press.

Roberts, R., and R. Youmans. 1993. Down the Jersey Shore. New Brunswick: Rutgers University Press.

Rose, T. F., H. C. Woolman, and T. T. Price. 1878. Historical and Biographical Atlas of the New Jersey Shore. Philadelphia: Woolman and Rose.

Teal, J., and M. Teal. 1969. Life and Death of the Salt Marsh. New York: Ballantine Books.

Tiner, R. W., Jr. 1987. A Field Guide to Coastal Wetland Plants of the Northeastern United States. Amherst: University of Massachusetts Press.

Worth, C. B. 1972. Of Mosquitoes, Moths, and Mice. New York: Norton & Company, Inc.

References for Individual Chapters

Suggested Readings for Chapter 1

Burger, J. 1991. Coastal landscapes, coastal colonies and seabirds. Aquatic Reviews 4:23–43.

Carlson, C., and J. Fowler. 1980. The Salt Marsh of Southern New Jersey. Pomona, N.J.: Stockton Center for Environmental Studies.

Daiber, F. C. 1977. Salt marsh animals: Distributions related to tidal flooding, salinity and vegetation. Pp. 70–108 in V. J. Chapman, ed., Wet Coastal Ecosystems. Amsterdam: Elsevier Scientific Publishing.

Ehrenfeld, J. G. 1990. Dynamics and processes of barrier island vegetation. Aquatic Sciences 2:437–480.

Nixon, S. W. 1982. The ecology of New England salt marshes: A community profile. U.S. Fish and Wildlife Service, FWS/OBS 81–55. Washington, D.C.

Orson, R. A., R. S. Warren, and W. A. Niering. 1987. Development of a tidal marsh in a New England River valley. Estuaries 10:20–27.

Redfield, A. C. 1972. Development of a New England salt marsh. Ecological Monographs 42:201–237.

Teal, J., and M. Teal. 1969. Life and Death of a Salt Marsh. New York: National Audubon Society.

Suggested Readings for Chapter 2

Burger, J. 1977. The role of visibility in the nesting behavior of 5 species of *Larus* gulls. Journal of Comparative Physiology and Psychology 91:1347–1358.

———. 1979. Salt marshes: Havens for waterbirds. New Jersey Outdoors 6:6–7, 26–27.

———. 1979b. Nest repair behavior in birds nesting in salt marshes. Journal of Comparative Physiology and Psychology 11:189–199.

Burger, J., and F. Lesser. 1980. Nest site selection in an expanding population of herring gulls. Bird Banding 51:270–280.

Burger, J., and J. Shisler. 1980. Colony site and nest selection in laughing gulls in response to tidal flooding. Condor 82:251–258.

Burger, J. 1985. Habitat selection in temperate marshes. Pp. 253–281 in M. Cody, ed., Nest Site Selection in Birds. New York: Academic Press.

———. 1991. Coastal landscapes, coastal colonies and seabirds. Aquatic Reviews 4:23–43.

Wander, W., and S. A. Brady. 1979. A closer look at New Jersey's wading birds. New Jersey Outdoors 6:10–11.

Suggested Readings for Chapter 3

Burger, J., ed. 1994. Before and after an oil spill: The Arthur Kill. New Brunswick: Rutgers University Press.

Burger, J., and M. Gochfeld. 1988. Metals in tern eggs in a New Jersey estuary: A decade of change. Environmental Monitoring and Assessment 11:127–135.

———. 1994. Behavioral impairments of lead-injected young herring gulls in nature. Fundamental and Applied Toxicology 23:553–561.

Burger, J., and J. Shisler. 1979. The effects of ditching a salt marsh on colony and nest site selection by herring gulls (*Larus argentatus*). American Midland Naturalist 100:54–63.

Burger, J., J. Shisler, and F. Lesser. 1982. Avian utilization in six New Jersey salt marshes. Biological Conservation 23:187–212.

Burger, J., K. Staine, and M. Gochfeld. 1993. Fishing in contaminated waters: Knowledge and risk perception of hazards by fisherman in New York City. Journal of Toxicology and Environmental Health 39:95–105.

Burger, J., M. Horoszewski Lavery, and M. Gochfeld. 1994. Temporal changes in lead levels in common tern feathers in New York and relationship of field levels to adverse effects in the laboratory. Environmental Toxicology and Chemistry 13:581–586.

Colborn, T., and C. Clement, eds. 1992. Chemically-induced Alterations in Sexual and Functional Development: The Wildlife/Human Connection. Princeton, N.J.: Princeton Scientific Publishing Co., Inc.

Halpert, H. 1983. The Folklore and Folklife of New Jersey. New Brunswick: Rutgers University Press.

Hegeman, H. R. 1977. The Barnegat Bay sneakbox. New Jersey Outdoors 4:4–5, 28–29.

Moonsammy, R. Z., D. S. Cohen, and L. E. Williams, eds. 1987. Pinelands Folklife. New Brunswick: Rutgers University Press.

Nixon, S. W. 1982. The ecology of New England salt marshes: A community profile. U.S. Fish and Wildlife Service, FWS/OBS 81–55. Washington, D.C.

Rose, T. F., H. C. Woolman, and T. T. Price. 1878. Historical and Biographical Atlas of the New Jersey Shore. Philadelphia: Woolman and Rose.

Talbot, C. W., K. W. Able, and J. K. Shisler. 1986. Fish species composition in New Jersey salt marshes: Effects of marsh alterations for mosquito control. Transactions of the American Fisheries Society 115:269–278.

Teal, J., and M. Teal. 1969. Life and Death of a Salt Marsh. New York: National Audubon Society.

Suggested Readings for Chapter 4

Burger, J. 1990. Seabirds, tropical biology, and global warming: Are we missing the ark? Colonial Waterbirds 13:81–84.

Cohn, J. P. 1989. Gauging the biological impacts of the greenhouse effect. BioScience 39:142–146.

Hackney, C. T., and W. J. Cleary. Saltmarsh loss in Southeastern North Carolina lagoons: Importance of sea level rise and inlet dredging. Journal of Coastal Research 3:93–97.

Houghton, J. T., B. A. Callander, and S. K. Varney. 1992. Climate Change 1992. Cambridge: Cambridge University Press

Orson, R., W. Panageotou, and S. P. Leatherman. 1985. Responses of tidal salt marshes of the U.S. Atlantic and Gulf coasts to rising sea levels. Journal of Coastal Research 11:29–37.

Pielke, R. A., and R. Avissar. 1990. Influence of landscape structure on local and regional climate. Landscape Ecology 4:133–155.

Titus, J. G. 1991. Greenhouse effect and coastal wetland policy: How Americans could abandon an area the size of Massachusetts at minimum cost. Environmental Management 15:39–58.

Suggested Readings for Chapter 5

Burger, J., and J. Shisler. 1978. Nest-site selection in willets. Wilson Bulletin 90:359–375.

Burger, J., and M. Gochfeld. 1991a. The Common Tern: Its Breeding Biology and Social Behavior. New York: Columbia University Press.

Lauro, B., and J. Burger. 1989. Nest-site selection in the American oystercatcher in salt marshes. Auk 106:185–192.

Suggested Readings for Chapter 6

Dunne, M. 1989. New Jersey toads. New Jersey Outdoors 11:40.

Garber, S. D. 1987. The Urban Naturalist. New York: Wiley & Sons, Inc.

Zappalorti, R. T. 1982. Spring voices in the night. New Jersey Outdoors 9:11–13.

Suggested Readings for Chapter 7

Bertness, M. D. 1985. Fiddler crab regulation of *Spartina alterniflora* production on a New England salt marsh. Ecology 66:1042–1055.

Burger, J. 1994. Immediate effects of oil spills on organisms in the Arthur Kill. Pp. 115–129 in Burger, J., ed., 1994, Before and after an Oil Spill: The Arthur Kill. New Brunswick: Rutgers University Press.

Burger, J., and M. Gochfeld. 1992. Effects of washing fiddler crabs (*Uca pugnax*) following an oil spill. Environmental Pollution 77:15–22.

Burger, J., J. Brzorad, and M. Gochfeld. 1991. Effects of an oil spill on emergence and mortality in fiddler crabs *Uca pugnax*. Environmental Monitoring and Assessment 22:107–115.

———. 1992. Immediate effects of an oil spill on behavior of fiddler crabs (*Uca pugnax*). Archives of Environmental Contamination and Toxicology 20:404–409.

———. 1994. Fiddler crabs (*Uca* spp.) as bioindicators for oil spills. Pp. 161–177 in Burger, J., ed., 1994, Before and after an Oil Spill: The Arthur Kill. New Brunswick: Rutgers University Press.

Crane, J. 1975. Fiddler Crabs of the World. Princeton: Princeton University Press.

Katz, L. C. 1980. Effects of burrowing by the fiddler crab, *Uca pugnax* (Smith). Estuarine and Coastal Marine Science 11:233–237.

Parsons, K. C. 1994. The Arthur Kill oil spills: Biological effects in birds. Pp. 215–237 in Burger, J., ed., 1994, Before and After an Oil Spill: The Arthur Kill. New Brunswick: Rutgers University Press.

Teal, J. M. 1958. Distribution of fiddler crabs in Georgia salt marshes. Ecology 39:185–193.

Suggested Readings for Chapter 8

Burger, J. 1978. The pattern and mechanism of nesting in mixed-species heronries. Pp. 45–58 in Wading Birds. National Audubon Report 7. New York.

———. 1978b. Competition between cattle egrets and native North American herons, egrets and ibises. Condor 80:15–23.

———. 1979b. Resource partitioning: Nest site selection in mixed-species colonies of herons, egrets and ibises. American Midland Naturalist 101:191–210.

———. 1981. A model for the evolution of mixed-species colonies of Ciconiiformes. Quarterly Review of Biology 56:143–167.

———. 1981b. Cattle egret: White robin of the future. New Jersey Outdoors 8:10–13.

Burger, J., and M. Gochfeld. 1983. Host selection as an adaptation to host-dependent foraging success in the cattle egret (*Bubulcus ibis*). Behaviour 79:212–229.

———. 1992b. Host-specific foraging behavior of cattle egrets *Bubulcus ibis*. Proceedings of Seventh Pan-African Ornithological Congress:413–419.

———. 1993. When is a heronry crowded?: A case study of Huckleberry Island, New York, U.S.A. Journal of Coastal Research 9:221–228.

Meyrriecks, A. J. 1960. Success story of a pioneering bird. Natural History 69:46–57.

Mock, D. W., and B. J. Ploger. 1987. Parental manipulation of optimal hatch asynchrony in cattle egrets: An experimental study. Animal Behavior 35:150–160.

Telfair, R. C., II, 1983. The cattle egret: A Texas focus and world view. College Station: Texas Agricultural Experiment Station.

———. 1994. Cattle egret (*Bubulcus ibis*). In Poole, A., and F. Gill, eds., The Birds of North America, No. 113. Philadelphia: The Academy of Natural Sciences; Washington D.C.: The American Ornithologists' Union.

Suggested Readings for Chapter 9

Carlson, C., and J. Fowler. 1980. The Salt Marsh of Southern New Jersey. Pomona, N.J.: Stockton Center for Environmental Studies.

Hillman, R. J., and M. J. Kennish. 1983. Commercial and sportfishing. Pp. 281–301 in Kennish, M. J., and R. A. Lutz, eds., 1984, Ecology of Barnegat Bay. New York: Springer-Verlag.

Safina, C., and J. Burger. 1985. Common tern foraging: Seasonal trends in prey fish densities and competition with Bluefish. Ecology 66:1457–1463.

———. 1988. Use of sonar and a small boat for studying foraging ecology of seabirds. Colonial Waterbirds 11:234–244.

———. 1988b. Prey dynamics and the breeding phenology of common terns (*Sterna hirundo*). Auk 105:720–726.

———. 1989. Population interactions among free-living bluefish and prey fish in an ocean environment. Oecologia. 79:91–95.

Talbot, C. W., and K. W. Able. 1984. Composition and distribution of larval fishes in New Jersey high marshes. Estuaries 7:434–443.

Tatham, T. R., D. L. Thomas, and D. J. Danila. 1983. Fishes of Barnegat Bay, New Jersey. Pp. 241–280 in Kennish, M. J., and R. A. Lutz, eds., Ecology of Barnegat Bay. New York: Springer-Verlag.

Kneib, R. T. 1988. Testing for indirect effects of predation in an intertidal soft-bottom community. Ecology 69:1795–1801.

Suggested Readings for Chapter 10

Botton, M. L., and R. E. Loveland. 1987. Orientation of the horseshoe crab, *Limulus polyphemus*, on a sandy beach. Biological Bulletin 173: 289–298.

———. 1989. Reproductive risk, high mortality associated with spawning by horseshoe crabs (*Limulus polyphemus*) in Delaware Bay, USA. Marine Biology 101:143–151.

Burger, J., and M. Gochfeld. 1991b. Vigilance and feeding behavior in large feeding flocks of laughing gulls, *Larus atricilla*, on Delaware Bay. Estuarine, Coastal, and Shelf Science 32:207–212.

Hall, W. R., Jr. 1990. The horseshoe crab—a reminder of Delaware's past. MAS Bulletin, University of Delaware, Newark, Delaware.

Loveland, R. E., and M. L. Botton. 1992. Sexual dimorphism and the mating system in horseshoe crabs, *Limulus polyphemus* L. Animal Behavior 44:907–916.

McLain, P. 1994. The living fossils of the Delaware Bay. New Jersey Outdoors 2:25–29.

Paladino, L. 1983. The horseshoe crab: A crab not a crab. The Conservationist 37:22–27.

Shuster, C. N., Jr., and M. L. Botton. 1985. A contribution to the population biology of horseshoe crabs, *Limulus polyphemus* (L) in Delaware Bay. Estuaries 8:363–372.

Sutton, C. C. 1994. State of the estuary. Estuary News 5:1–15.

Suggested Readings for Chapter 11

Botton, M. L., and R. E. Loveland. 1993. Predation by herring gulls and great black-backed gulls on horseshoe crabs. Wilson Bulletin 105:518–521.

Botton, M. L., R. E. Loveland, and T. R. Jacobsen. 1994. Site selection by migratory shorebirds in Delaware Bay, and its relationship to beach characteristics and abundance of horseshoe crab (*Limulus polyphemus*) eggs. Auk 111:605–616.

Burger, J. 1986. The effect of human activities on shorebirds in two coastal bays in Northeastern United States. Environmental Conservation 13:123–130.

Burger, J., and J. Galli. 1987. Factors affecting distribution of gulls (*Larus*) on two New Jersey coastal bays. Environmental Conservation 14:59–65.

Burger, J., and M. Gochfeld. 1991b. Vigilance and feeding behavior in large feeding flocks of laughing gulls, *Larus atricilla*, on Delaware Bay. Estuarine, Coastal, and Shelf Science 32:207–212.

Burger, J., M. Gochfeld, and L. J. Niles. 1994. Ecotourism and birds in coastal New Jersey: Contrasting responses of birds, tourists and managers. Environmental Conservation 22:56–64.

Burger, J., K. L. Clark, and L. Niles. 1996. Importance of beach, mudflat, and marsh for migrant shorebirds on Delaware Bay: Integration of beach, mudflat and marsh habitats. Biological Conservation (in press).

Clark, K. E. 1991. Jersey: A way station for migratory birds. New Jersey Outdoors 18:28–31.

Clark, K. E., L. J. Niles, and J. Burger. 1993. Abundance and distribution of migrant shorebirds in Delaware Bay. Condor 95:694–705.

Harrington, B. 1983. The migration of the red knot. Oceanus 26:44–48.

McLain, P. 1985. Delaware Bay shorebirds. New Jersey Outdoors 12:25–29.

McLain, P. 1987. Sanderlings. New Jersey Outdoors 14:23–25.

Myers, J. P. 1989. Delaware Bay: A spectacle of spring passage. The Nature Conservancy Magazine, March/April (no vol. no.): 6 pp.

Nyman, R., ed. 1995. Habitat Requirements of Animals in Delaware Bay. New York: EPA Harbor Estuary Program.

Wagner, L., and J. Burger. Ms. Nutrient requirements of laughing gulls.

Suggested Readings for Chapter 12

Burger, J. 1976. Daily and seasonal activity patterns in breeding laughing gulls, *Larus atricilla.* Auk 93:308–323.

———. 1978b. Nest-building behavior in laughing gulls. Animal Behavior 26:856–861.

Burger, J., and C. Beer. 1975. Territoriality in laughing gulls. Behaviour 55:301–320.

Burger, J., and M. Gochfeld. 1983b. Feeding behavior of laughing gulls: Compensatory site selection by young. Condor 85:467–473.

Burger, J., and K. Staine. 1993. Nocturnal behavior of gulls in coastal New Jersey. Estuaries 16:809–814.

Griffin, W. D. 1982. Gulls of the salt marsh. New Jersey Outdoors 9:12.

Nyman, R., ed. 1995. Habitat Requirements of Animals in Delaware Bay. New York: EPA Harbor Estuary Program.

Suggested Readings for Chapter 13

Worth, C. B. 1972. Of Mosquitoes, Moths, and Mice. New York: Norton & Company, Inc.

Suggested Readings for Chapter 14

Burger, J. 1981c. Sexual differences in parental activities of breeding black skimmers. American Naturalist 117:975–984.

———. 1982. The role of reproductive success in colony-site selection and abandonment in black skimmers (*Rynchops niger*). Auk 99:109–115.

Burger, J., and M. Gochfeld. 1990. The Black Skimmer: Social Dynamics of a Colonial Species. New York: Columbia University Press.

———. 1991. The Common Tern: Its Breeding Biology and Social Behavior. New York: Columbia University Press.

———. 1992c. Terns for the better. Natural History 6/92:45–47.

Burger, J., and F. Lesser. 1978. Selection of colony sites and nest sites by common terns *Sterna hirundo* in Ocean County, New Jersey. Ibis 120:433–449.

Burger, J., F. Lesser, and M. Gochfeld. 1992. Brown pelicans attempt nesting in New Jersey. Records of New Jersey Birds 18:78–79.

Erwin, R. M. 1977. Black skimmer breeding ecology and behavior. Auk 94:709–717.

Gochfeld, M., and J. Burger. 1994. Black skimmer (*Rynchops niger*). In Poole, A., and F. Gill, eds., The Birds of North America, No. 108. Philadelphia: The Academy of Natural Sciences; Washington D.C.: The American Ornithologists' Union.

Safina, C., and J. Burger. 1985. Common tern foraging: Seasonal trends in prey fish densities and competition with Bluefish. Ecology 1457–1463.

Weidner, D. S. 1991. Champagne Island, Hereford Inlet. New Jersey Audubon 17:20–21.

Suggested Readings for Chapter 15

Burger, J. 1984. Least terns in New Jersey. New Jersey Outdoors. 11:133–35.

———. 1987. Physical and social determinants of nest-site selection in piping plover in New Jersey. Condor 89:811–818.

———. 1991b. Foraging behavior and the effects of human disturbance on the piping plover (*Charadrius melodus*). Journal of Coastal Research 7:39–52.

———. 1994b. The effect of human disturbance on foraging behavior and habitat use in Piping Plover (*Charadrius melodus*). Estuaries 17:695–701.

Burger, J., and D. Jenkins. 1986. Our endangered beach nesting birds. New Jersey Outdoors 13:14–16.

Burger, J., C. D. Jenkins, Jr., and K. Staine. 1992. Beach nesting birds: Optimism for the future. New Jersey Audubon 18 (Summer 1992):9–11.

Burger, J., M. Gochfeld, and L. J. Niles. 1994. Ecotourism and birds in coastal New Jersey: Contrasting responses of birds, tourists and managers. Environmental Conservation 22:56–64.

Dyer, R. W. 1993. The piping plover: Conservation needs in the Eastern United States. Underwater Naturalist 21:19–22.

Haig, S. M. 1990. Piping plover. In Poole, A., and F. Gill, eds., The Birds of North America, No. 2. Philadelphia: The Academy of Natural Sciences; Washington D.C.: The American Ornithologists' Union.

Haig, S. M., and J. H. Plissner. 1993. Distribution and abundance of piping plovers: Results and implications of the 1991 international census. Condor 95:145–156.

Nicholls, J. L., and G. A. Baldassarre. 1990. Habitat associations of piping plovers wintering in the United States. Wilson Bulletin 102:581–590.

U.S. Fish and Wildlife Service. 1994. Atlantic Coast piping plover revised recovery plan. Boston, Mass.: Fish and Wildlife Service.

Suggested Readings for Chapter 16

Clark, K. E. 1995. Research and management of the peregrine falcon. Unpublished report to the New Jersey Endangered and Nongame Species council. Trenton, New Jersey.

Hickey, J. J., ed. 1969. Peregrine Falcon Populations: Their Biology and Decline. Madison: University of Wisconsin Press.

Segars, H. 1986. The osprey. New Jersey Outdoors 13:28–30.

Valent, M. 1993. Endangered and Nongame Species Program: Annual Report 1992. N.J. Department of Environmental Protection. Trenton, N.J.

Worth, C. B. 1972. Of Mosquitoes, Moths, and Mice. New York: Norton & Company, Inc.

Wiemeyer, S., T. G. Lamont, C. M. Bunck, C. R. Sindelar, F. J. Gramlich, J. D. Fraser, and M. A. Byrd. 1984. Organochlorine pesticide, polychlorobiphenyl, and mercury residues in bald eagle eggs 1969–1979 and their relationships to shell thinning and reproduction. Archives Environmental Contamination and Toxicology 13:529–549.

Suggested Readings for Chapter 17

Bertness, M. D. 1984. Ribbed mussels and *Spartina alterniflora* production in a New England salt marsh. Ecology 65:1794–1807.

Burger, J., and M. Gochfeld. 1991c. Predation, vigilance, and antipredator behavior. Pp. 168–247 in: Burger, J., and M. Gochfeld. 1991. The Common Tern: Its Breeding Biology and Social Behavior. New York: Columbia University Press.

Carlson, C., and J. Fowler. 1980. The Salt Marsh of Southern New Jersey. Pomona, N.J.: Stockton Center for Environmental Studies.

Chanda, D. 1989. Mink. New Jersey Wildlife Profiles I:66–67.

Suggested Readings for Chapter 18

Anderson, K. 1984. Turtles: The reptiles of New Jersey. New Jersey Outdoors 11:17–20.

Burger, J., and W. A. Montevecchi. 1975. Nest site selection in the terrapin, *Malaclemys terrapin*. Copeia 1975:113–119.

Burger, J. 1976. Behavior of hatchling diamondback terrapin, *Malaclemys terrapin terrapin*. Copeia 1976:742–748.

———. 1977b. Determinants of hatching success in diamondback terrapin, *Malaclemys terrapin*. American Midland Naturalist 97:444–464.

———. 1982b. Diamondback terrapins: Between laying and hatching. New Jersey Outdoors 9:2–3, 30–31.

———. 1989. Diamondback terrapin protection. Plastron Papers 19:35–40.

Garber, S. D. 1988. Diamondback terrapin exploitation. Plastron Papers 1718–22.

Hurd, L. E., G. W. Smedes, and T. A. Dean. 1979. An ecological study of a natural population of diamondback terrapins (*Malaclemys t. terrapin*) in a Delaware salt marsh. Estuaries 2:28–33.

Suggested Readings for Chapter 19

Crans, W. J. 1977. The status of *Aedes sollicitans* as an epidemic vector of eastern equine encephalitis in New Jersey. Mosquito News 37:85–89.

Crans, W. J., J. McNelly, T. L. Schulze, and A. Main. 1986. Isolation of eastern equine encephalitis virus from *Aedes sollicitans* during an epizootic in southern New Jersey. Journal of the American Mosquito Control Association 2:68–72.

Crans, W. J., L. J. McCuiston, and D. A. Sprenger. 1990. The blood-feeding habits of *Aedes sollicitans* (Walker) in relation to eastern equine encephalitis virus in coastal areas of New Jersey I. Hose selection in nature determined by precipitin tests on wild-caught specimens. Bulletin of the Society of Vector Ecology 15:144–148.

Headlee, T. J. 1936. Possibility of malarial outbreaks in New Jersey. New Jersey Agricultural Experiment Station: Circular 368.

Worth, C. B. 1972. Of Mosquitoes, Moths, and Mice. New York: Norton & Company, Inc.

Suggested Readings for Chapter 20

Burger, J. 1986. The effect of human activities on shorebirds in two coastal bays in Northeastern United States. Environmental Conservation 13:123–130.

———. 1988. Jamaica Bay studies VIII: An overview of abiotic factors affecting several avian groups. Journal of Coastal Research 4:193–205.

Burger, J., and M. Gochfeld. 1983c. Jamaica Bay studies V: Flocking associations and behavior of shorebirds at an Atlantic Coastal estuary. Biology of Behavior 8:289–318.

Burger, J., M. A. Howe, D. C. Hahn, and J. Chase. 1977. Effects of tide cycles on habitat selection and habitat partitioning by migrating shorebirds. Auk 94:743–758.

Suggested Readings for Chapter 21

Dickerson, M. C. 1901. Moths and Butterflies. Boston: Athenaeum Press.

Garber, S. D. 1987. The Urban Naturalist. New York: Wiley & Sons, Inc.

Gochfeld, M., and J. Burger. 1996 (in press). Butterflies of New Jersey. New Brunswick: Rutgers University Press

Urquhart, F. A. 1987. The Monarch Butterfly: International Traveler. Chicago: Nelson-Hall.

Suggested Readings for Chapter 22

Burger, J., M. Gochfeld, and L. J. Niles. 1994. Ecotourism and birds in coastal New Jersey: Contrasting responses of birds, tourists and managers. Environmental Conservation 22:56–64.

Clark, K. E. 1991. Jersey: A way station for migratory birds. New Jersey Outdoors 18:28–31.

Dunne, P. J., and W. S. Clark. 1977. Fall hawk movement at Cape May Point, N.J.—1976. New Jersey Audubon 3:114–124.

Dunne, P. J., D. Sibley, and C. Sutton. 1988. Hawks in Flight. Boston: Houghton Mifflin Co.

Dunne, P., and C. Sutton. 1986. Population trends in coastal raptor migrants over ten years of Cape May Point autumn counts. Records of New Jersey Birds 12:39–43.

Kerlinger, P. 1989. Flight Strategies of Migrating Hawks. Chicago: University of Chicago Press.

Suggested Readings for Chapter 23

Burger, J. 1988b. Effects of demolition and beach clean-up on birds on a coastal bay. Estuaries 27:97–108.

Burger, J., M. Gochfeld, and L. J. Niles. 1994. Ecotourism and birds in coastal New Jersey: Contrasting responses of birds, tourists and managers. Environmental Conservation 22:56–64.

Kerlinger, P., M. R. Lein, and B. J. Sevick. 1985. Distribution and population fluctuations of wintering snowy owls (*Nyctea scandiaca*) in North America. Canadian Journal of Zoology 63:1829–1834.

Parmelee, D. F. 1992. Snowy owl. In Poole, A., P. Stettenheim, and F. Gill, eds., Birds of North America, No. 10. Philadelphia: The Academy of Natural Sciences; Washington D.C.: The American Ornithologists' Union.

No Suggested Readings for Chapter 24

Suggested Readings for Chapter 25

Buchsbaum, R., J. Wilson, and I. Valiela. 1986. Digestibility of plant constituents by Canada geese and Atlantic brant. Ecology 67:386–393.

Burger, J. 1988. Jamaica Bay studies VIII: An overview of abiotic factors affecting several avian groups. Journal of Coastal Research 4:193–205.

Burger, J., R. Trout, W. Wander, and G. Ritter. 1983. Jamaica Bay studies IV: Abiotic factors affecting abundance of brant and Canada geese on an East Coast estuary. Wilson Bulletin 95:384–403.

Chanda, D. 1989b. Gray fox. New Jersey Wildlife Profiles. 1:62–63.

Kirby, R. E., and F. Ferrigno. 1980. Winter, waterfowl, and the saltmarsh. New Jersey Outdoors 7:10–13.

Niles, L. J., K. Clark, and D. Ely. 1991. Breeding status of bald eagles in New Jersey. Records of New Jersey Birds 17:2–5.

Smith, T. J., and W. E. Odum. 1981. The effects of grazing by geese on coastal salt marshes. Ecology 62:98–106.

Suggested Readings for Chapter 26

Burger, J. 1963. Comparative behavior of the killdeer and spotted sandpiper. Kingbird 13:14–17.

Garber, S. D. 1987. The Urban Naturalist. New York: Wiley & Sons, Inc.

Suggested Readings for Chapter 27

Burger, J. 1977c. Nesting behavior of Herring gulls: Invasion into *Spartina* salt marsh areas of New Jersey. Condor 79:162–169.

———. 1978. Herring gulls invade New Jersey. New Jersey Outdoors. 5:6–7, 26–27.

———. 1980. Nesting adaptations of Herring gull (*Larus argentatus*) to salt marshes and storm tides. Biology of Behavior 5:147–162.

——— 1984b. Pattern, mechanism, and adaptive significance of territoriality in Herring gulls (*Larus argentatus*). Ornithological Monographs No. 34:1–92.

———. 1986b. Selection for equitability in some aspects of reproductive investment in herring gulls *Larus argentatus*. Ornis Scandinavica 18:17–23.

Pierotti, R. J., and T. P. Good. 1994. Herring gull (*Larus argentatus*). In Poole, A., and F. Gill, eds., The Birds of North America, No. 113. Philadelphia: The Academy of Natural Sciences; Washington D.C.: The American Ornithologists' Union.

Suggested Readings for Chapter 28

Burger, J. 1978. The pattern and mechanism of nesting in mixed-species heronries. Pp. 45–58 in Wading Birds. National Audubon Report 7. New York.

———. 1978b. Competition between cattle egrets and native North American herons, egrets and ibises. Condor 80:15–23.

———. 1979b. Resource partitioning: Nest site selection in mixed-species colonies of herons, egrets and ibises. American Midland Naturalist 101:191–210.

———. 1981d. On becoming independent in herring gulls: Parent-young conflict. American Naturalist 117:444–456.

Burger, J., and M. Gochfeld. 1993. When is a heronry crowded?: A case study of Huckleberry Island, New York, U.S.A. Journal of Coastal Research 9:221–228.

Hancock, J., and J. Kushlan. 1984. The Herons Handbook. New York: Harper and Row.

Parsons, K. C. 1994. The Arthur Kill oil spills: Biological effects in birds. Pp. 215–237 in Burger, J., ed., 1994, Before and After an Oil Spill: The Arthur Kill. New Brunswick: Rutgers University Press.

Wander, W., and S. A. Brady. 1979. A closer look at New Jersey's wading birds. New Jersey Outdoors 6:10–11.

General Index

Species Index

About the Author

Joanna Burger is Professor of Biological Sciences at Rutgers University, where she teaches animal behavior, ecology, and ecological risk. As a child she began watching salamanders, snakes, butterflies, and birds on her parent's farm in Niskayuna, New York. She has written over 350 scientific papers as well as essays for the general reader in *Natural History, Explorer's Journal,* and *New Jersey Outdoors.* Her seven books include *Before and After an Oil Spill: The Arthur Kill* (Rutgers University Press). Although her research has taken her all over the world, no place has proved more interesting or challenging to her than the Jersey Shore. She lives in Somerset, New Jersey, with her family on her own nature preserve.